I0799918

IMAGES
of America

NASHVILLE
FROM THE COLLECTION OF CARL AND OTTO GIERS

James Hoobler

ARCADIA
PUBLISHING

ISBN 978-0-7385-0295-3

Published by Arcadia Publishing
Charleston, South Carolina

Printed in the United States of America

Library of Congress Catalog Card Number applied for.

For all general information contact Arcadia Publishing at:
Telephone 843-853-2070
Fax 843-853-0044
E-Mail sales@arcadiapublishing.com
For customer service and orders:
Toll-Free 1-888-313-2665

Visit us on the Internet at www.arcadiapublishing.com

This book is dedicated to the two women who preserved the work of Carl C. Giers and Otto B. Giers, Hunter Giers Hicks and Sarah Hunter Hicks Green.

IMAGES
of America

NASHVILLE
FROM THE COLLECTION OF CARL AND OTTO GIERS

Contents

Introduction

These photographs are the work of Carl and Otto Giers, German-American citizens of Nashville. Carl Casper Giers was born on April 28, 1828, in Bonn, Germany. He came to the United States in 1845 and made Nashville his home in 1852. In Nashville, he first worked as a conductor on the Chattanooga rail line, and he took out the first regular passenger train to Murfreesboro. In 1855 he began his career as a photographer. During the Civil War, he photographed soldiers from both sides as Nashville changed hands. In 1864 he was issued a military pass to leave occupied Nashville and to go to Louisville and return. On October 10, 1864, he was permitted to ship himself supplies from Louisville. In 1865 he was issued a military permit to pass on any pike in and out of the city. All of which reflects the trust that the Federal occupation had in him.

He was also held in high regard by his neighbors in Nashville, because in 1874 both the Democrats and the Republicans nominated him as a candidate for the Tennessee General Assembly's House of Representatives. Carl Giers easily won and was seated in the legislature. He worked to promote immigration. In 1873 he served as Tennessee's delegate to the world exposition in Vienna. On his way home, he had his photograph made in Munich. In 1876 he put together Tennessee's exhibition at the United States Centennial Exposition in Philadelphia. Peter Burkhardt was born in 1845 and married Barbara Zimmerman, who had been born in 1837. They had two children, Otto and Katie. On August 25, 1868, Barbara died of influenza. Then on February 13, 1870, Peter also died of influenza. Carl and Pauline Giers were childless, and they adopted their neighbors orphaned children. The 1860 census shows Carl, Pauline, and Carl's mother, Gertrude, all living together and having three tenants as well. In the 1870 census, Gertrude is no longer there, nor are the tenants. Now the Giers have 6-year-old Katie Burkhardt Giers and 12-year-old Otto Burkhardt Giers living with them. Carl introduced Otto into the community. Both of them were members of the Knights Templar. In that Masonic brotherhood, they met Edward Hicks II, and Carl became his good friend. They frequently visited Ed Hicks at his home, Devon Farm. Otto Giers's daughter, Hunter, would marry Ed Hicks's grandson, Edward Hicks IV, and live with him at Devon Farm after 1920.

Carl Giers's obituary states that he died at his Granny White Pike home, 3 miles from the city, after a long and painful illness. He was 49 years old when he died on May 24, 1877.

When Carl died, his widow and children needed money, so the photography business was sold. Otto had been born on January 25, 1858, so he was 19 years old when his second father died. In 1883, at age 25, Otto decided to try his hand as a photographer. He went to work with some other German-American Nashvilleans to form Thuss, Koellein, and Giers. Late the next year, he began a remarkable series of documentary photographs of Nashville's streets, schools, churches, homes, and government facilities. He worked on it into 1885. This series gives us a remarkable view of Nashville as it was developing as a New South city.

Between these two generations of photographers, they have passed on to us a treasury of images of Nashville at war, rebuilding as a new culture emerging from defeat, and as a prosperous New South city eagerly developing industry, yet maintaining a fine quality of life. They would photograph numerous individuals, great and humble, and important events, such as the first industrial exposition held in Nashville, in 1871, and the Tennessee Centennial Exposition in 1897. They would document such estates as Belmont, Belle Meade, and the Hermitage. They photographed Andrew Jackson's former slave, Alfred Jackson, as well as troops mustering in for the Spanish-American War, children at play, the family on outings, and Civil War officers.

Otto's only child, Hunter, was photographed as any doting father would his daughter. But, being a professional, Otto was able to repeatedly capture her as she grew up. Here you can see that happen.

When Otto died on March 13, 1940, Hunter inherited the works of Carl and Otto. She had married Edward Dickson Hicks IV and would live at Devon Farm, a property in his family since the 1790s and one in which the daughter, Sarah Marks, lives today.

Otto had done extensive work for *Confederate Veteran* magazine and made hundreds of portrait photographs of old veterans. He also collected Native American pottery, points, tools, and effigy pieces, and around 1930, he gave them to the Heye Foundation in New York City. He was living at 1619 Eighteenth Avenue South at the time of his death, and his next door neighbor, the author and educator Alfred L. Crabb, served as one of his pallbearers. Otto was a member of the Episcopal Church of the Advent.

Hunter and her daughter, Sarah Hunter Hicks Green, have continued to preserve these treasures, and now they are handed on to you after over 100 years. We hope that you will enjoy—and learn from—them.

All of these images are the work of Carl and Otto Giers, and all are from the family collection of Sarah Hunter Hicks Green, Otto's granddaughter. Most have never before been published.

One

The Giers Family: Four Generations of Nashvilleans

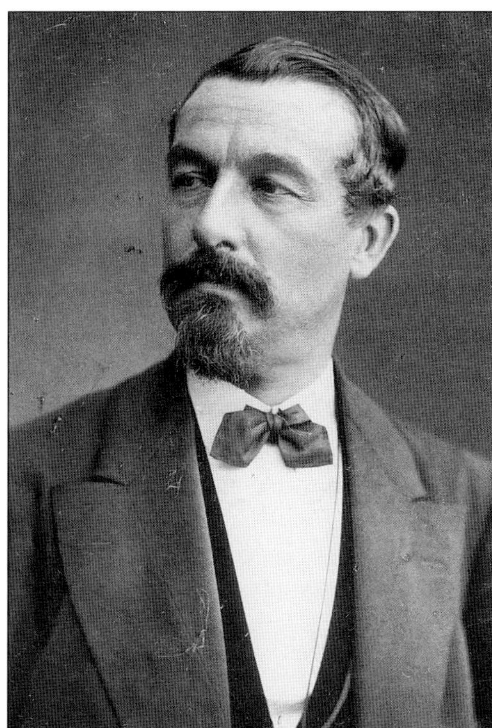

Carl Casper Giers lived from April 28, 1828, to May 24, 1877. Born in Bonn, Germany, he came to the United States in 1845. In 1852 he moved to Nashville and was employed as a conductor on the Chattanooga railroad. He took the first regular passenger train to Murfreesboro. In 1855 he opened a photographic business.

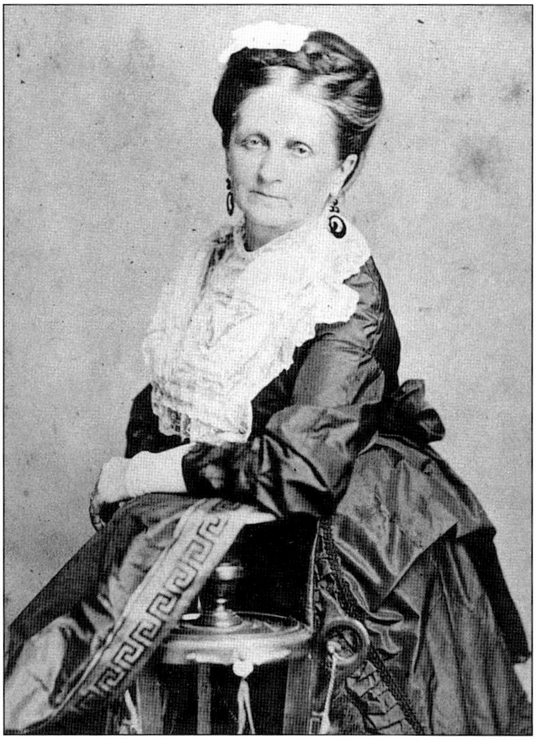

Pauline Giers, wife of Carl C. Giers, was born in 1835 in Wurttemberg, Germany.

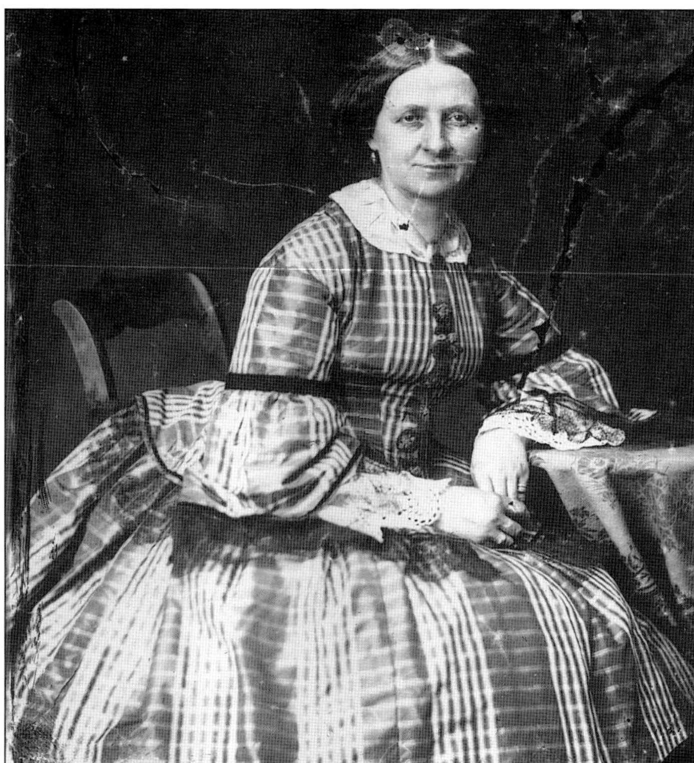

Meeting and marrying Carl Giers in Nashville's German immigrant community, Pauline Giers was the subject of numerous photographs by her husband.

The Giers adopted the orphaned children of their German neighbors and raised Otto and Katie as their own.

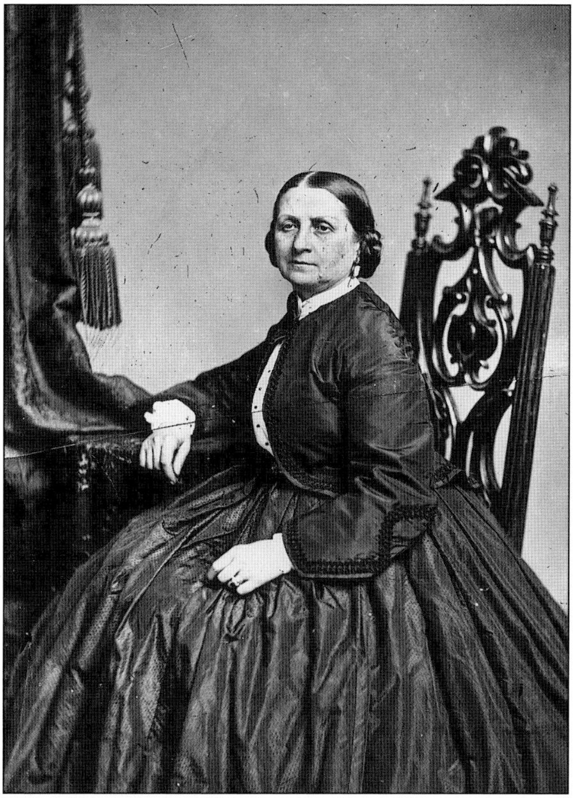

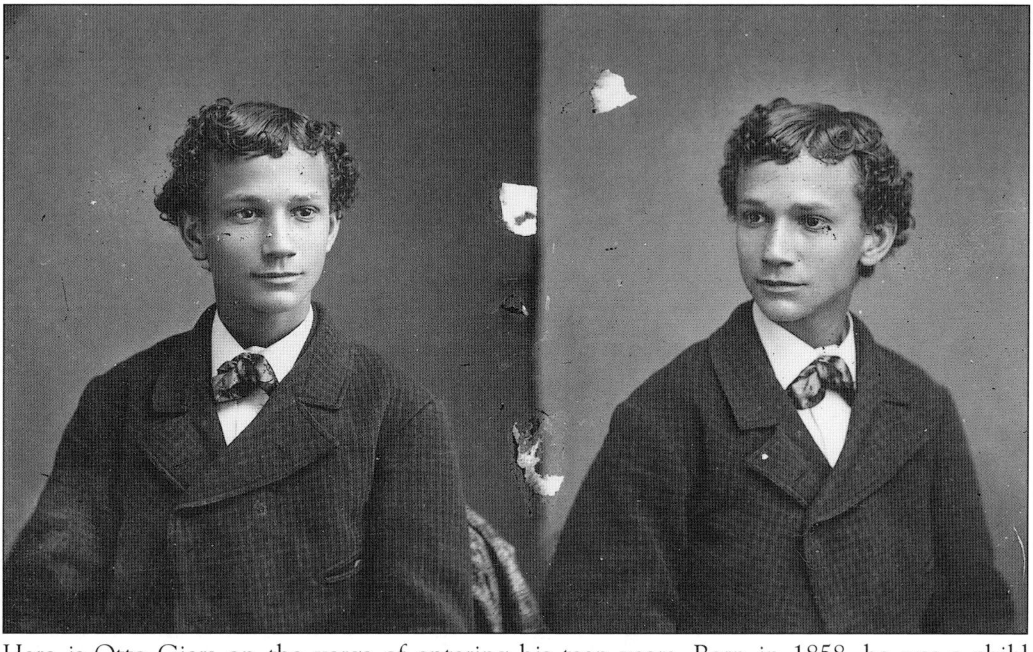

Here is Otto Giers on the verge of entering his teen years. Born in 1858, he was a child during the Civil War years. This photograph was probably made about the time of his adoption in 1870.

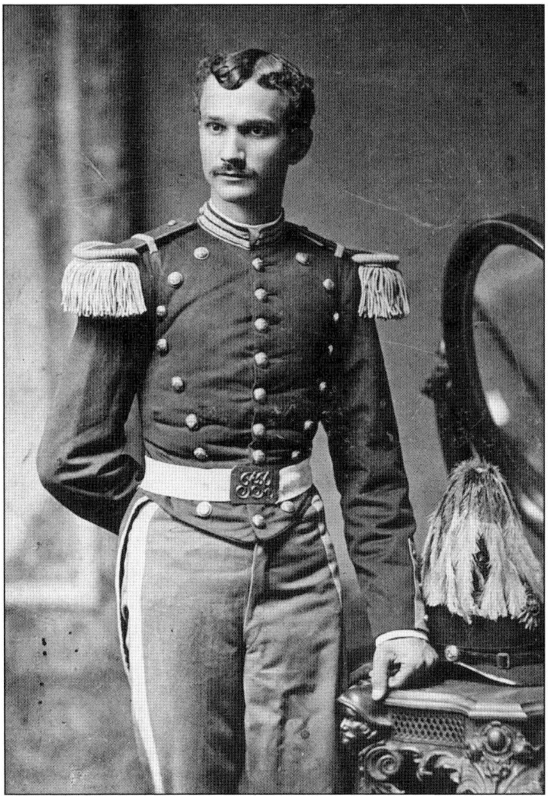

As a member of the Porter Rifles military drill squad, Otto Giers posed for this portrait in the 1870s.

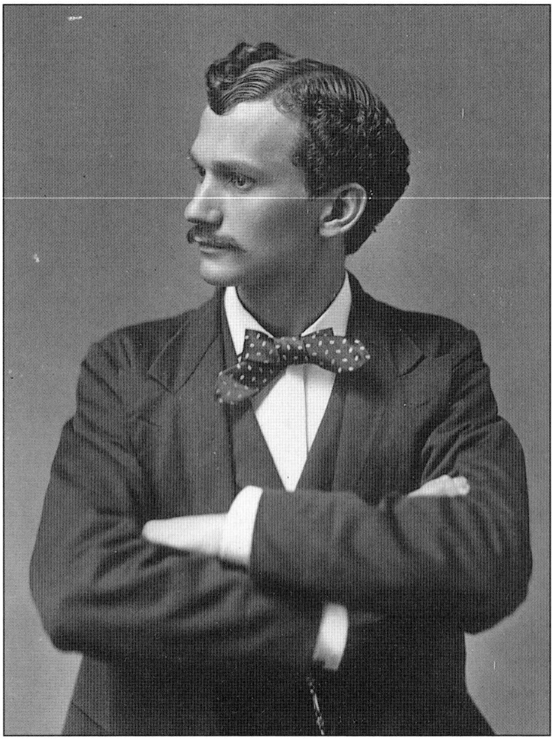

With the death of Carl Giers in 1877, Otto became responsible, at age 19, for his mother and sister's care. In 1883, at age 25, Otto followed in Carl's footsteps and became a photographer. The family lived at 534 South Summer Street.

Sallie Hunter married Otto Giers and became the frequent subject of his photography.

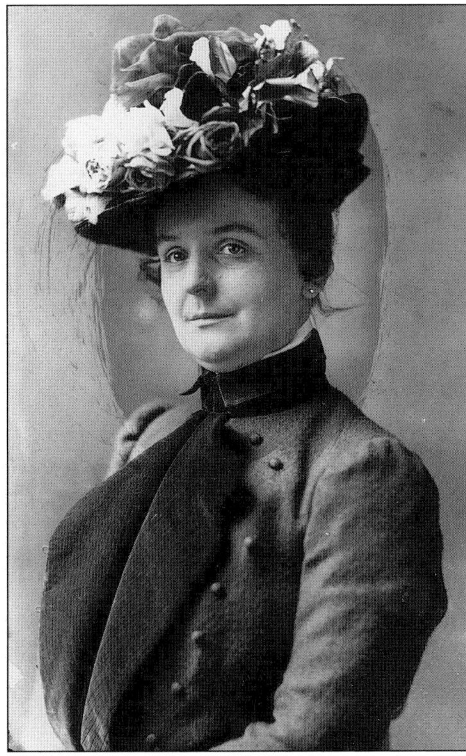

The William Hunter residence was at 445 Chestnut Street, in South Nashville. Sallie's widower father lived here, and she and Otto joined him. Here, a group gathers on the front porch.

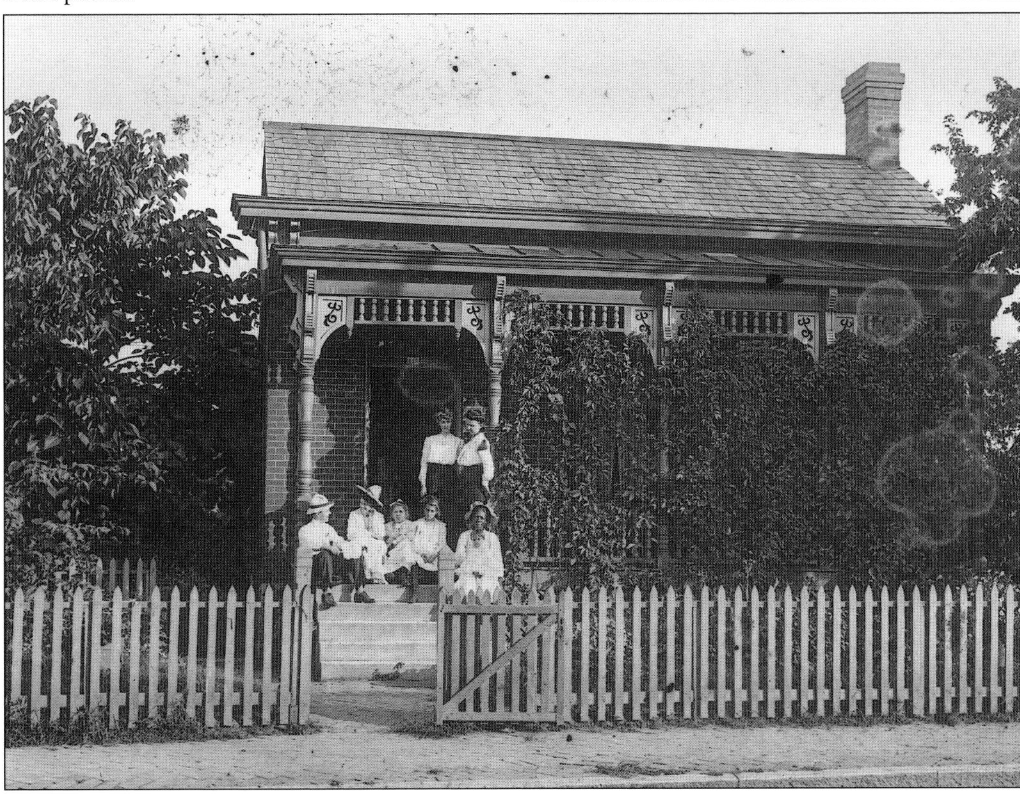

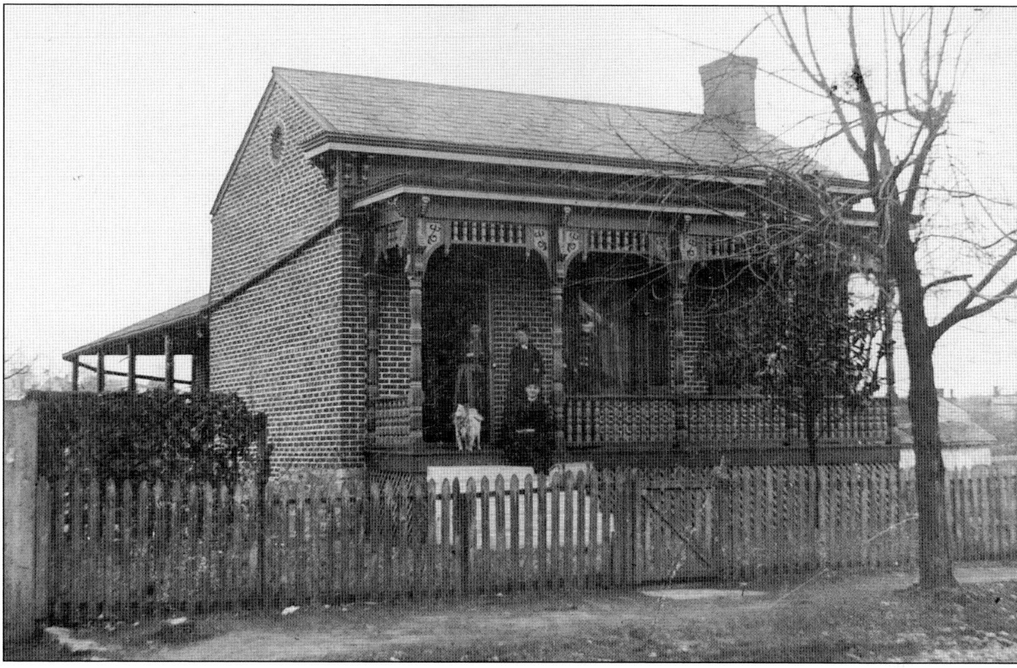
This is the William Hunter residence at 445 Chestnut Street, in the 1880s.

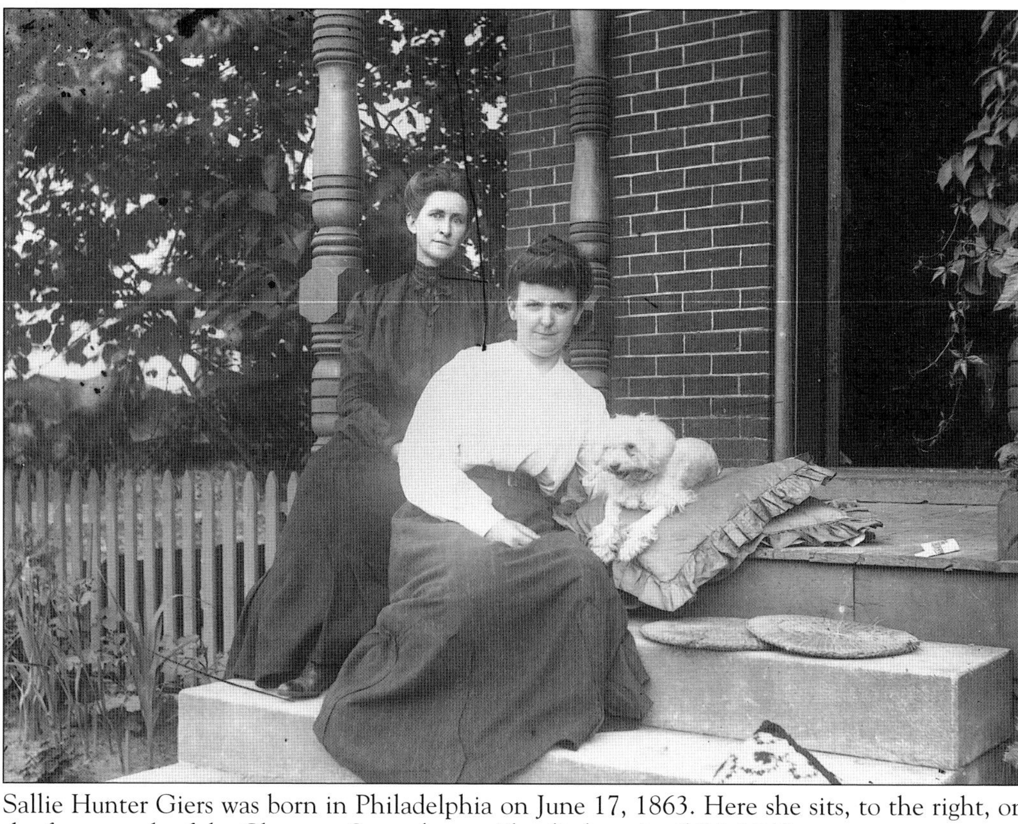
Sallie Hunter Giers was born in Philadelphia on June 17, 1863. Here she sits, to the right, on the front porch of the Chestnut Street home. She died on April 26, 1940.

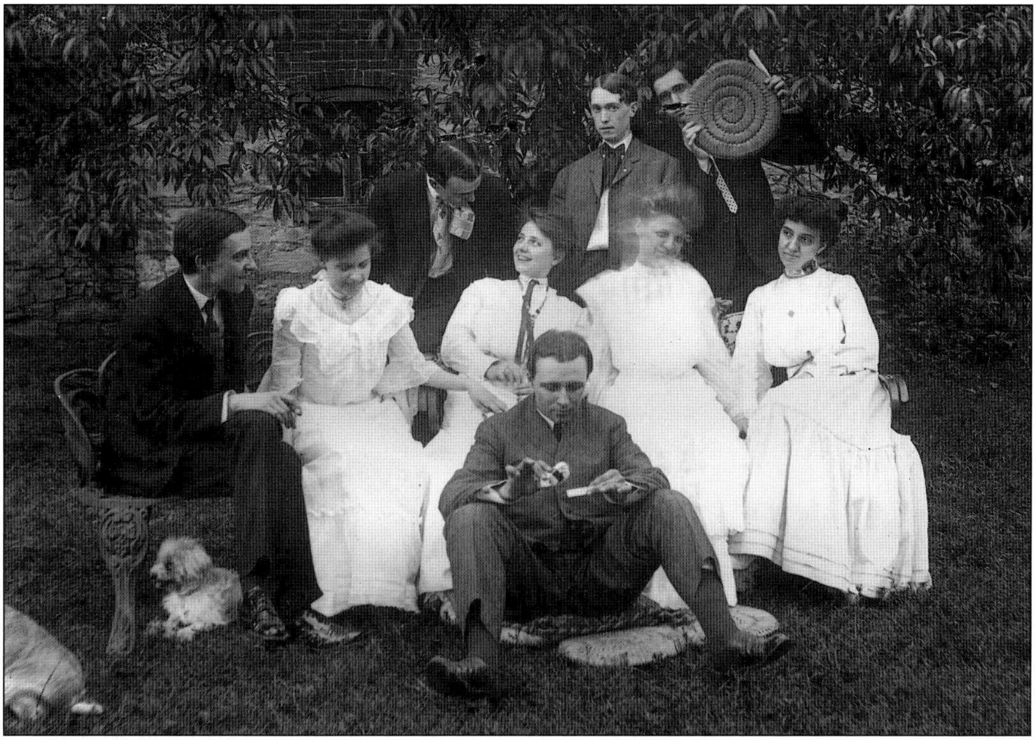

In the backyard of the Chestnut Street home, a group of friends poses for Otto Giers's camera.

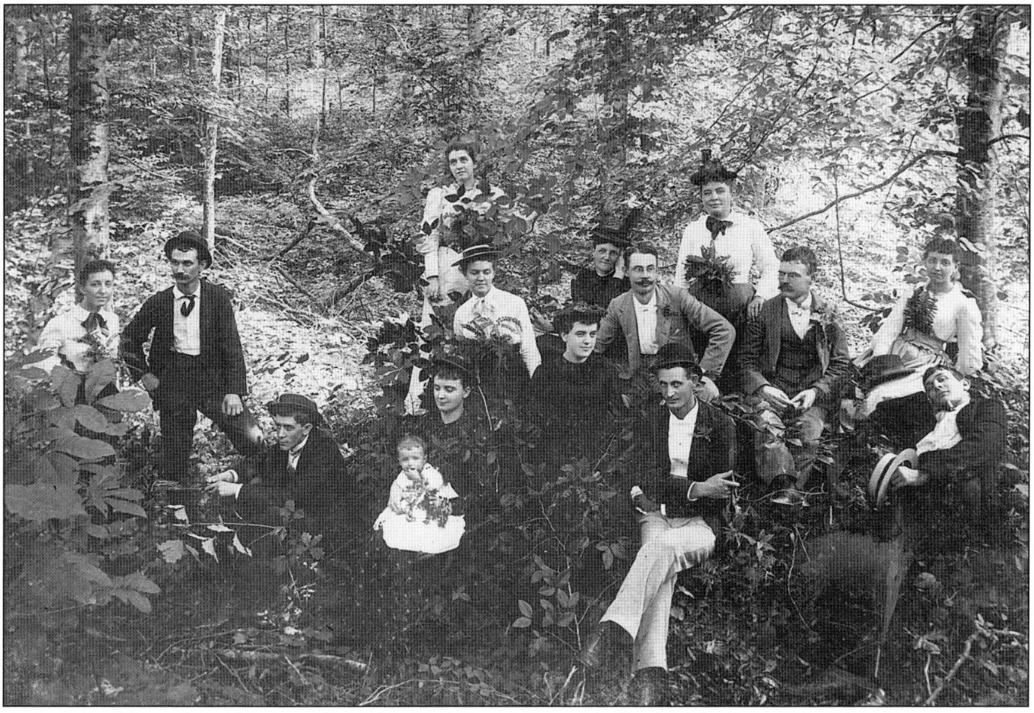

A group of friends gathers with Sallie and Otto Giers. Sallie holds their baby daughter, Hunter, at center, while Otto stands to the left. A friend took the photograph for Otto.

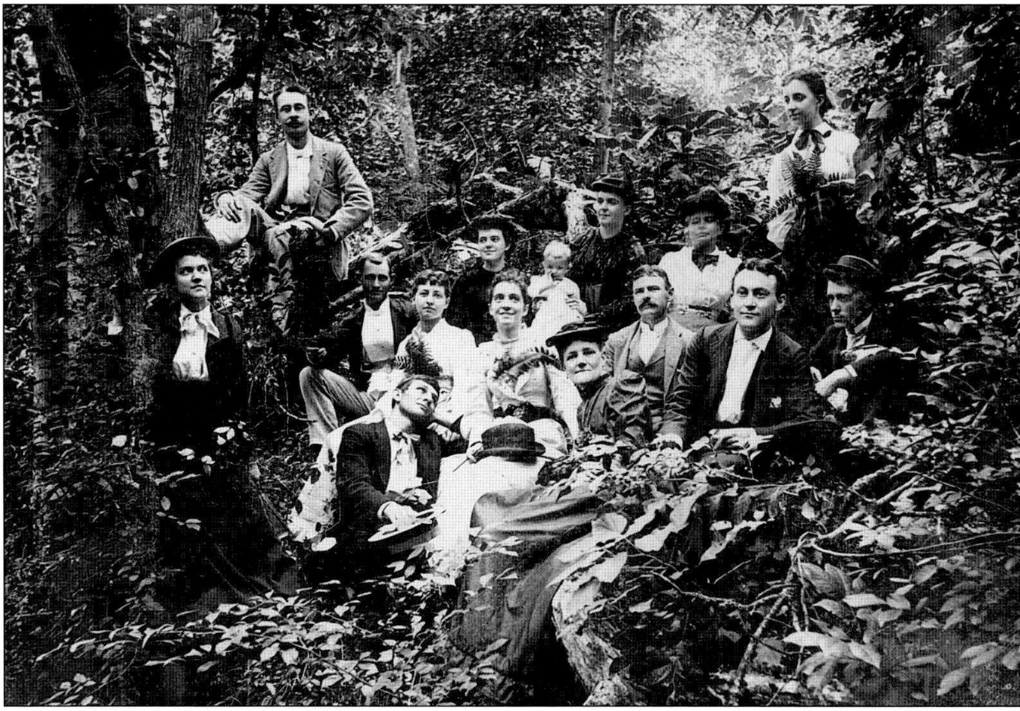

Here, the same group poses for Otto, who is now taking the photograph. Sallie and Hunter are again at the center. This is probably 1892, as Hunter was born in August 1891.

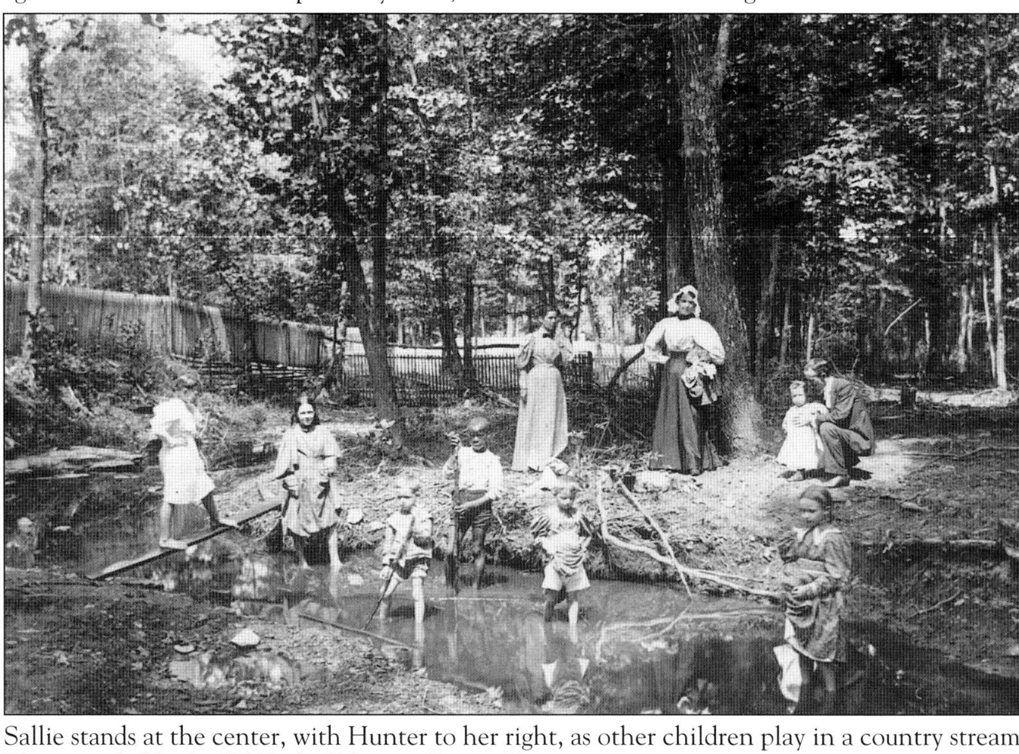

Sallie stands at the center, with Hunter to her right, as other children play in a country stream. This is probably the Ed Hicks II home, Devon Farm.

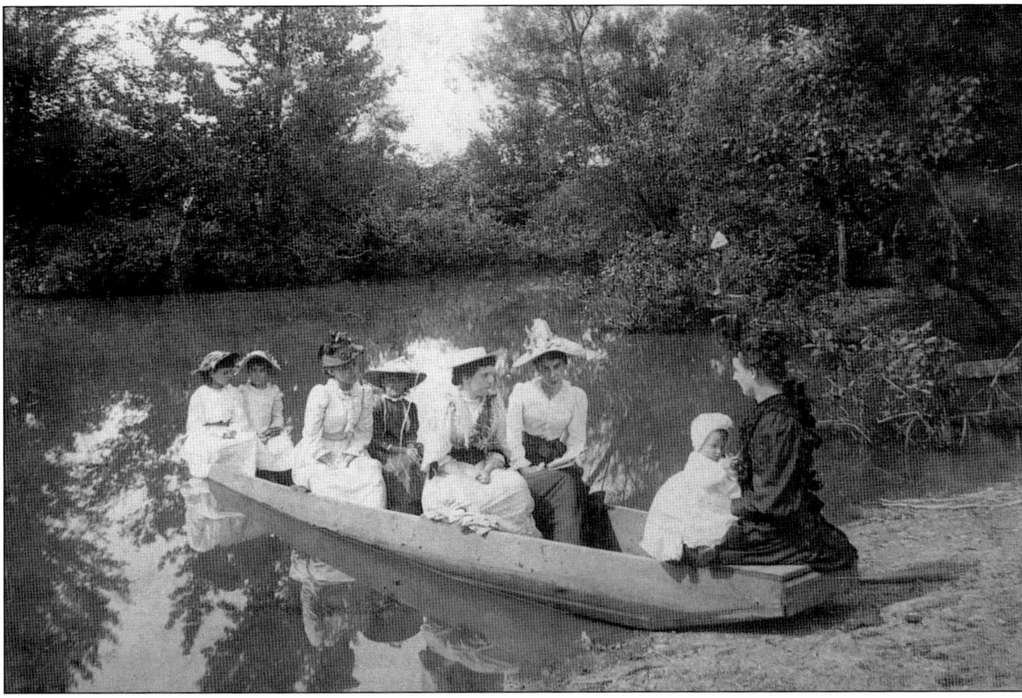

Sallie and Hunter pose with six other women friends in a pirogue. This again is probably at Devon Farm, along the Harpeth River.

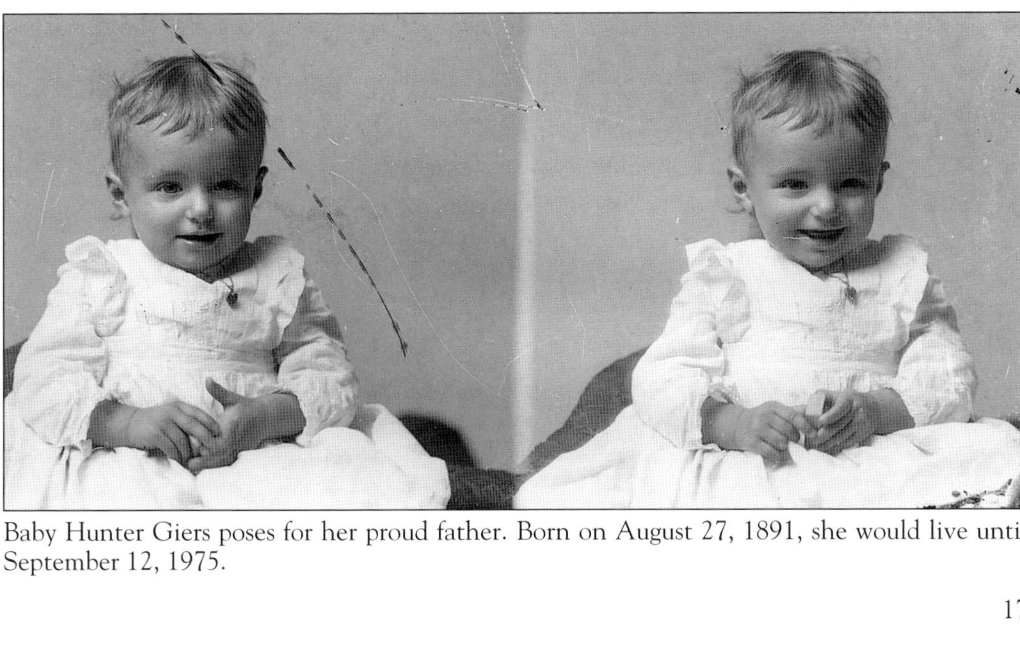

Baby Hunter Giers poses for her proud father. Born on August 27, 1891, she would live until September 12, 1975.

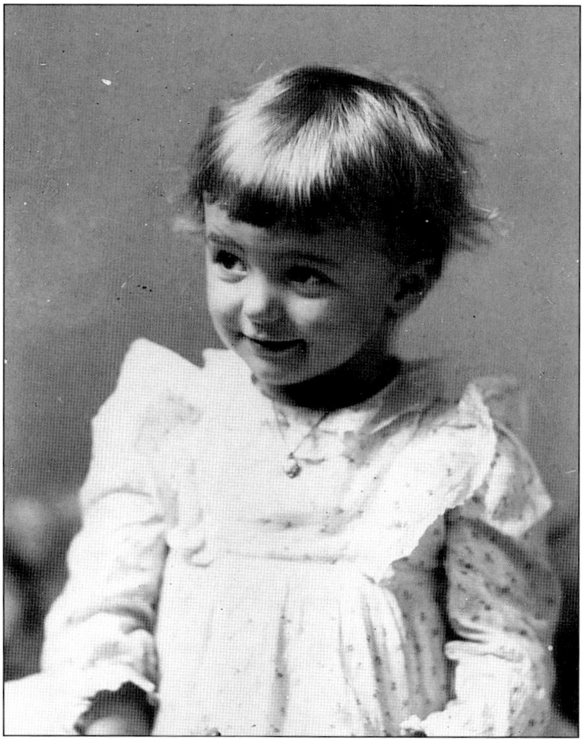

Because Hunter is frequently the subject of her adoring father's camera, there is an opportunity to watch her grow up through her father's eyes.

Here, Hunter has a tea party with a friend.

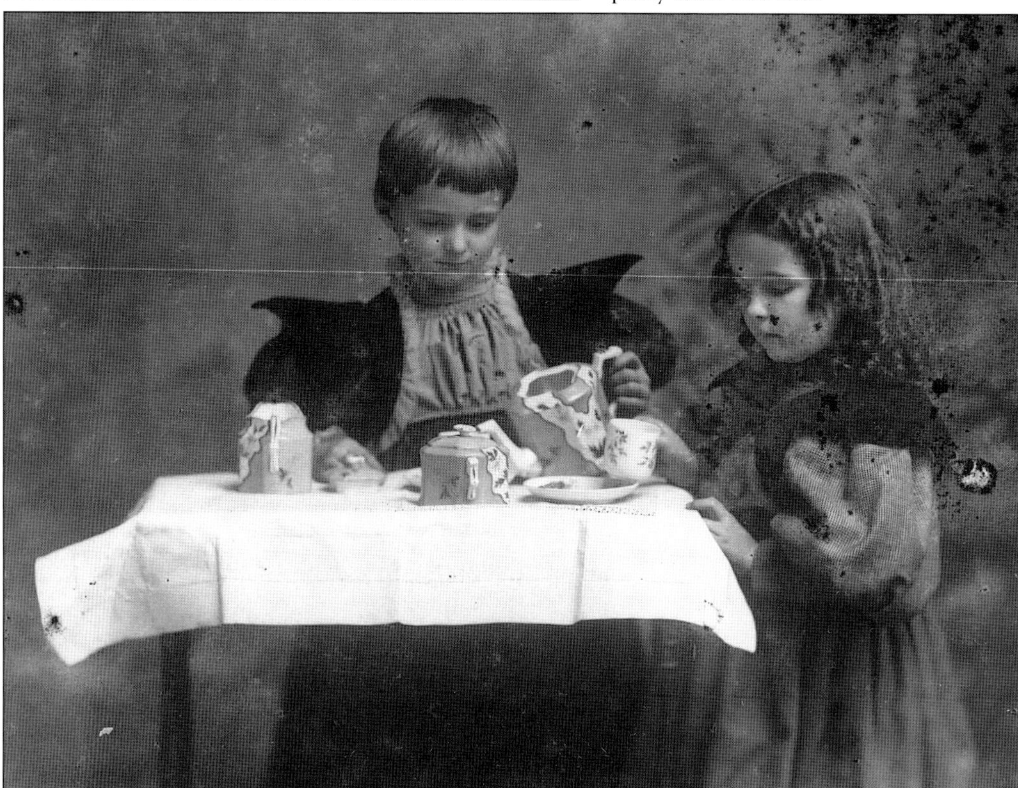

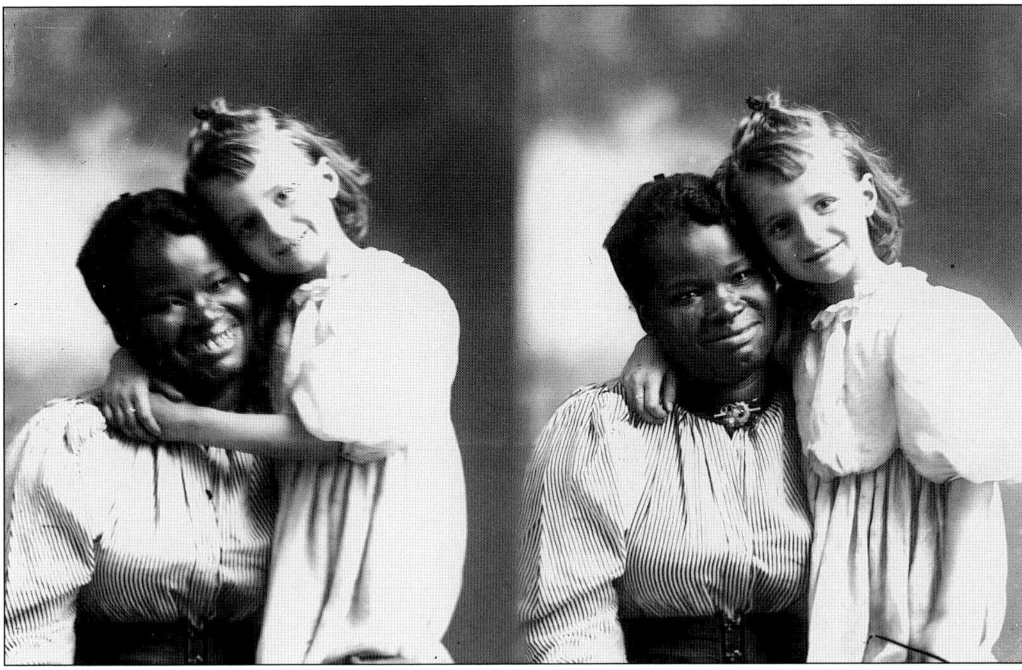

In this image, Hunter is hugging her beloved nurse Mime.

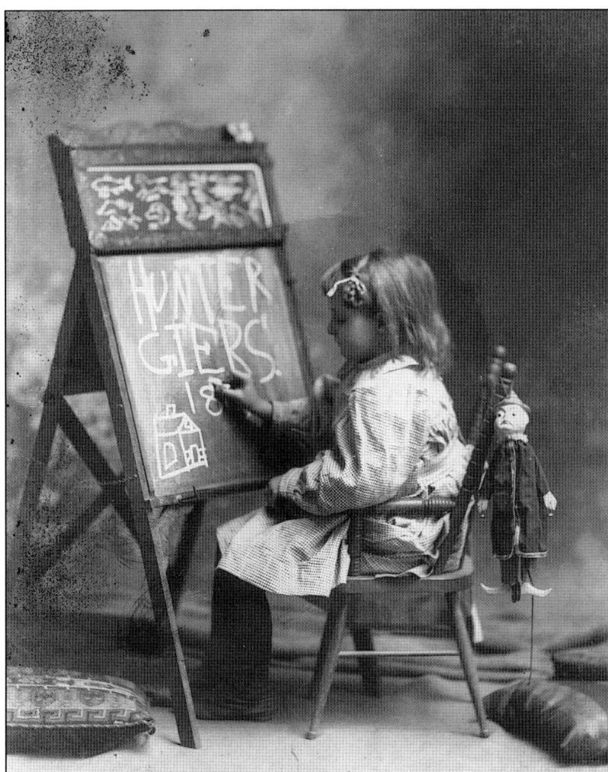

Hunter poses here before a chalkboard with her name upon it, and she has a marionette hanging on the knob of her chair.

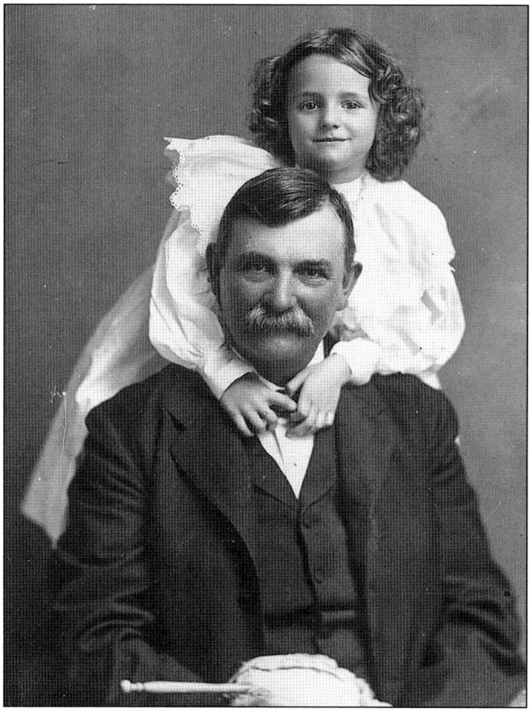

Here, Hunter hugs her grandfather, William Hunter. William Hunter was born in Philadelphia on December 18, 1836. He was a Southern sympathizer and moved to Nashville. He died on July 6, 1912.

Playing with her friends, Hunter poses with the Crutchfield brothers in a tree behind her home.

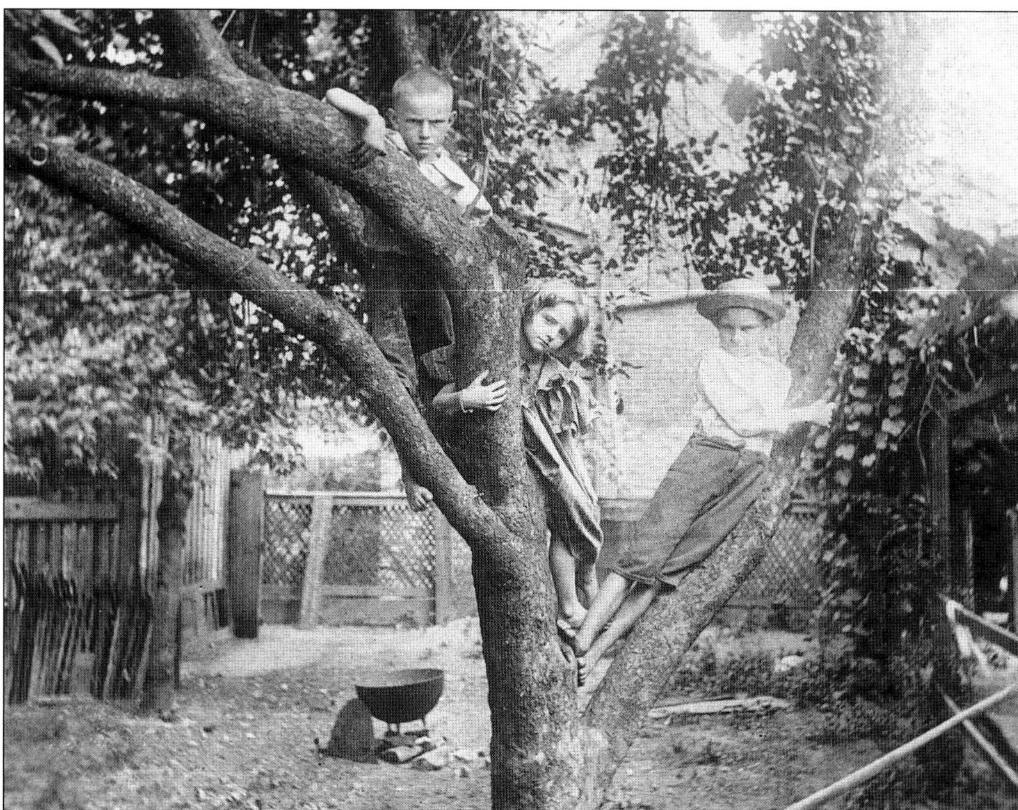

For the Tennessee Centennial Exposition, a floral parade was organized by a women's committee. Here, Hunter sits in her tricycle, decorated for the parade.

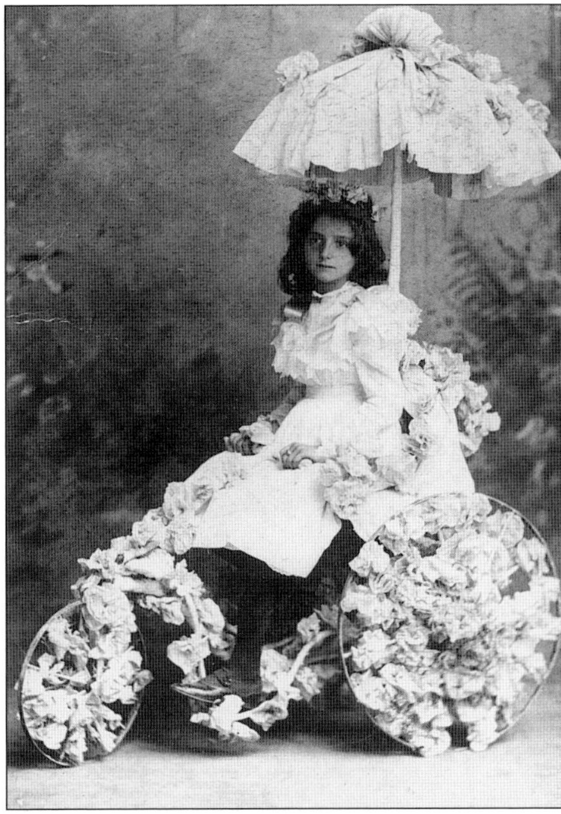

In a scene reminiscent of Thomas Eakins's *The Swimming Hole*, Giers captures three boys swimming at the turn of the century.

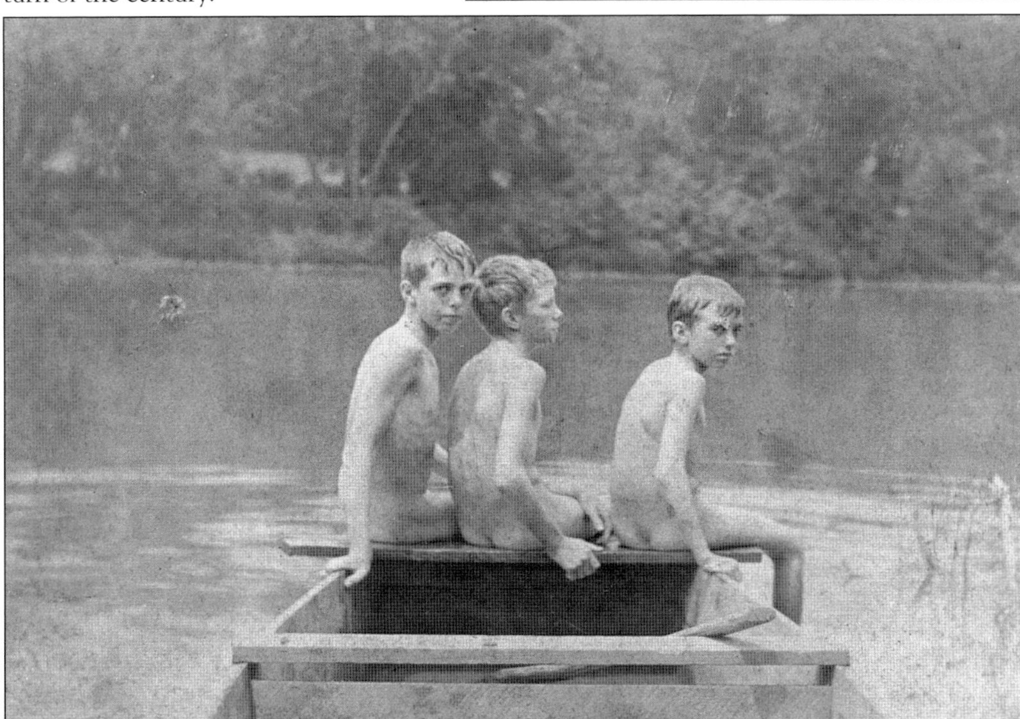

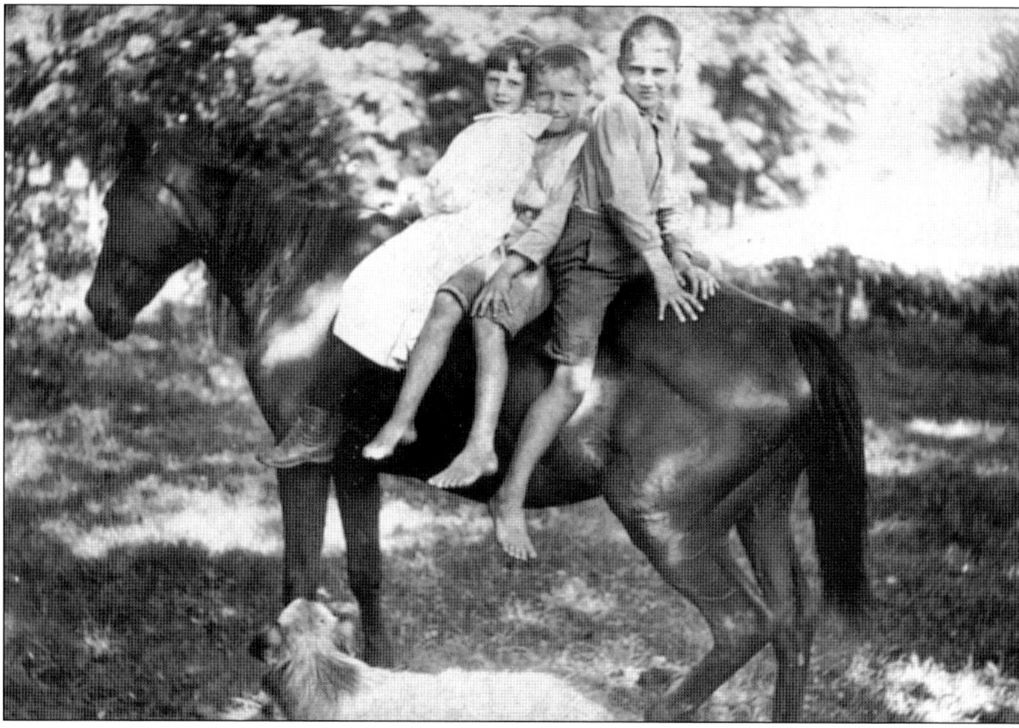

The Crutchfield brothers pose with another friend of Hunter in this scene from a child's summer at the turn of the 20th century.

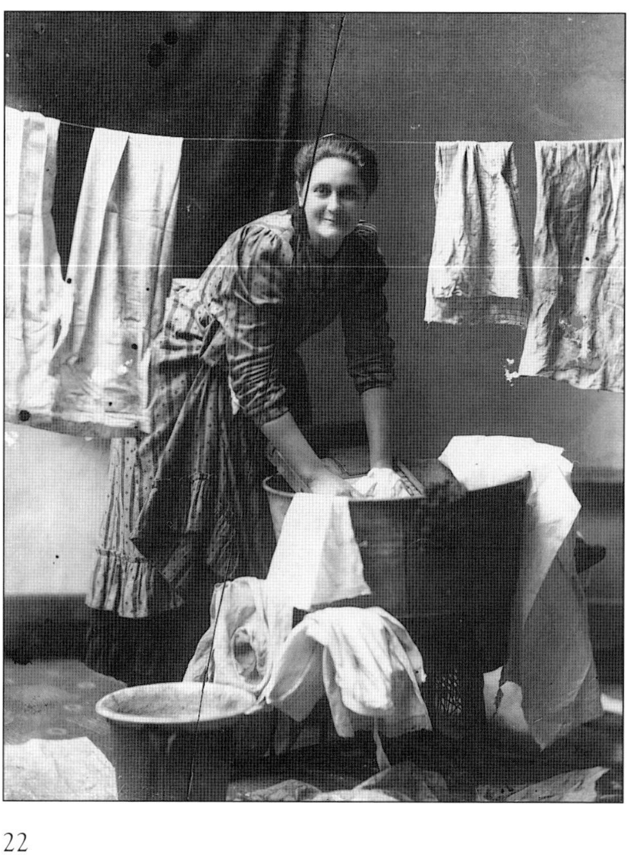

Minnie Hempstead Hunter, the second wife of William Hunter, poses here for Otto as a laundress. She lived from 1862 to 1952.

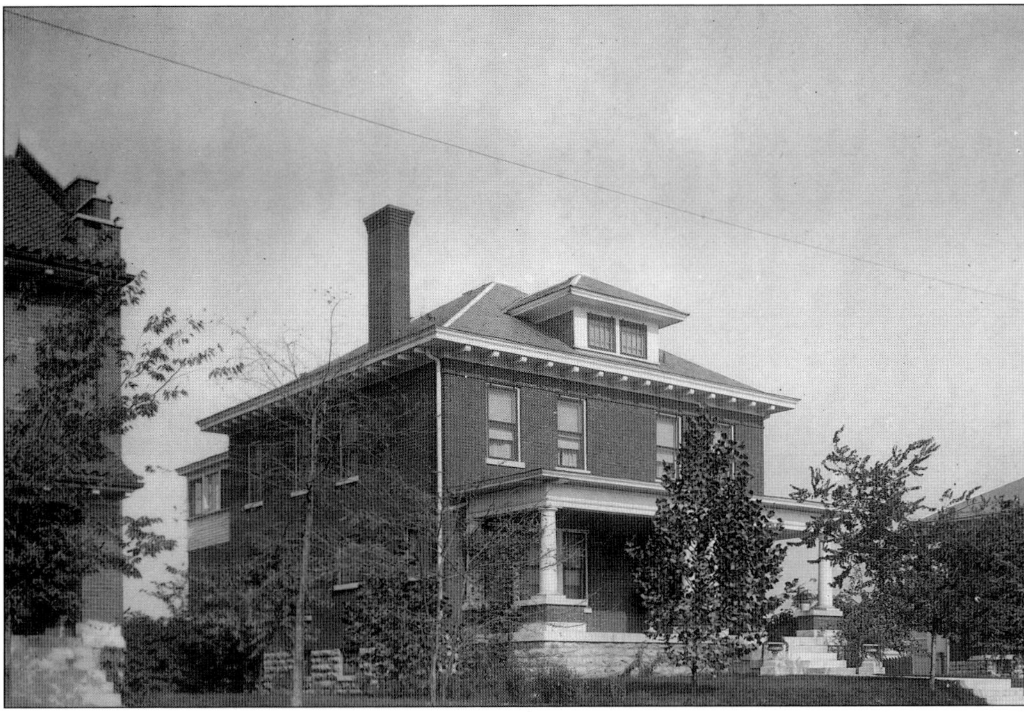

The house to the center was the home of Otto, Sallie, and Hunter. It stands at 1619 Eighteenth Avenue South. This was where Otto lived until his death in 1940. The house to its left was the home of Dr. Alfred Leland Crabb, Nashville educator and novelist/historian.

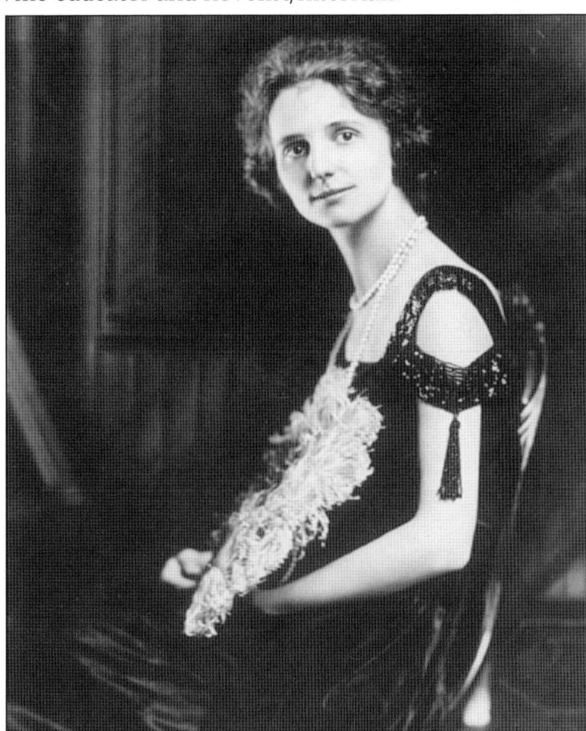

Hunter poses here at about the time of her wedding in 1920.

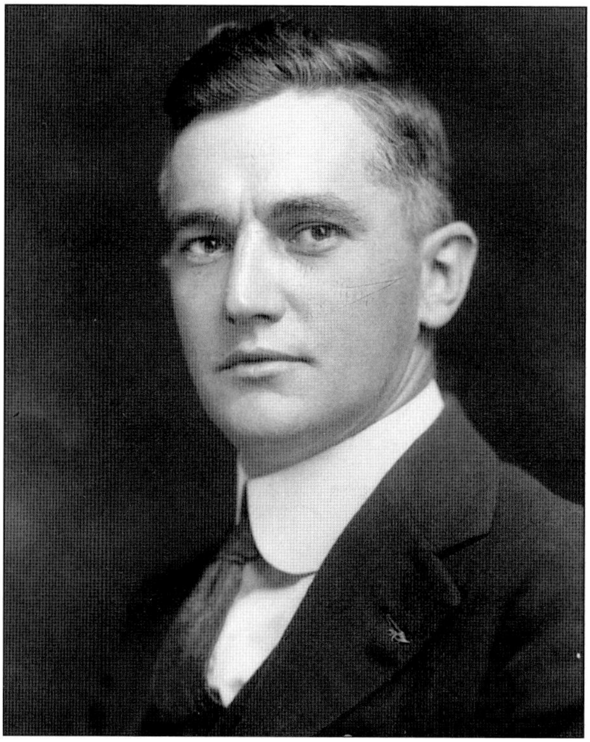

Hunter's husband, Edward Dickson Hicks IV (1892–1961), is seen here around the time of his marriage to Hunter Giers on February 11, 1920.

The home of Ed Hicks is photographed here, with some of the Mississippian artifacts that he dug up along the Harpeth River near Devon Farm, his family home. Note the man looking in the window.

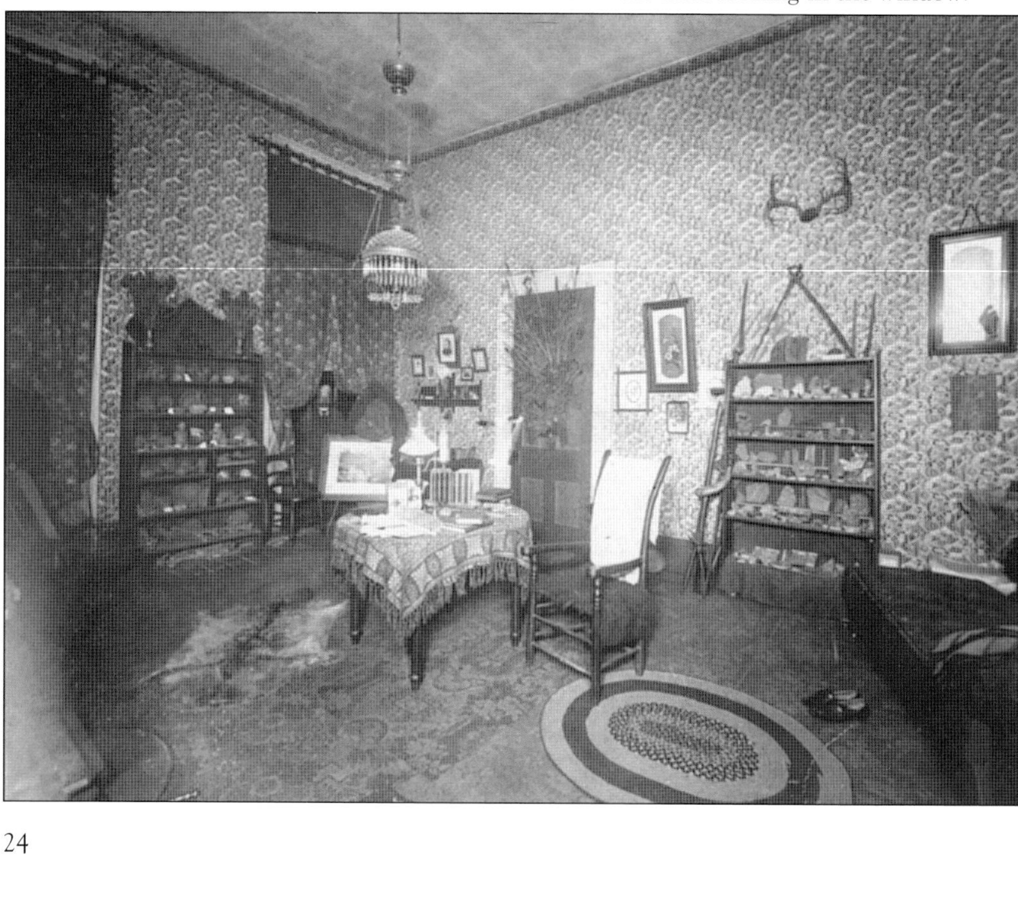

Two

Coming to Town

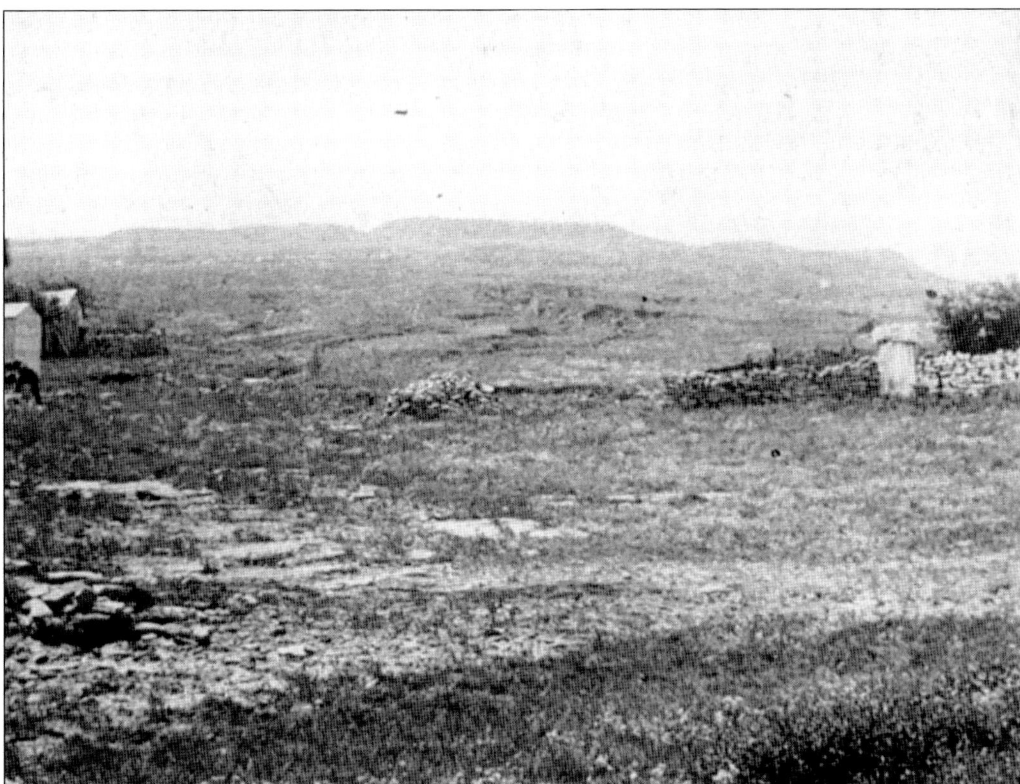

Fort Negley was built by the U.S. Army during the military occupation of Nashville during the Civil War. It was begun in 1862. On December 15, 1864, the opening salvo of the Battle of Nashville was fired from this fort. In 1884 Otto Giers began a personal photographic project. He set out to document his hometown, and he did so in several hundred views. Here we begin a look at Otto Giers's Nashville. All of the subsequent views were made by him in 1884–1885.

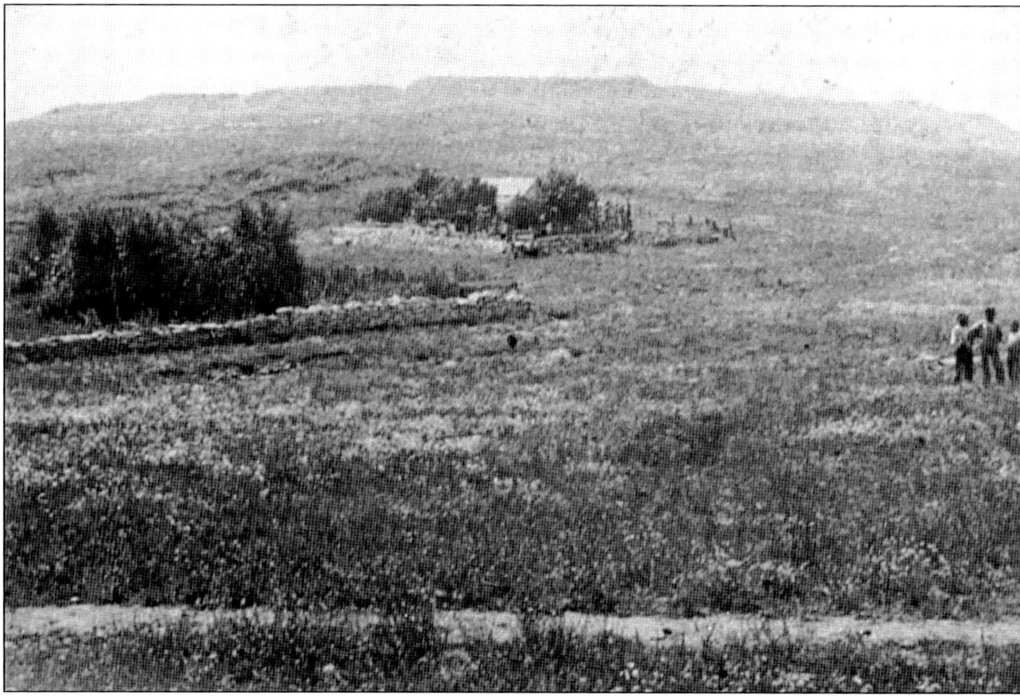

The profile of Fort Negley is visible atop St. Cloud Hill, south of Nashville, above present-day Greer Stadium.

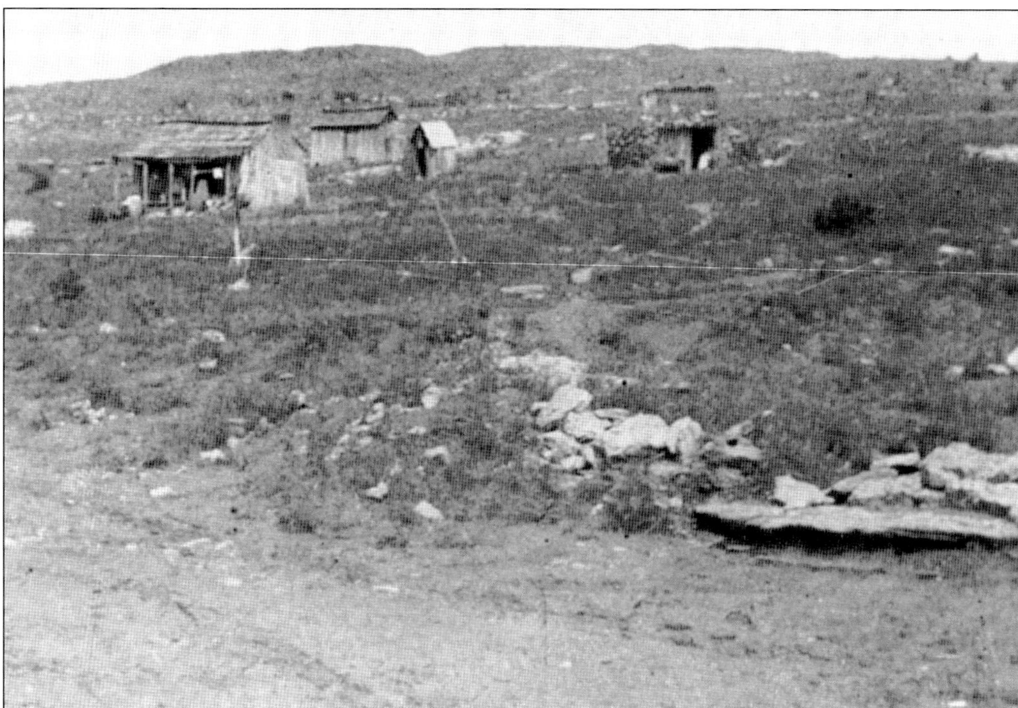

Ex-slaves took up residence in the areas around the federal garrisons in occupied Nashville and continued to live there after the war.

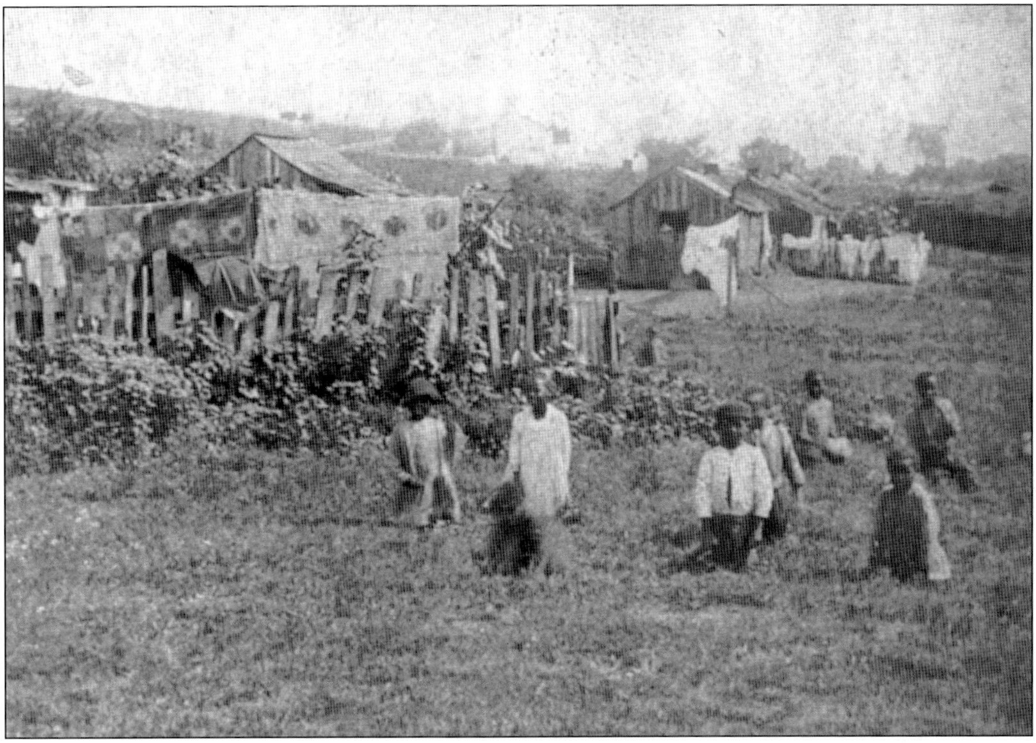

These descendants of "contrabands," who were ex-slaves seeking the protection of U.S. troops during the Civil War, are living here below Fort Negley, in 1884.

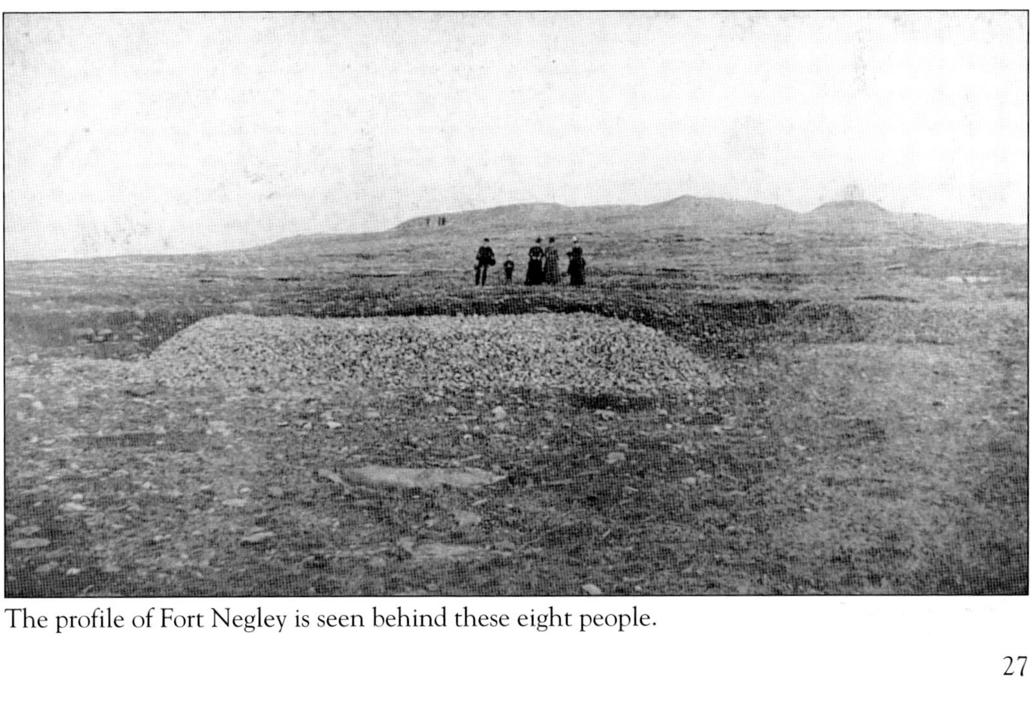

The profile of Fort Negley is seen behind these eight people.

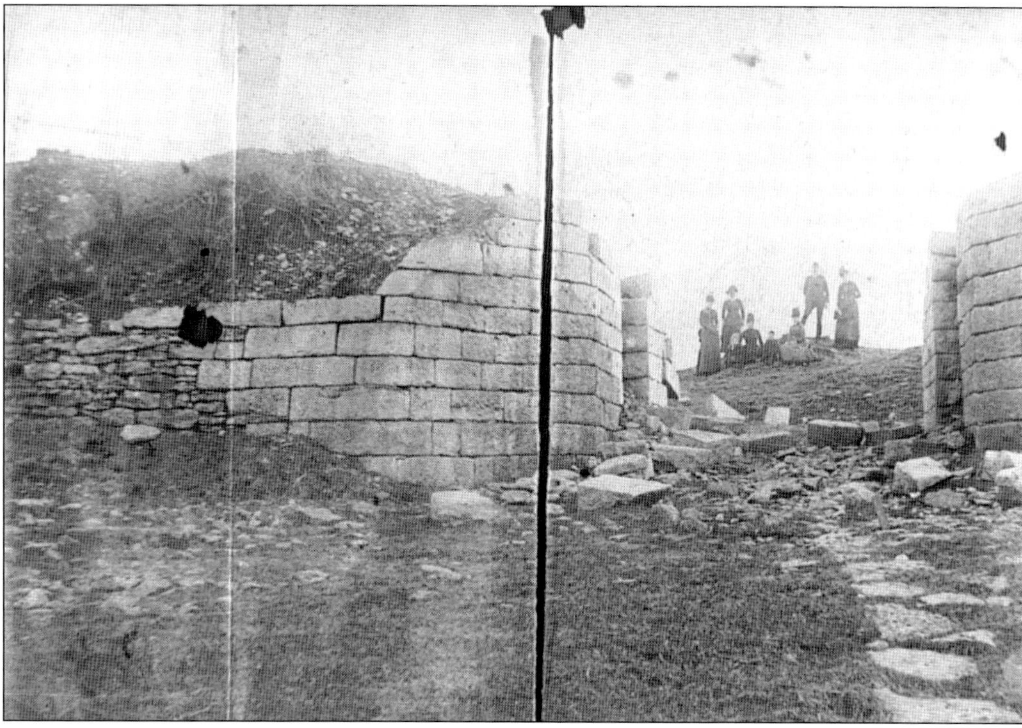

The gateway to Fort Negley is seen here with the same group of eight people. Metro Nashville is now talking about restoring the fort.

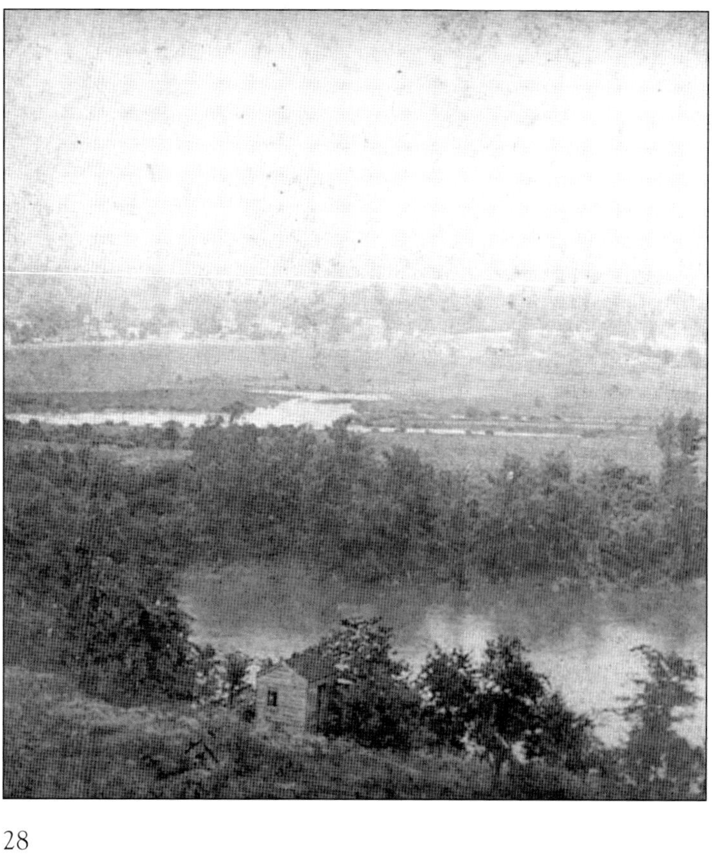

Shelby's Pond is seen across the Cumberland River from the Tennessee School for the Blind. Shelby Bottoms Park is in this area today.

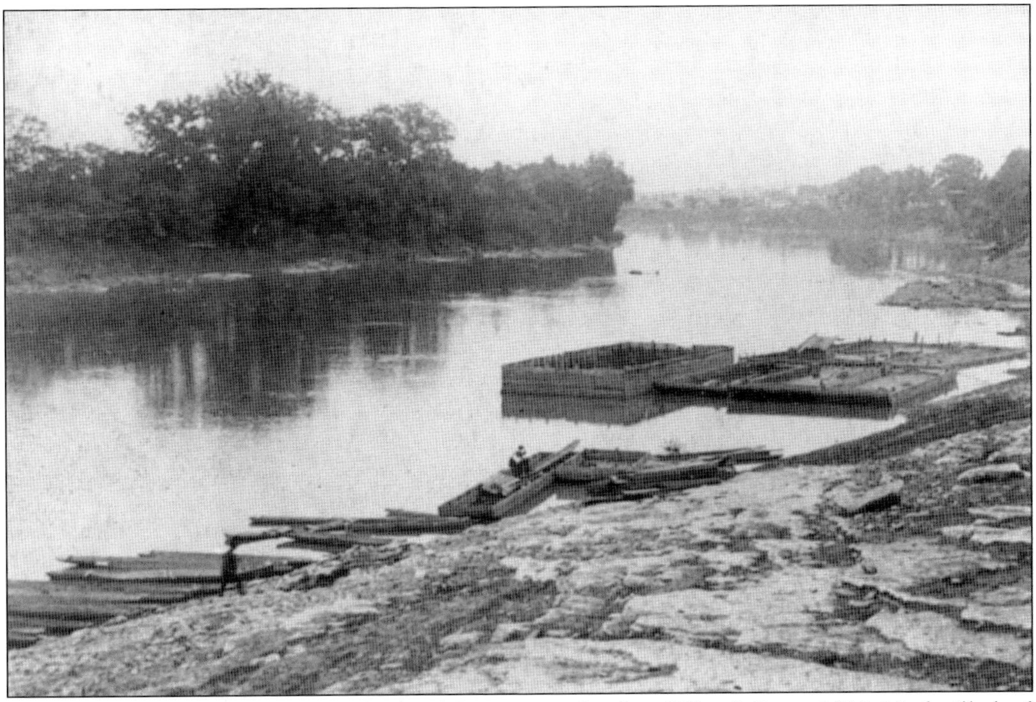

Captured in this view is the Cumberland River near the City Wharf. Since 1819, Nashville had been receiving riverboats at the landing.

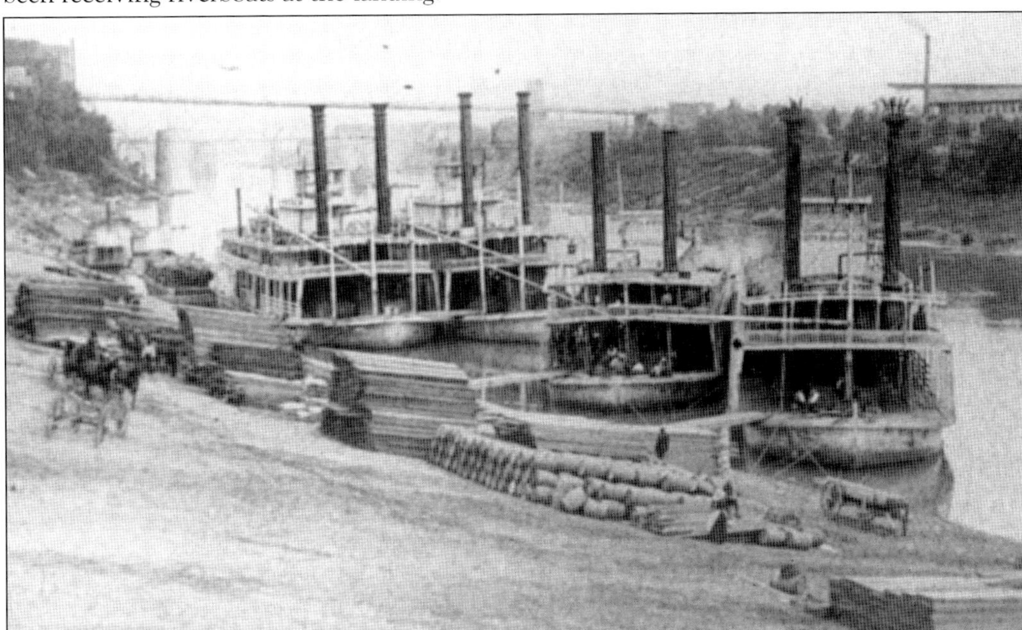

By 1884 the City Wharf was a bustling place. The *City of Nashville*, whose master was W.S. Bowman, is docked to the right. With A.T. Armstrong as its master, the *L.P. Ewald* is docked next to it. As can be seen from the landing, lumber was becoming a big industry in the Cumberland River valley. Trees were cut upstream, floated to Nashville, and milled in Edgefield on the east bank of the river.

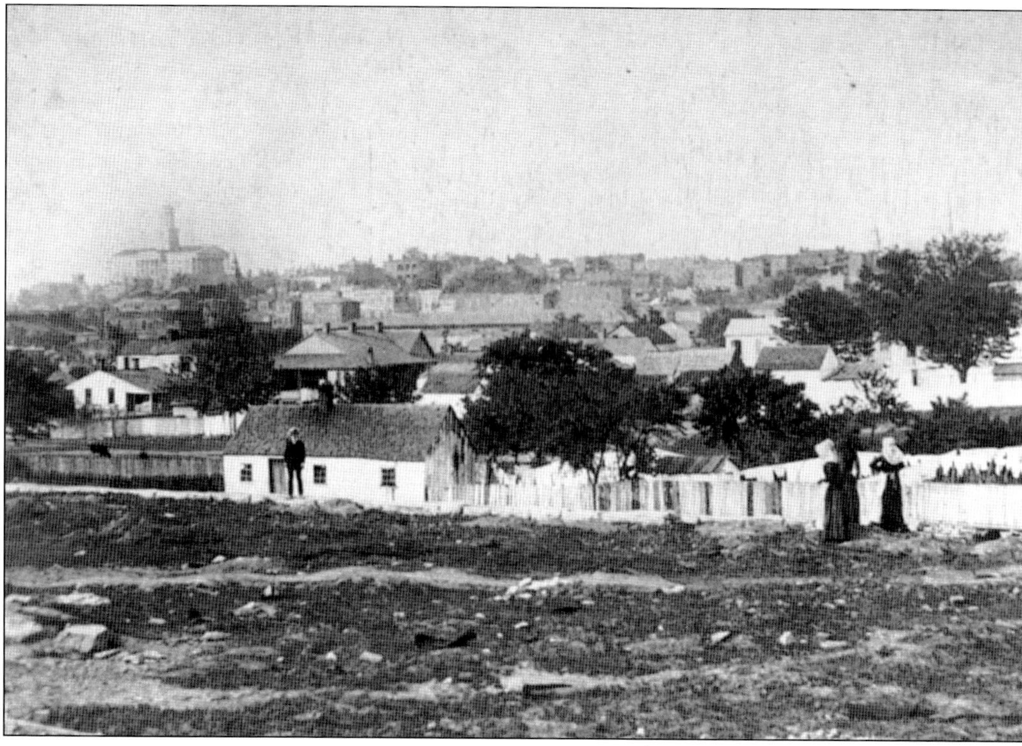

This is a view of Nashville from near Demonbreun and Mulberry (Tenth), about 1884. The Tennessee State Capitol dominated the city as its largest building. Two women in sunbonnets have just hung out their laundry.

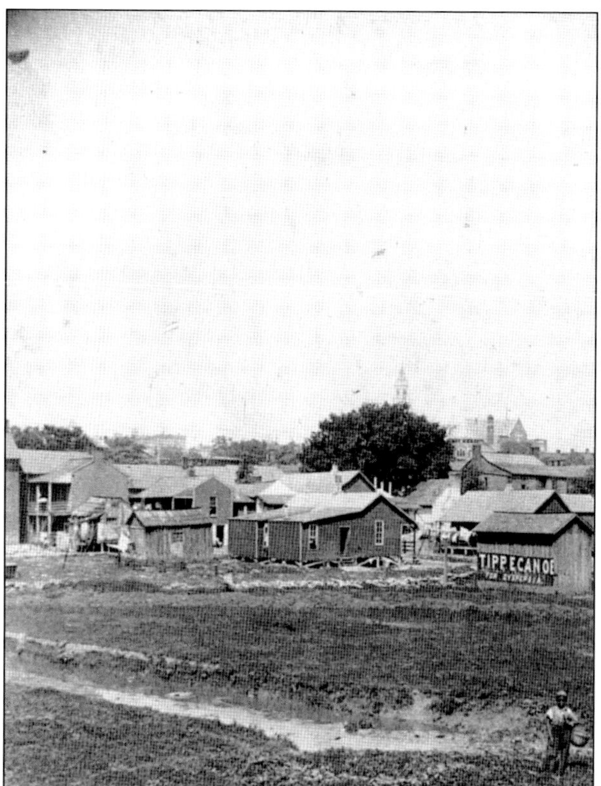

Located south of Broad, the U.S. Customs House tower is visible at the center. To its right, First Baptist Church is under construction. A small boy poses in the right foreground. This view was made probably near Walnut (Tenth), along the rail line.

This is the Louisville & Nashville (L & N) Railroad bridge across the Cumberland River. The stone piers to this swing-span bridge were built in the 1850s, and they still support the main rail line into town from the north. The bridge was made capable of swinging open in the center so that the smoke stacks of riverboats could pass.

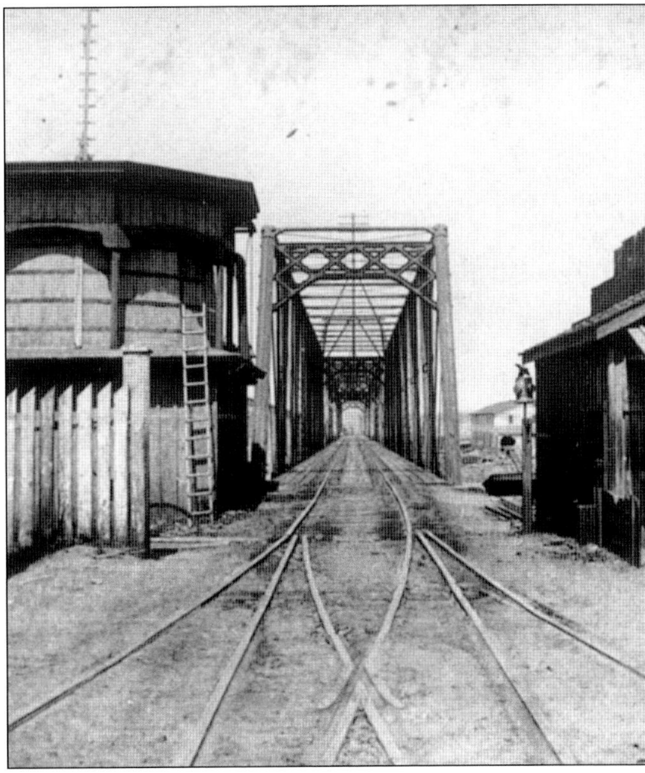

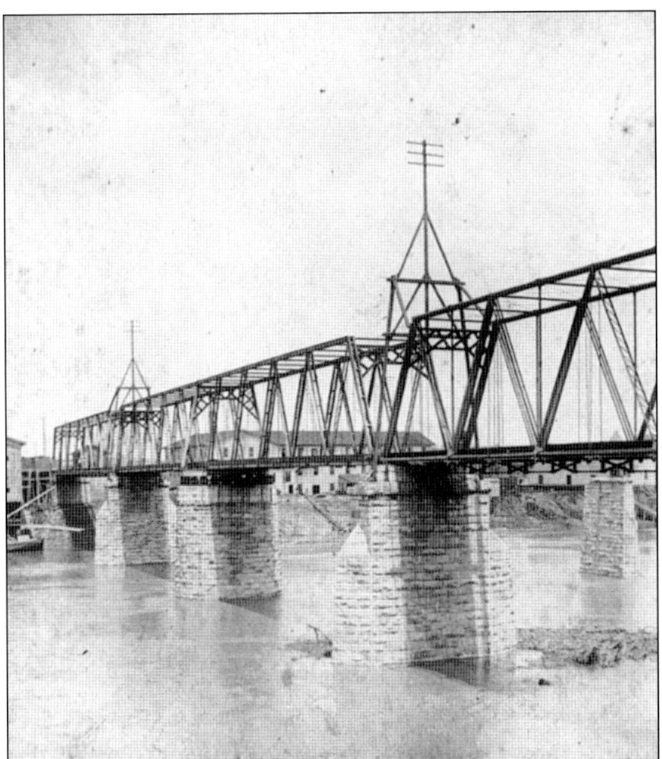

This is a side view of the L & N Railroad bridge. One of the swing-span supporting piers, for when the bridge was open, is visible to the right.

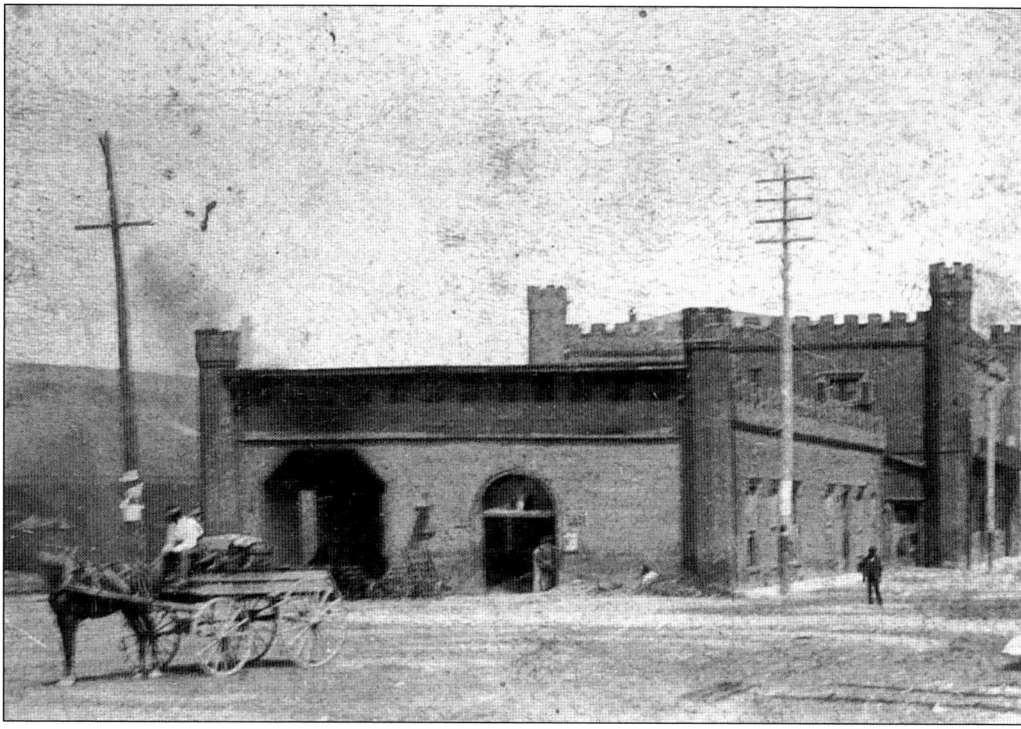

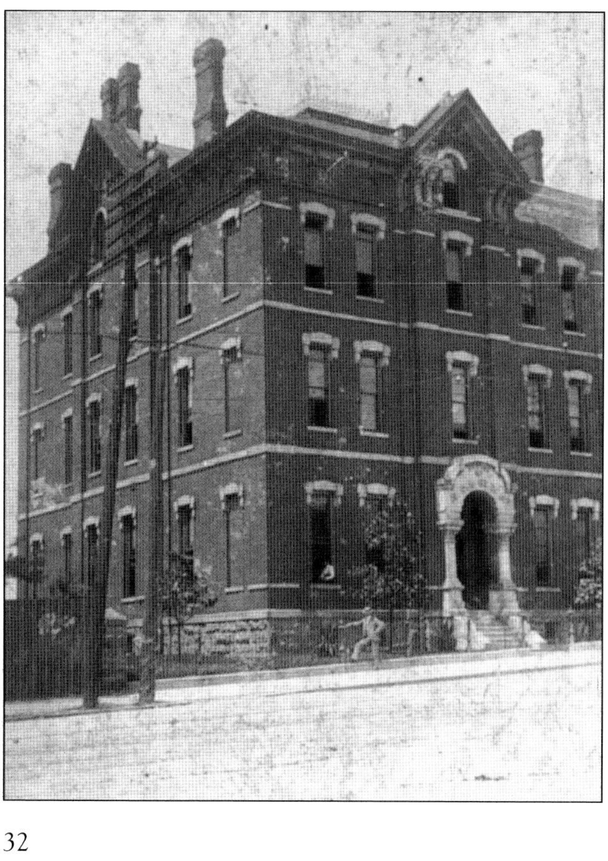

Erected in the 1850s, the Nashville, Chattanooga & St. Louis Railroad depot was located in the rail valley west of downtown, between Church Street and Union Street on the west side of Walnut Street (Tenth). Railroads were beginning to compete heavily for the same trade that used riverboats in this period.

This is the office of the Nashville, Chattanooga & St. Louis Railroad, on the north side of Broad near Walnut (Tenth). The Baptist Bookstore is there now.

The one-carriage, foot, and horseback bridge across the Cumberland River connected the towns of Edgefield and Nashville. It was located where the Woodland Street Bridge crosses the river now, in front of the Davidson County Courthouse. This is the view from Edgefield.

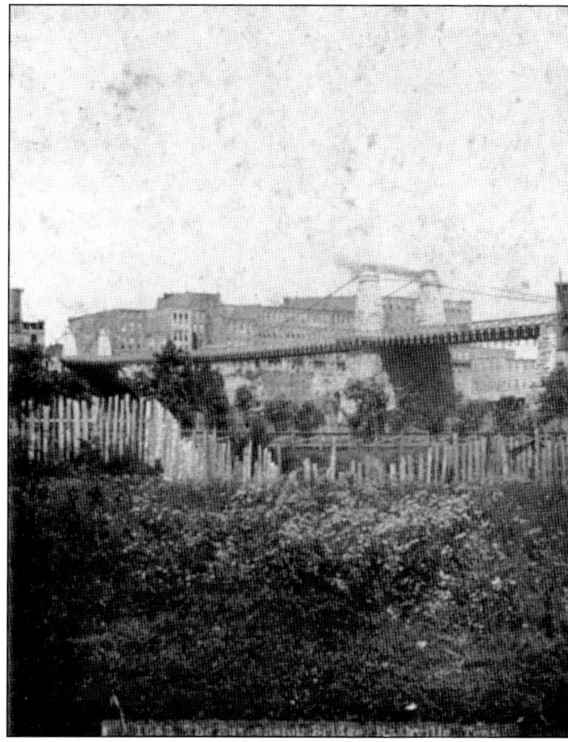

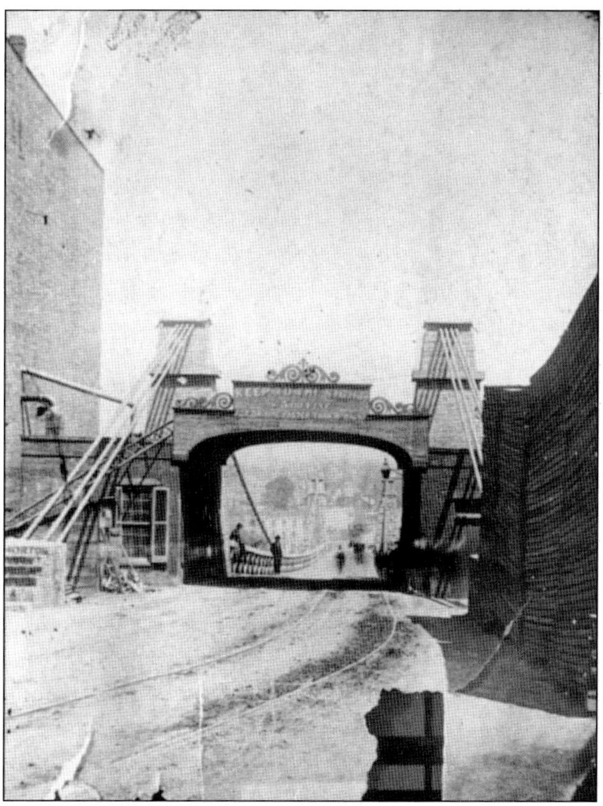

The sign above the bridge entrance reads as follows: "Keep To The Right. $5.00 Fine For Driving Faster Than A Walk." The city of Edgefield is visible across the river.

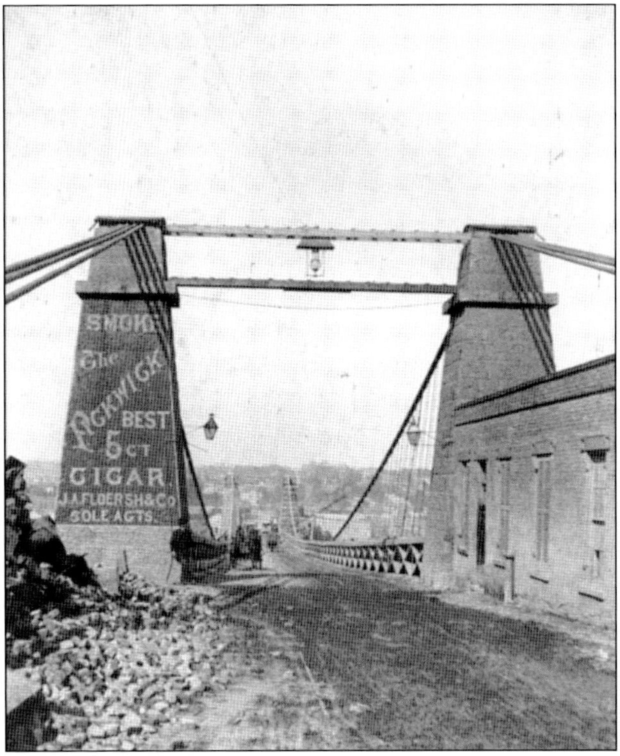

Demolition is beginning for a steel truss bridge to replace the cable and plank suspension bridge.

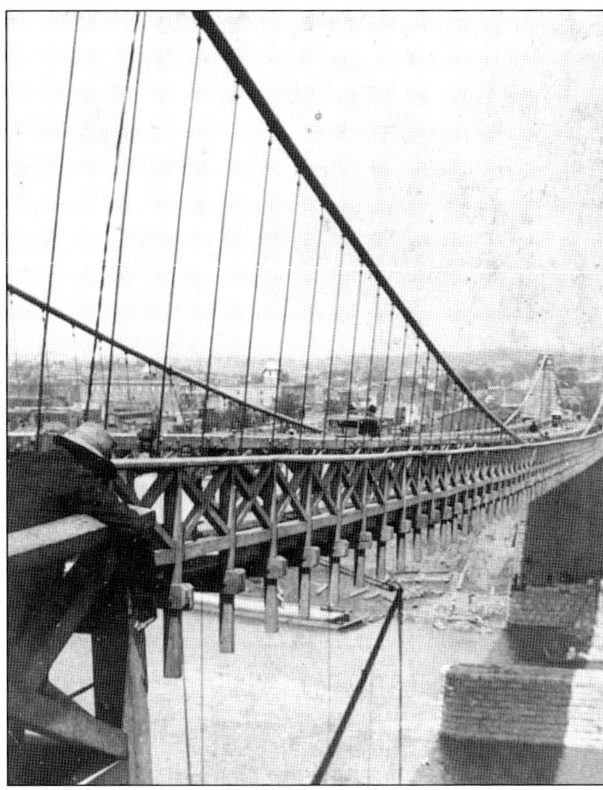

In 1884 work began on the construction of a new bridge to replace the 1866 suspension bridge across the Cumberland. Here, someone leans over the railing to watch the work on the new stone piers rising up out of the river.

While the bridge was being replaced, a pontoon bridge was operated by Tom Ryman from 1885 to 1886. Captain Ryman had just moved into a new home atop College Hill. From that location, he had an excellent view of the river and of his steamboats and pontoon bridge.

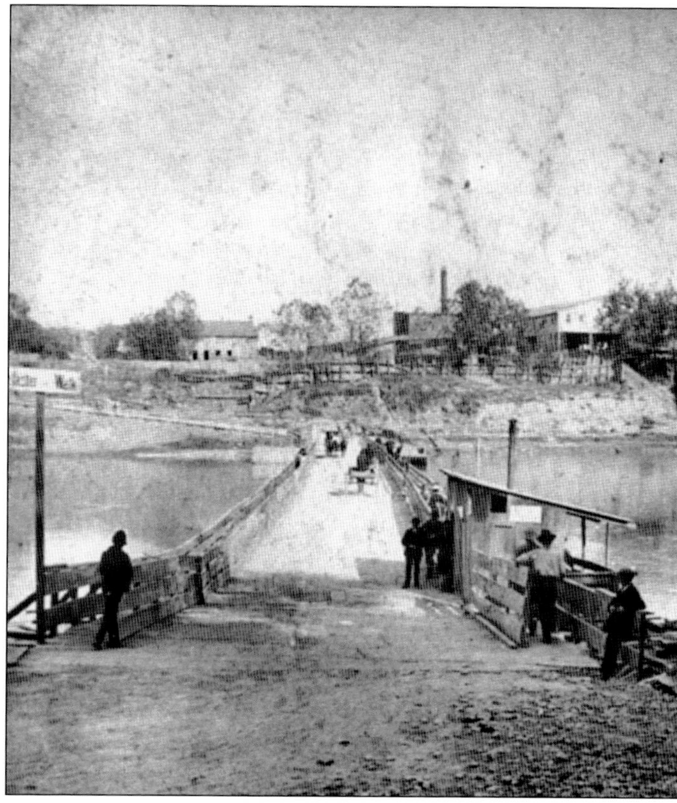

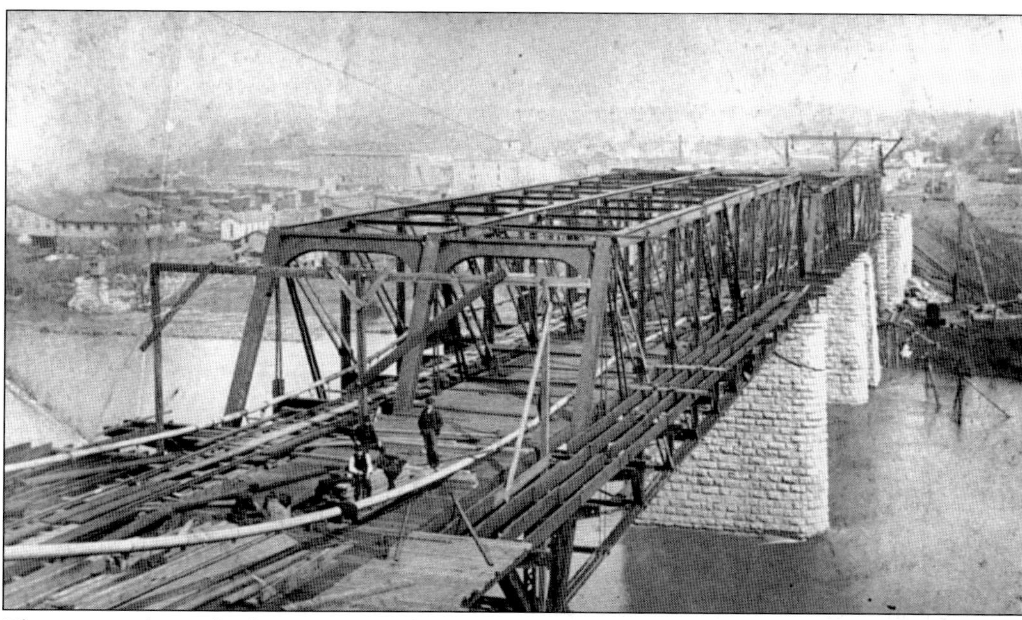

The new steel truss bridge nears completion on its new stone piers across the Cumberland River in 1886. The bridge remained in use until it was replaced in 1965.

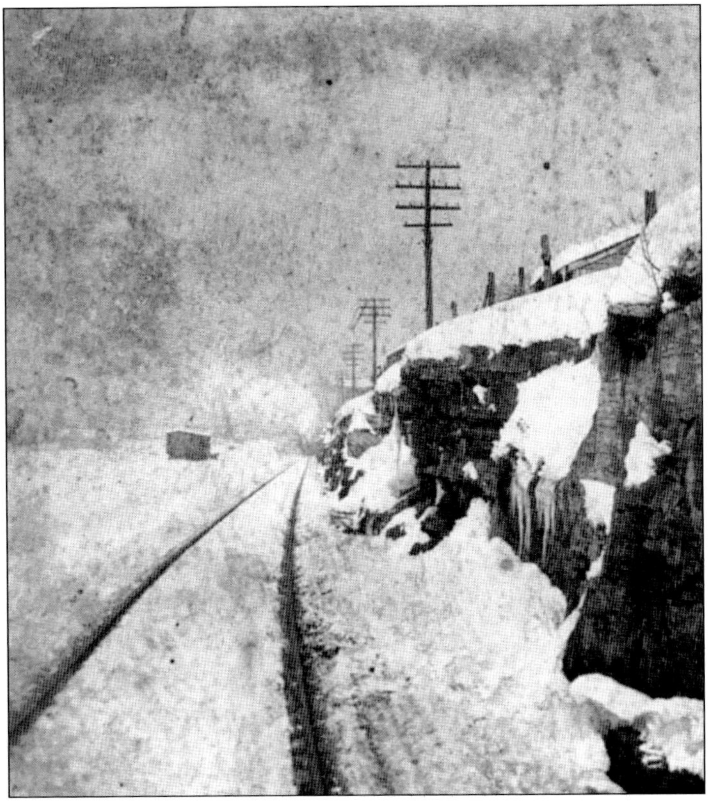

A heavy snow fell in the winter of 1884–1885. Here is a view along the Nashville, Chattanooga & St. Louis Railroad tracks near Broad.

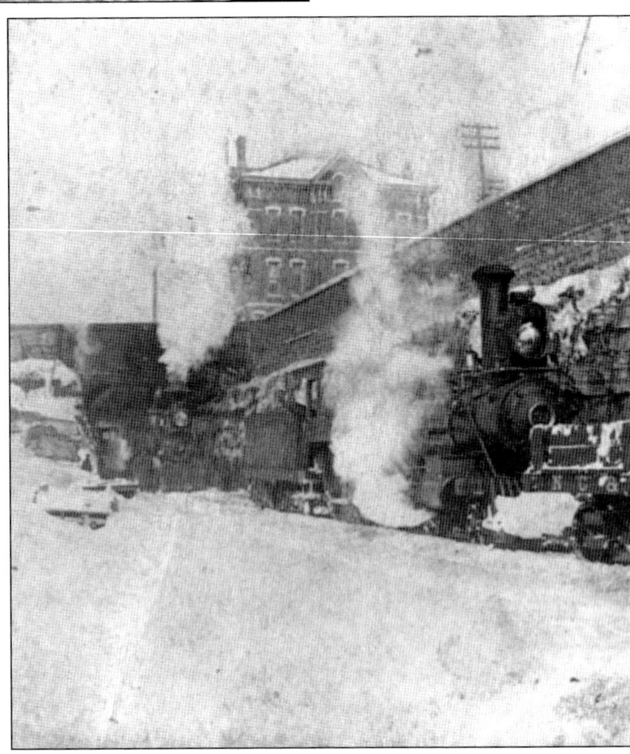

Looking up through steam and snow at the Nashville, Chattanooga & St. Louis Railroad office on Broad, we see more of the heavy snowfall of 1884–1885.

An engine has just arrived with its cowcatcher covered in snow by the blizzard of 1884–1885.

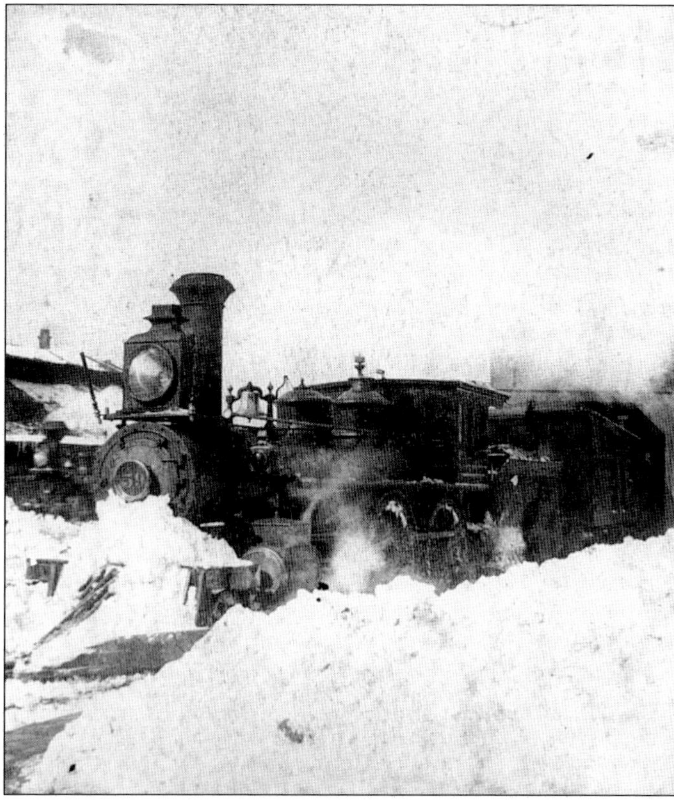

The Gilchrist Hotel, at Walnut (Tenth) and Church Streets, is seen here in the blizzard of 1884–1885.

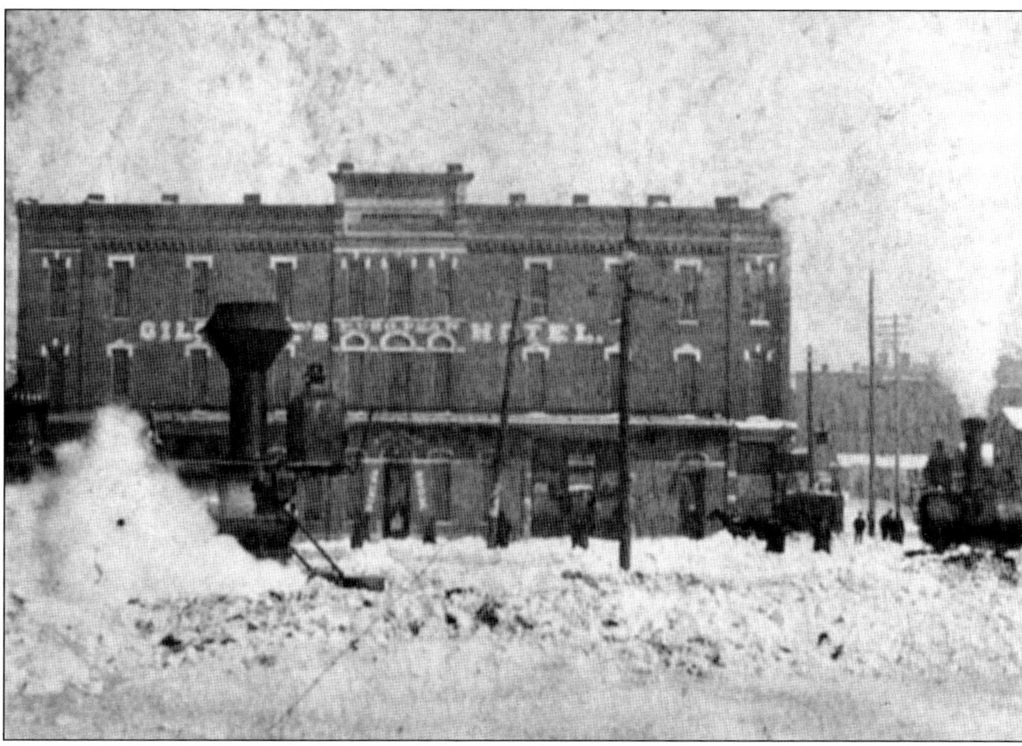

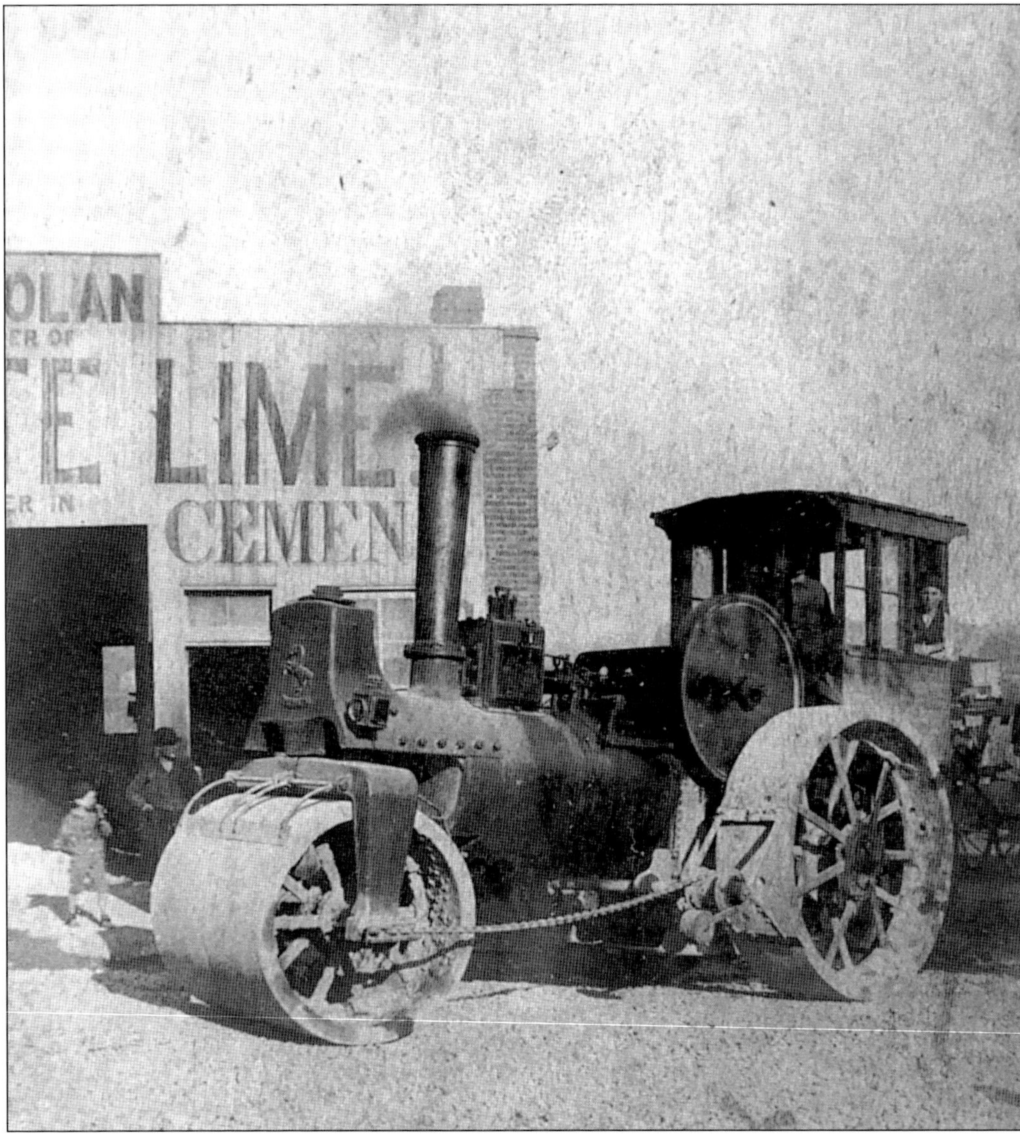

In 1883 Nashville purchased a new steamroller to roll crushed stone on the streets of the city. Here, a man and boy inspect the new machine, used to improve the streets of the city.

Three

A New South City

The parapet above the cornice to the west portico is gone in this photograph of the Davidson County Courthouse. Also, the trees are more mature than in the next image. So, it is a few years later than the second view. Built in 1857 by Francis Strickland, William Strickland's son, the county courthouse was reminiscent of the Tennessee State Capitol, upon which both Stricklands had worked. A third floor, marring the structure, was added in 1910. The building was demolished in 1937 for the present courthouse.

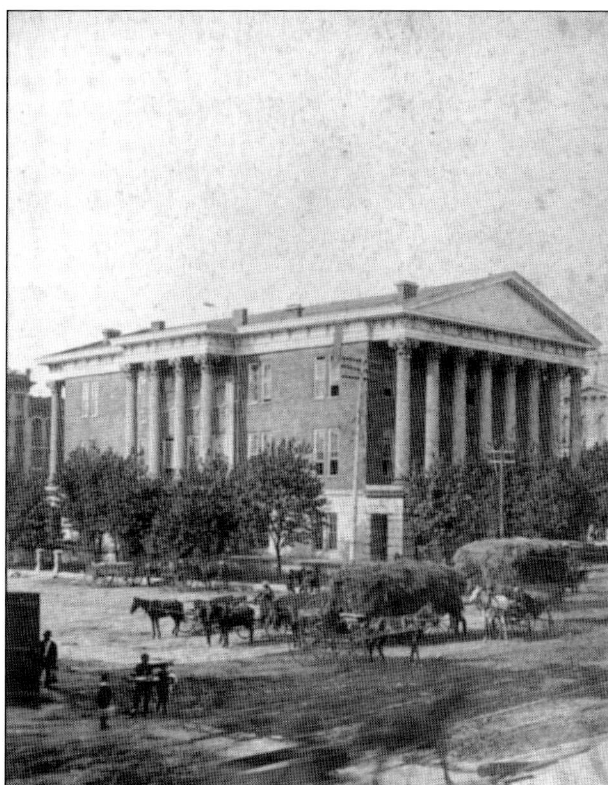

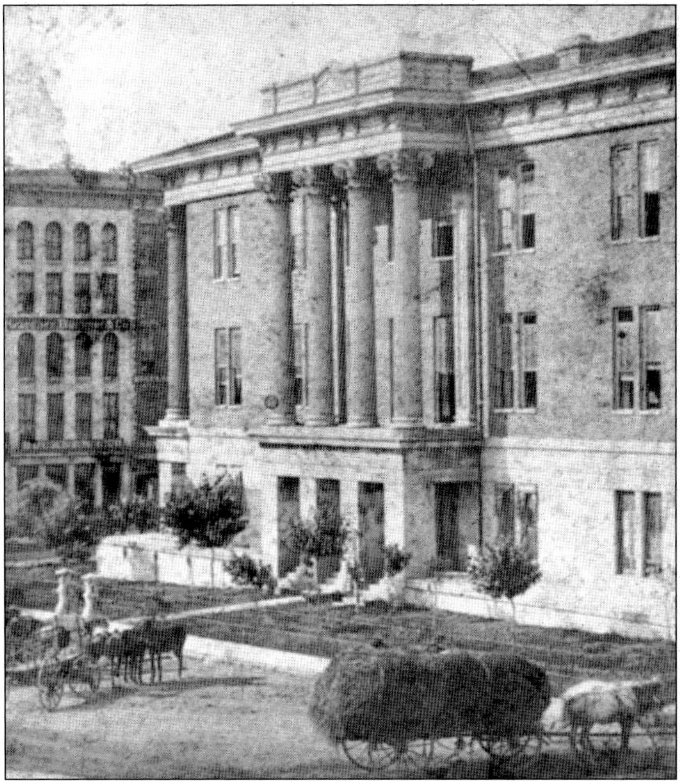

Here, the original parapet is still in place. Also the trees are younger, so this is an earlier view of the courthouse. Market Street (Second) ran through the Square and is seen here to the left, with hay wagons parked along it. On the other side of Market Street was the City Hall and Market, where farmers brought their produce to sell.

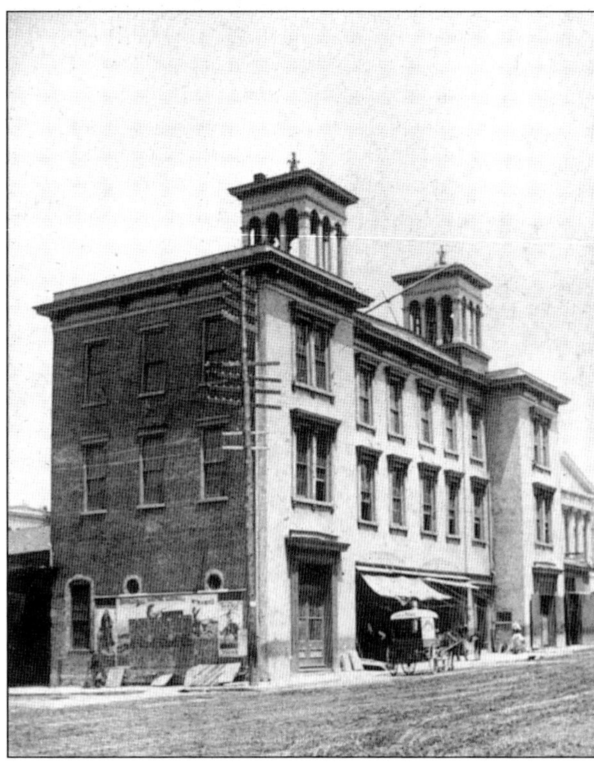

In 1884 the City Hall and Market stood on the west side of the Public Square. This view is from the southwest corner of the building, looking east toward the Southern Methodist Publishing House and the Cumberland River. The south portico to the Davidson County Courthouse is visible to the right of the City Hall and Market. On the end of the building, closest to the viewer, is a large poster advertising Buffalo Bill Cody's Wild West Show, which played in Nashville several times. He performed here on November 25–26, 1884.

The Davidson County Jail was erected at 31 North Front Street, along the river bank, in late 1884. It stood between Clark Street and Union Alley.

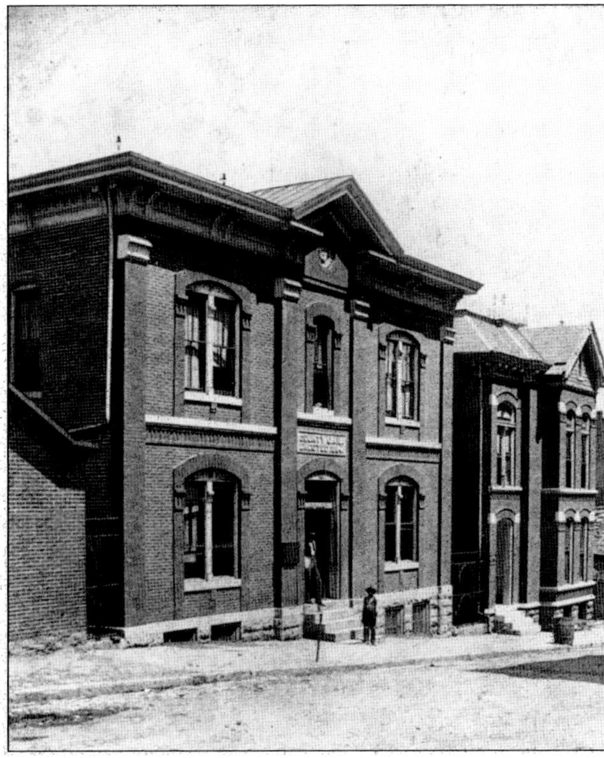

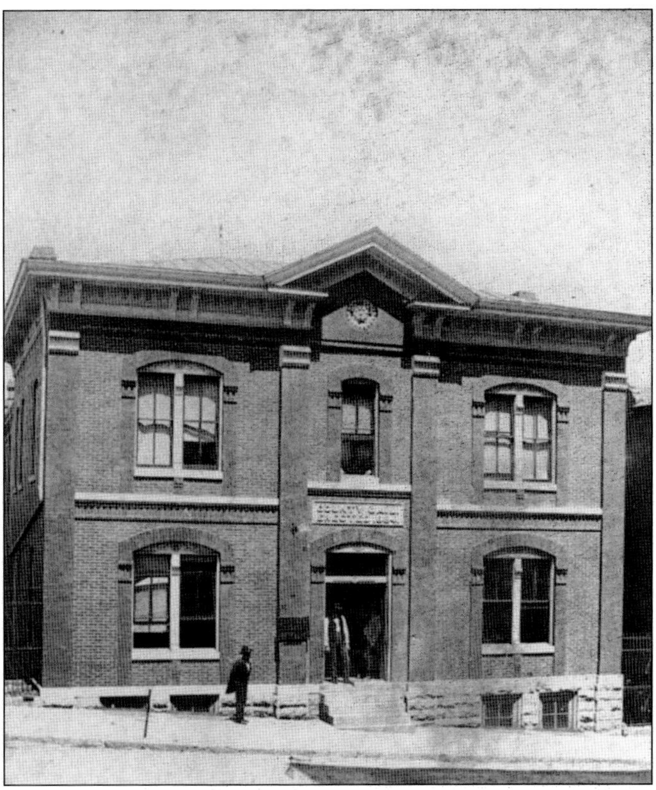

Also located in the Davidson County Jail was the County Health Office. Such diseases as cholera, smallpox, malaria, and typhus made the area unhealthy. As knowledge improved as to the causes of these diseases, the new County Health Office could work to eliminate them. A city water works had opened in 1880.

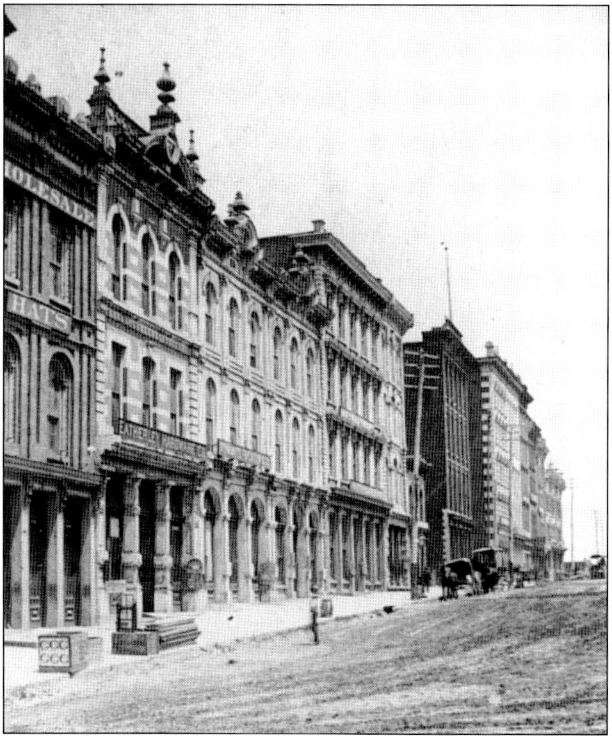

The Public Square was the heart of Nashville throughout most of the city's history. Here was the seat of local government, the farmer's market, and the retail stores the citizens needed. The northwest corner is seen here, looking toward the river. The Hicks Building, built in 1857 by architect Harvey Akeroyd, stands to the extreme left, shorn of its fourth floor and cornice. It was 89 feet wide. The Morgan Building, the fifth building from the left, was the dry goods store of merchant/industrialist Samuel Dold Morgan. Spanning 42.4 feet, it was four stories high. It was demolished in July 1974, and the remainder of the block was pulled down shortly thereafter.

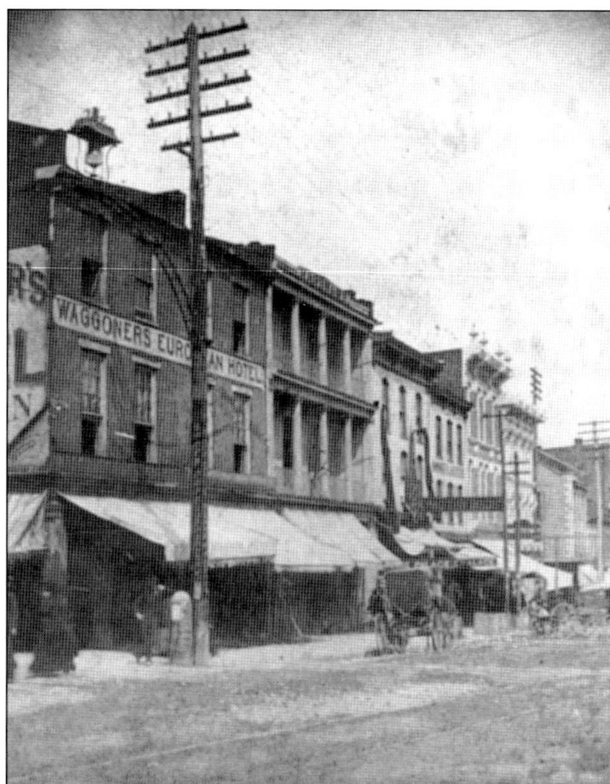

The western side of the Public Square is shown here. Deaderick Street is to the left, and the buildings face College Street (Third). Waggoner's European Hotel and restaurant are in the building to the left, at 26 Public Square. A hardware store, the J.M. Hamilton & Co., is next door at 23 Public Square. Beside it stands the Timothy Brothers dry goods store at 11–14 Public Square.

Looking up Deaderick Street from the Public Square, one can see that the street only ran for two blocks from College (Third) to Summer (Fifth). Carl Giers's old studio is the corner building to the left. He opened up there in 1855. Note the skylight in the roof, which enabled Carl to shoot in his studio. Jacob Herstein, photographer, was working there in 1884. He lived in Edgefield, at 303 Main Street. Charles Breyer operated a barbershop and Turkish bath at 124–126 Deaderick Street. You can see his barber pole on the sidewalk, on the left side of the street. He lived at 322 North Market Street, around from the Public Square.

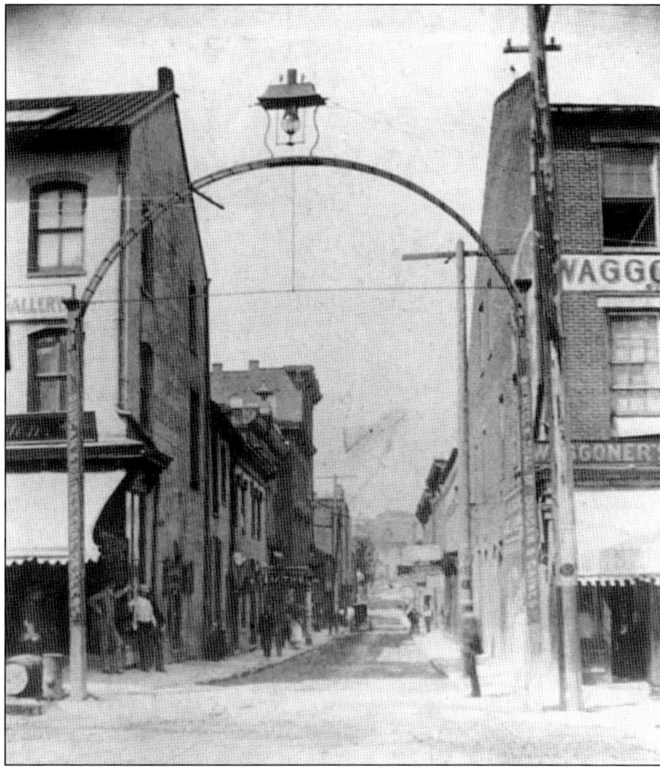

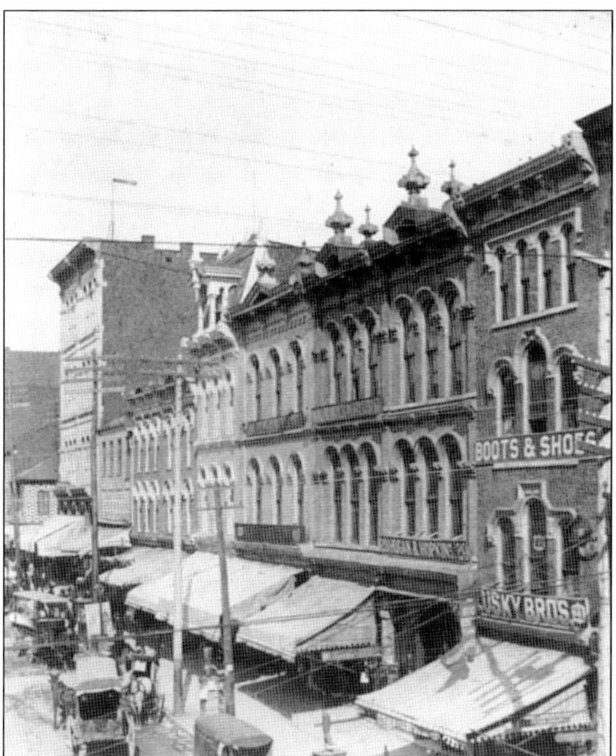

The south side of the Public Square is seen here. The tallest building is the Ensley Building to the extreme left. Market Street (Second) meets the Public Square between the four-story building and the checkerboard-patterned brick building. The Lusky Brothers, sellers of boots and shoes, operated at 21 Public Square in 1883. Louis Lusky boarded at North Summer near Cedar. Isaac Lusky boarded at 91 Broad. Hogan & Hopkins was to the left, at 20 Public Square. They also sold boots and shoes. J.W. Lawless & Co., sellers of boots and shoes, was at 19 Public Square, and Oliver & Co., also merchants of boots and shoes, was at 16 Public Square.

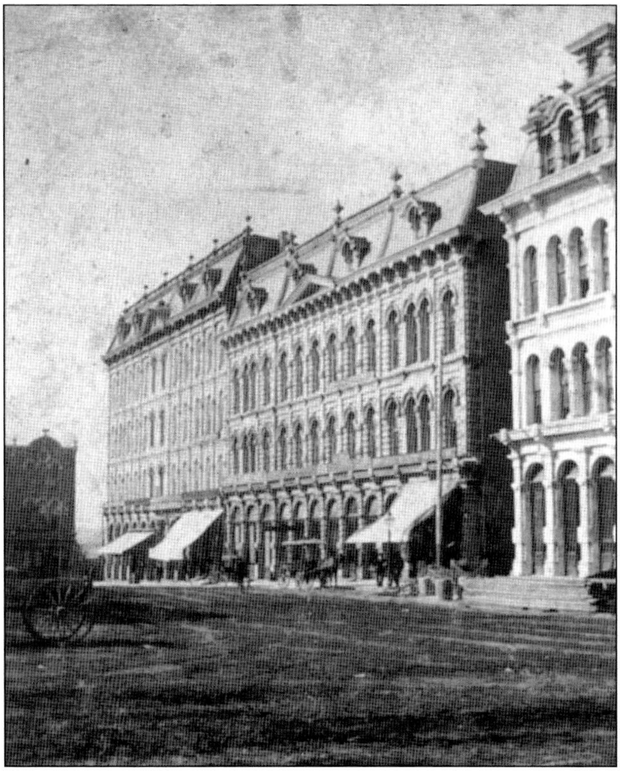

Perhaps the grandest compliment of buildings on the Public Square was along the east side, near the river bluff. The Second Empire–style buildings housed the Southern Methodist Publishing House in the four-story building to the far left, designed by John L. Smith. P.J. Williamson's City Hotel Block building is the handsome structure in the center. Sadly, they were demolished in 1974.

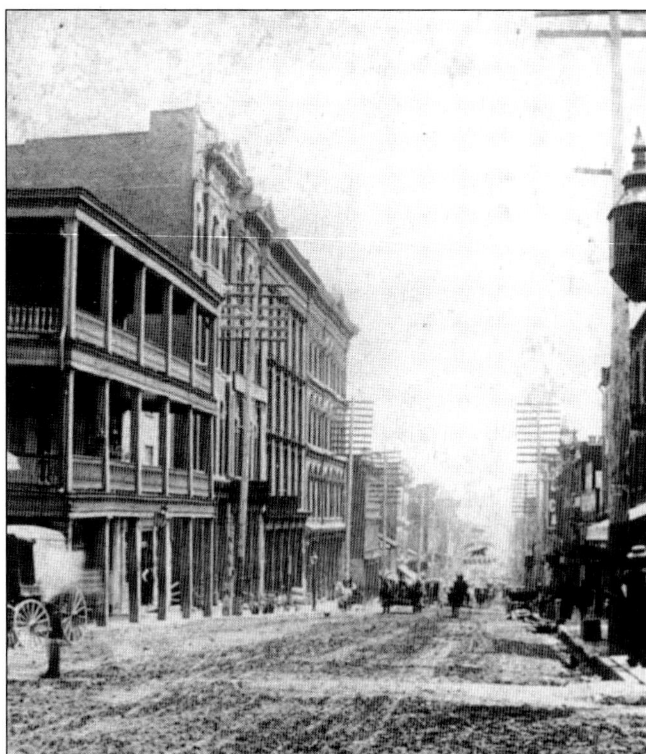

Located at 3 North Market Street, a Corbett Brothers Harness sign hangs across Market Street (Second) in this view. The old Watson House Hotel is the galleried, three-story structure to the left. Three doors down from it at 4 North Market Street is the old Morris and Stratton wholesale grocers building. Of all of these structures pictured here, only the facade of the Morris and Stratton business remains. The French Building at Clark and Market, also visible, was burned down by an arsonist in October 1985. The wagon to the left is parked beside Union Alley.

D. Weil & Co., located at the northwest corner of Market and Broad Streets, is largely intact today. The parapet, bay windows, and last two windows toward the Market Street end of the building are now gone. In 1934 the west side of Market Street was widened for truck traffic between Broad and Commerce Streets. All of the Victorian facades were removed on that side of the street. Weil & Co., 71–79 Broad Street, were wholesale dry goods, boot, and shoes merchants.

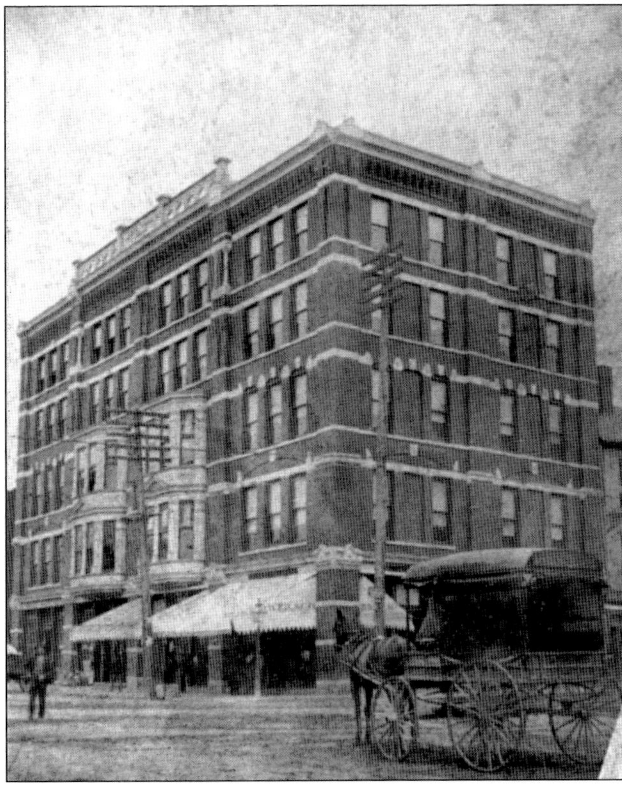

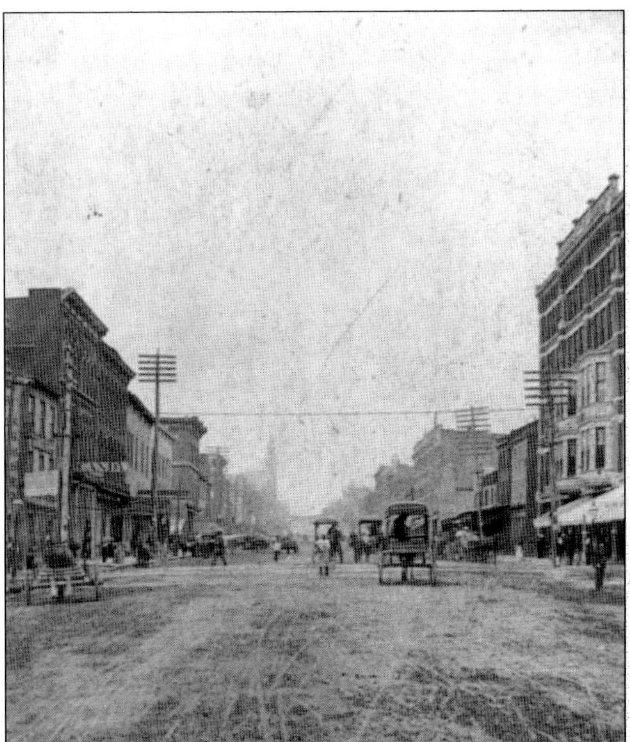

This is a view, looking west, up Broad from Market in 1884. Weil & Co. is to the right, and the tower on the U.S. Customs House is visible above the flood plain, atop the hill. Notice the electrical lines and the unpaved streets.

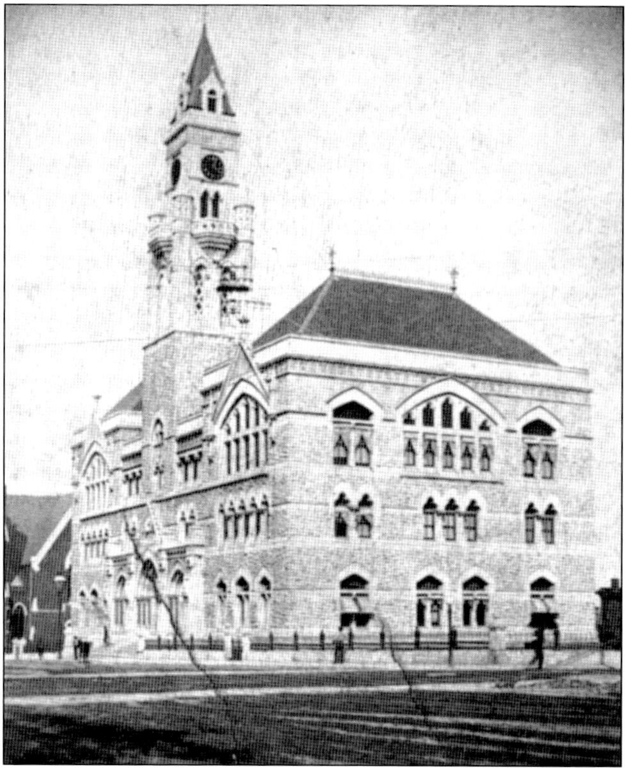

The cornerstone to the U.S. Customs House was laid in 1877 by President Rutherford B. Hayes. He had won a reversal of Southern Electoral College votes, and he won the presidency by pledging to the South that he would resume Federal construction in the region, which had ended in 1861. He also pledged to end Reconstruction.

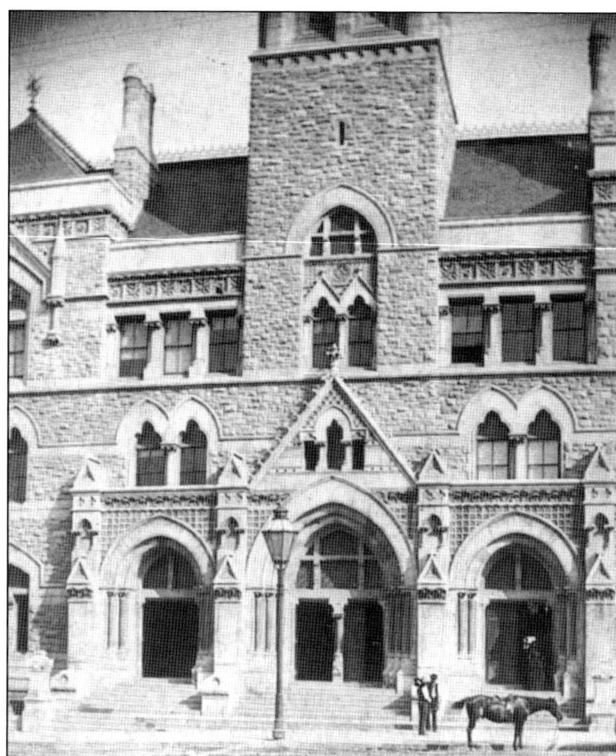

This is the main entrance to the U.S. Customs House in Nashville. The building's main block was completed in 1882. Additions were added to the rear (1902–1909) and sides (1916–1919) in the same style. The architect of the original portion was William Appleton Potter, supervising architect of the U.S. Treasury.

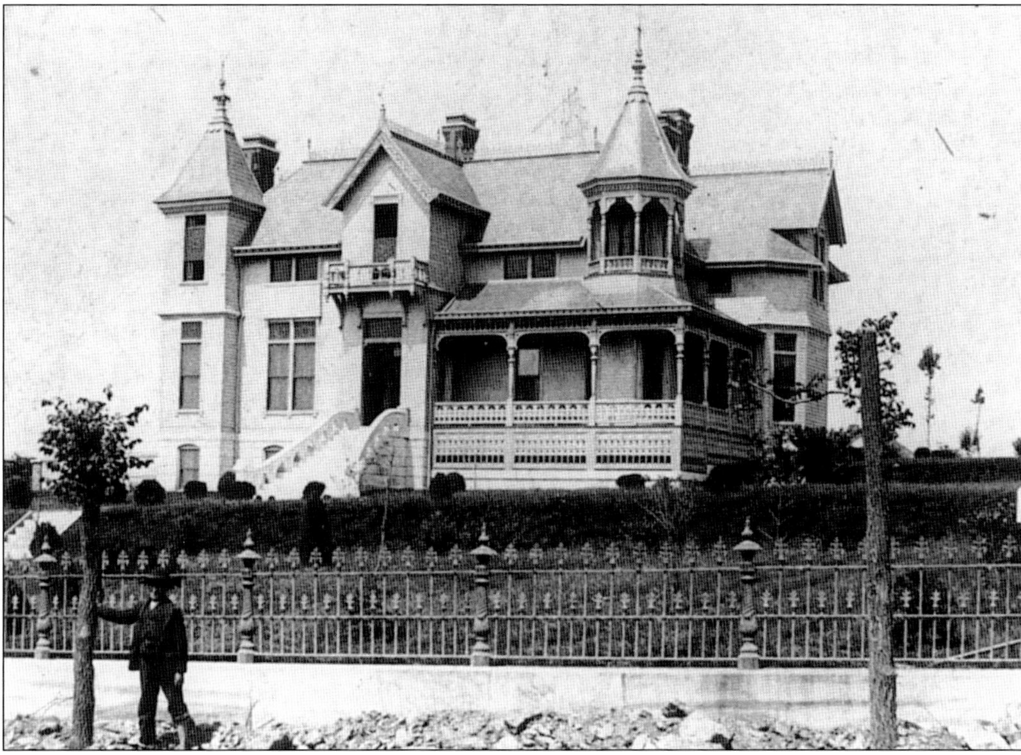

Riverboat Captain Thomas Green Ryman moved into this impressive home in 1885. Facing Highland Street, it was located at South Market and Highland, in South Nashville, on College Hill. Captain Ryman was the president and superintendent of the Nashville and Cairo Packet Co. He was the largest riverboat operator on the Cumberland River. Notice the terraced yard and the sidewalk construction.

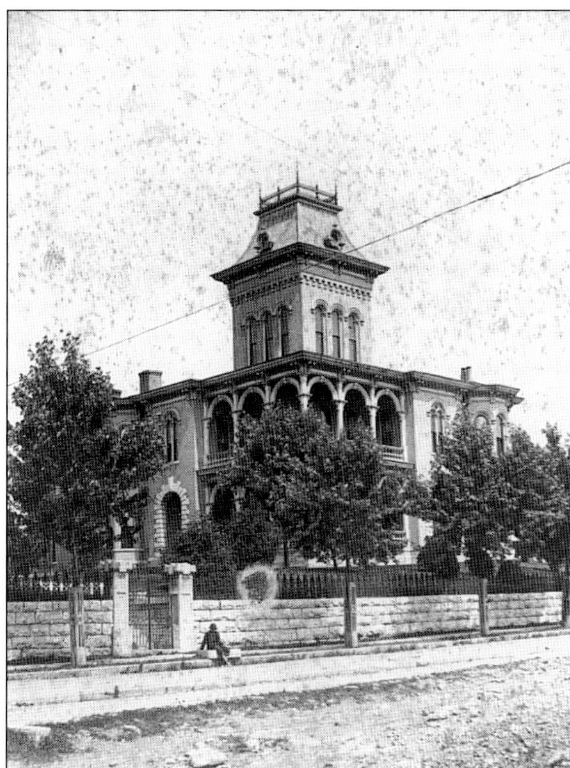

The residence of William Morrow was next door to Captain Ryman's home. Facing Peabody, it was downhill toward Broad, at the corner of South Market and Peabody. Cherry, Morrow & Co. ran the Tennessee Wagon Works and were lessees of the work crews at the Tennessee State Penitentiary. Cornell, Morrow & Co. were wholesale dry goods and boot and shoe merchants at 68 South Market Street.

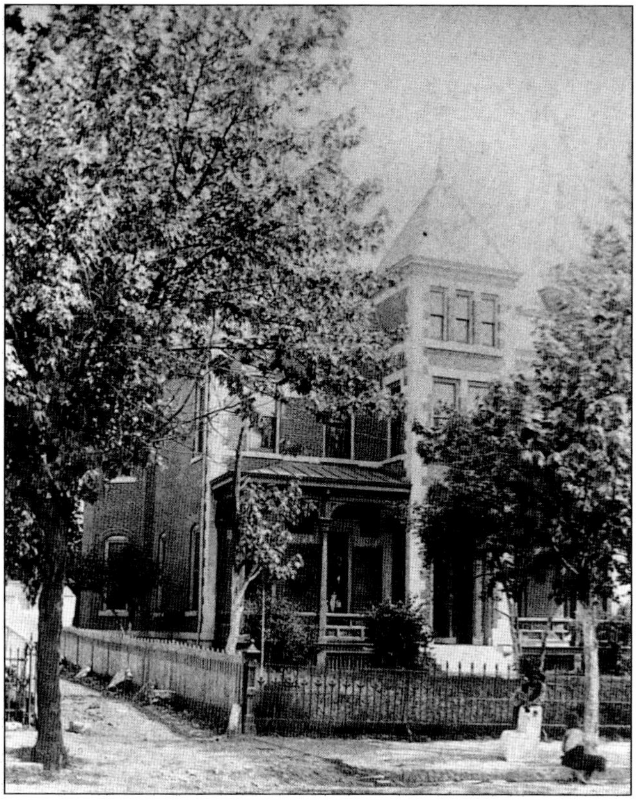

J.W. Thomas was in business with his son, W.D., as J.W. Thomas & Son. They ran the Nashville spice, coffee, and tea mills at 35 South Market Street and lived at 7 Lindsley Avenue on College Hill near the Normal School. The son was a boarder at his father's home. Note the mounting block that the two African-American boys are beside in front of the house. These were used to mount and dismount a riding horse or carriage.

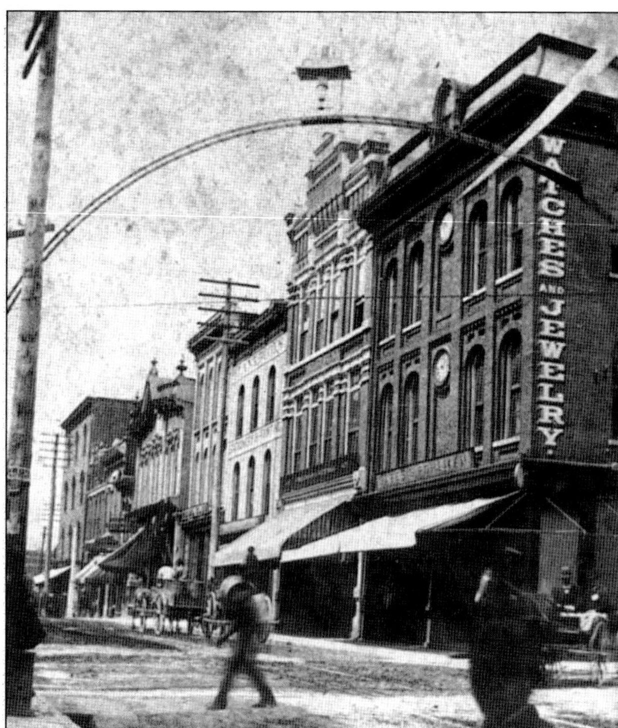

This is a view of College Street (Third) north from Union. The W.T. Gates & W.H. Pohlman Jewelers, located at 45 North College, sold watches and jewelry. A pair of clocks are mounted to the front of the building. Freeman & Keesee & Decorators worked from 47 North College in 1885. They specialized in wallpaper, pictures, and frames. Marshall & Bruce were at 49 North College and sold books and stationery. The City Hall and Market on the Public Square are one block away.

This photograph captures a view of the east side of College Street South (Third) from Union. On the corner stands the First National Bank. N. Baxter was president, and J.P. Williams was cashier. The third building is the Fourth National Bank, located at 35 North College. S.J. Keith was president, and W.M. McCarthy was cashier. Arrington, Farrer & Weakley Real Estate was at 35 1/2 North College. Hecla Coal & Mining Co. was located at 34 North College, and the Barnes & Co. auction and commission agents were at 33 North College.

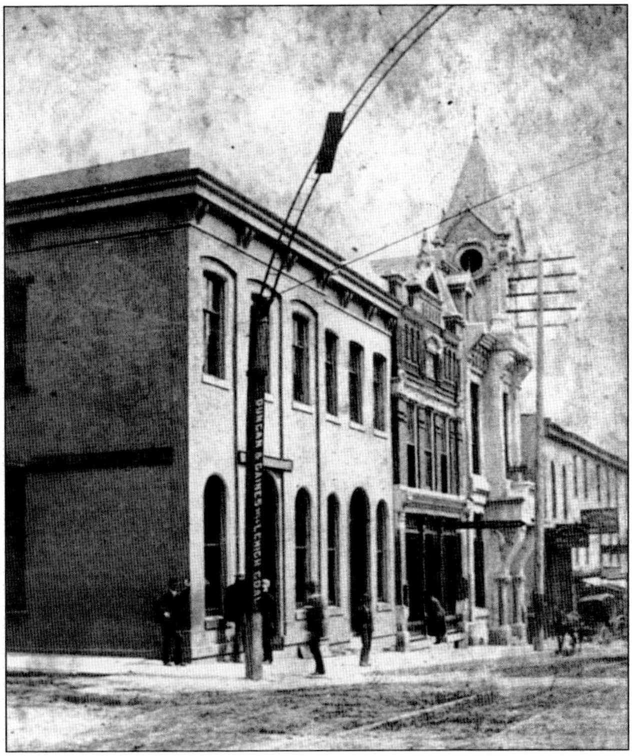

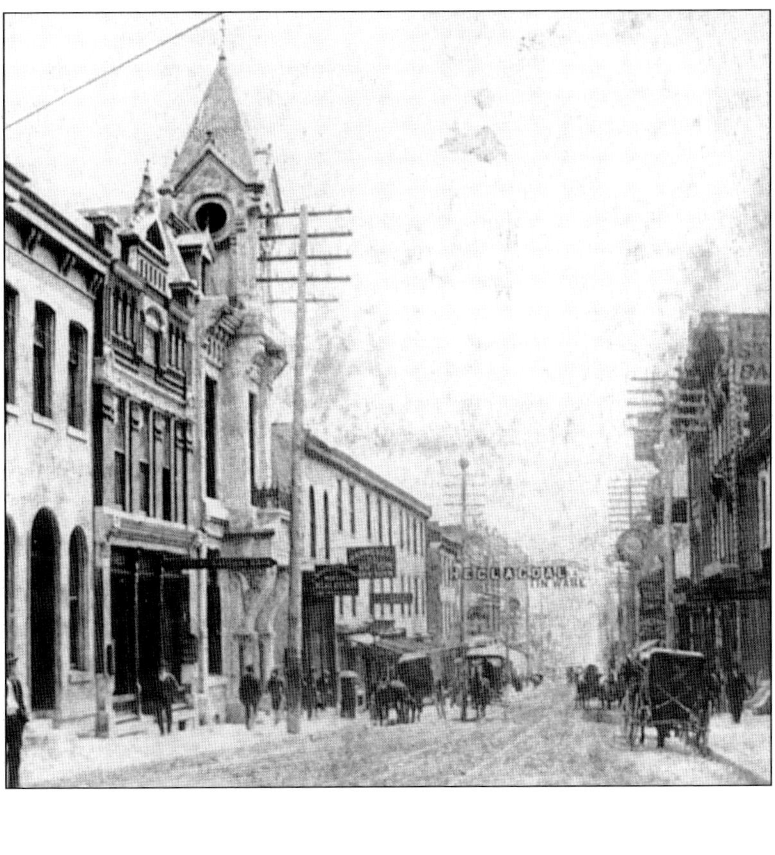

This is another view of College Street (Third), looking south toward Union. The Fourth National Bank is the building with the tower. Hecla Coal has a banner hanging across the street.

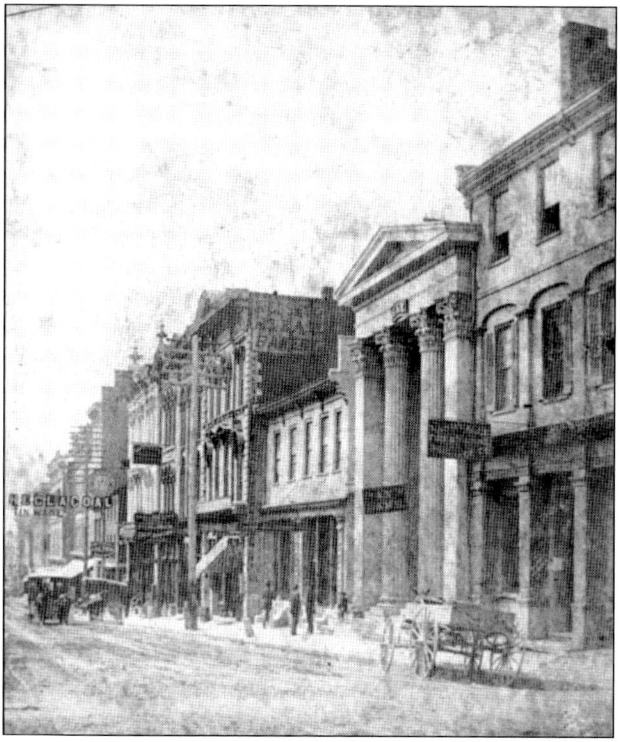

This view is of College Street (Third) looking south from Union, along the west side. Nashville Fire & Marine Insurance Co. is at 40 North College. Sax's Nashville Savings Bank is at 38 North College, and Wessel Bread Bakery is located at 32 North College.

The Cole Building at Cherry (Fourth) and Union, the northwest corner, was a hive of business activity. The city directory lists the following tenants: Dismukes & Guild, architects; Smith & Gible, architects; Calvert Bros., artists; H.L. Hillyer, artist. The following were attorneys with offices there: E. Baxter, J. Baxter, C.W. Beale, J.C. Bradford, M.T. Bryan, R.L. Campbell, Champion & Head, Covington & Atchison, B.F. DeBow, J.W. Gaines Jr., J.C. & J.M. Gaut, H.H. Harrison, J.W. Horton Jr., G.C. Hunt, P. Kinnaird, J. Lellyett, N.D. Malone, W.A. Milliken, E.T. Morris, J.L. Nolen, W.M. Spencer, E.R. Thurman, James Trimble, and S. Watson. These are also listed: N.W. Taylor, auctioneer; the American National Bank, John Kirkman, president, in the corner of the building; the Safe Deposit, Trust & Banking Co.; H.C. Gardner, civil engineer; Myer & Jackson, retail dry goods, notions and white goods; R.S. Ross, electrician (one of three in the whole city); the Nashville Electric Time Co.; Nashville Board of Underwriters, insurance; National Beneficial Association, insurance; Bishop & Webb Merchandise, brokers; Tennessee and Los Cerrillos Gold & Silver Mining Co.; J.W. Gaines, notary public; Steels & Caldwell, real estate; and the Tennessee Co., real estate. Poole's Photographic Art Gallery, whose proprietor was Rodney Poole, was located at 43 North Cherry.

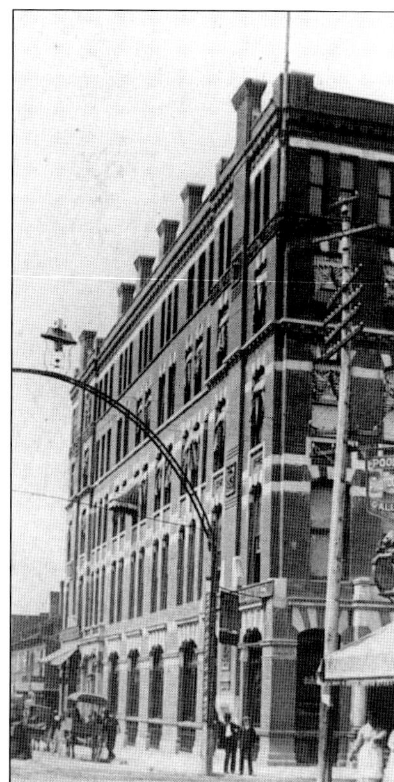

This is a view of Cherry Street (Fourth) looking south from Union. George R. Calhoun, diamonds and watches, is next door to Poole's Photographic Art Gallery on the left. The large building in the center is the McGavock Block. These attorneys were tenants: N. Cohn, H.E. Jones, A.H. Lusk, W.K. McAllister, P.D. Maddin, T. Steger, and A.W. Wills.

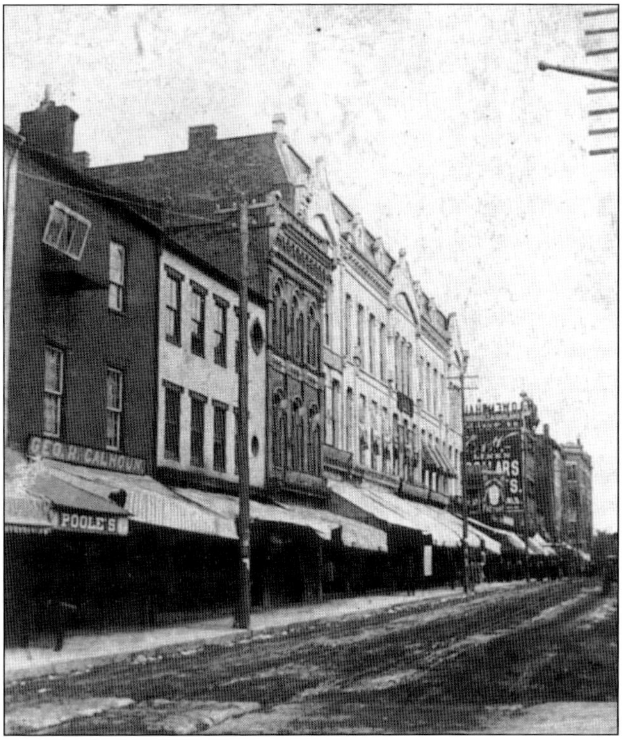

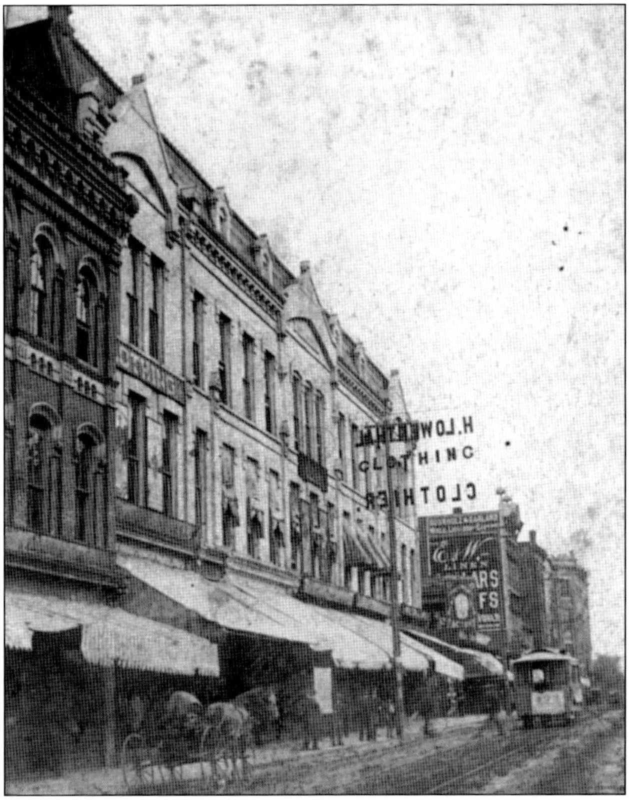

The McGavock Block was located on the east side of Cherry Street, between Church and Union. Herman Lowenthal clothing is located at 33 North Cherry.

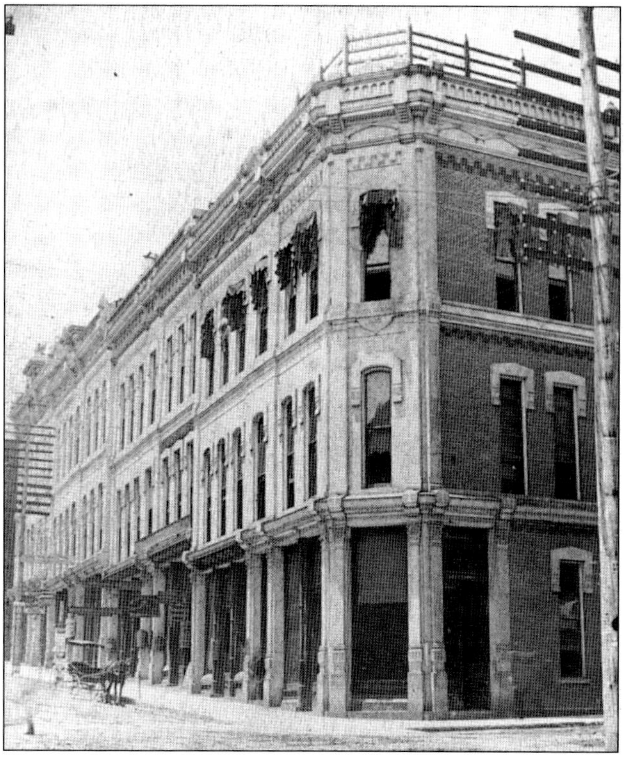

The Noel Block is seen here at the northeast corner of College (Third) and Church. Attorneys, stock and bond agents, a civil engineer, insurance agents, shipping agents, coal, iron and lumber dealers, the Western Union Telegraph Co., the Baltimore & Ohio Telegraph Co., Royal Insurance Co., and Southwestern Publishing House were among its tenants.

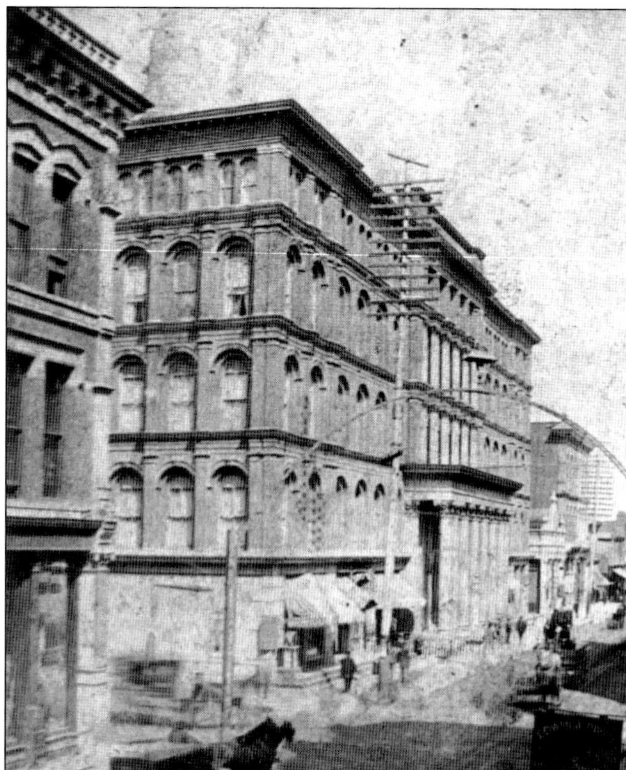

This view shows the Maxwell House Hotel, located on the northwest corner of Cherry and Church Streets, looking north from Church. Begun in 1859, the Civil War interrupted its construction, and the hotel was completed in 1869. It was the city's finest hotel and later burned down in 1961. A locally developed coffee was named for it.

This is a photograph showing Church Street looking west from Cherry (Fourth). The side of the Maxwell House Hotel is to the right. Across an alley from the rear of the hotel is the Nashville Masonic Hall. Carl Giers and Ed Hicks II were Knights Templar together. T.E. Winstead & Co., boots and shoes, is located at 154 Church, and Ready & Fitzwilliam, books and stationery, could be found at 158 Church Street.

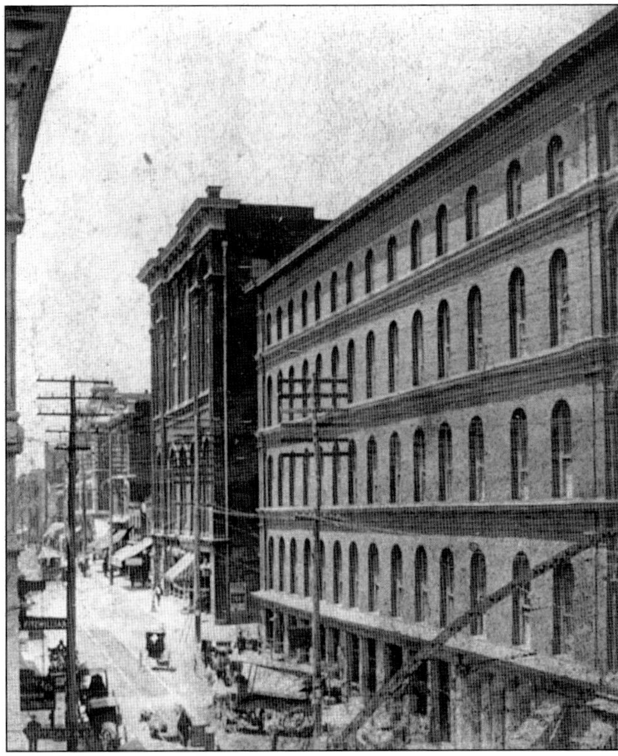

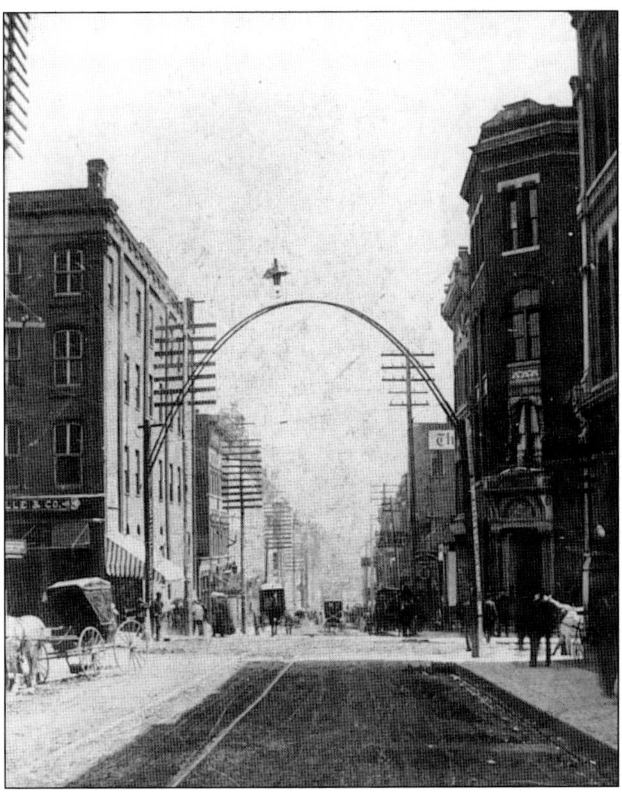

This is a view of Church Street at Cherry (Fourth), looking east. *The American* newspaper office published a daily and a weekly edition here, by the Union & American Publishing Co. The edge to the *The Nashville Banne*r newspaper sign is seen beyond the *American*'s office. The *Banner* also had a daily and a weekly edition, and it was published by the Nashville Banner Publishing Company, whose offices were located at 122 Church Street. The building still stands and is located along Printer's Alley. The alley got its name from the location of these two newspapers, as well as the nearby *Tennessean*.

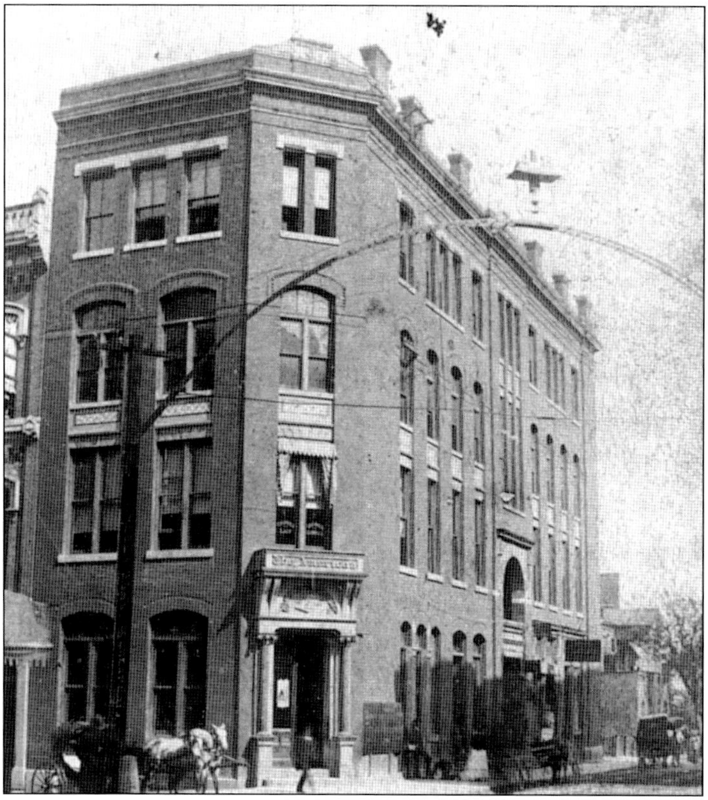

This is a photograph of *The American* newspaper office at Cherry (Fourth) and Church.

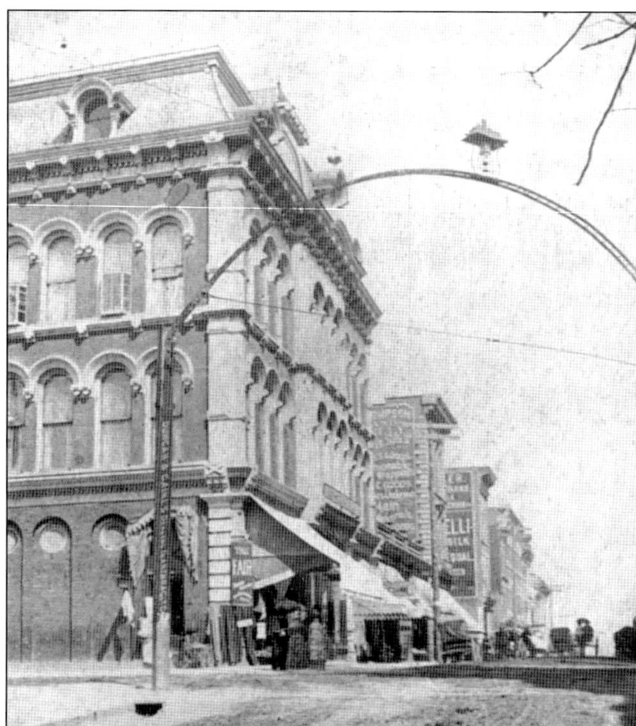

This is a view of the St. Cloud Block at the corner of Summer (Fifth) and Church. The building was named for a hotel that had stood there. Both military governor Andrew Johnson and General George Thomas stayed in the hotel during the Civil War. Thompson & Kelly dry goods store is located at 14 North Summer. Mr. Thompson traveled to Europe each year to buy silver, crystal, and linens for resale.

The Watkins Institute building, at the corner of Church and High (Sixth) Streets, was located on the southwest corner. Samuel Watkins, a brick maker, had bequeathed his estate to found this school for adults. The ground floor was leased out as commercial space. The Watkins Institute continued at this location until 1999, when it was relocated. In 1885 the Tennessee Historical Society would also move into this facility. W.C. Collier, grocer, confectioner, and coffee roaster, is advertising on the corner.

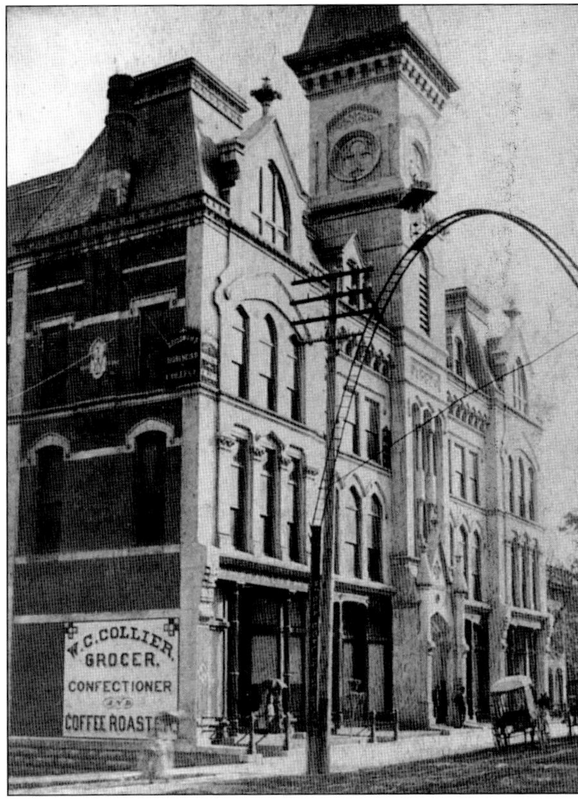

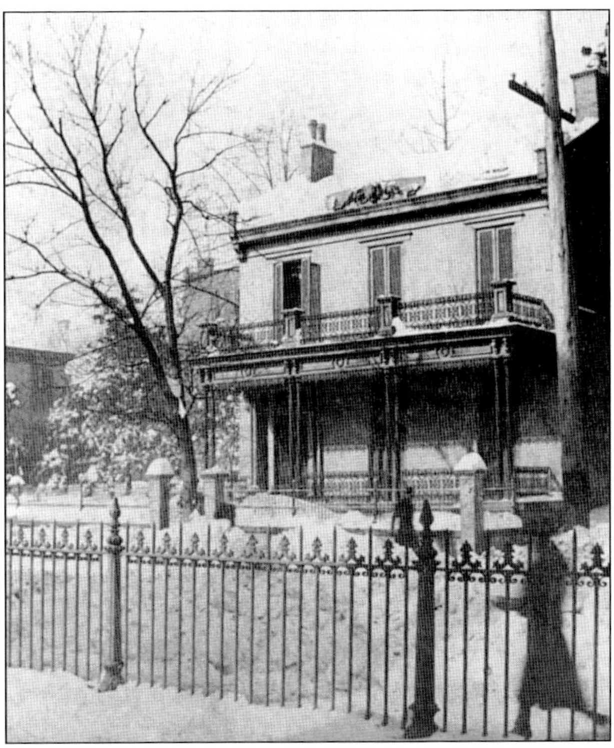

The Great Snow of 1884–1885 left the city blanketed and gave Otto Giers an opportunity for a rare sight. Here, he is showing the residence of J.M. Hill at 267 Church Street, which was located between High (Sixth) and Vine (Seventh) Streets. Built in the 1840s, it had a garden to the east side of it. In the center of the garden were a fountain and a summerhouse. Located where Capitol Boulevard enters Church Street, the summerhouse was octagonal, two stories high, and had an aquarium on the ground floor, surrounded by cast-iron seats. A cast-iron stair led up to the second floor.

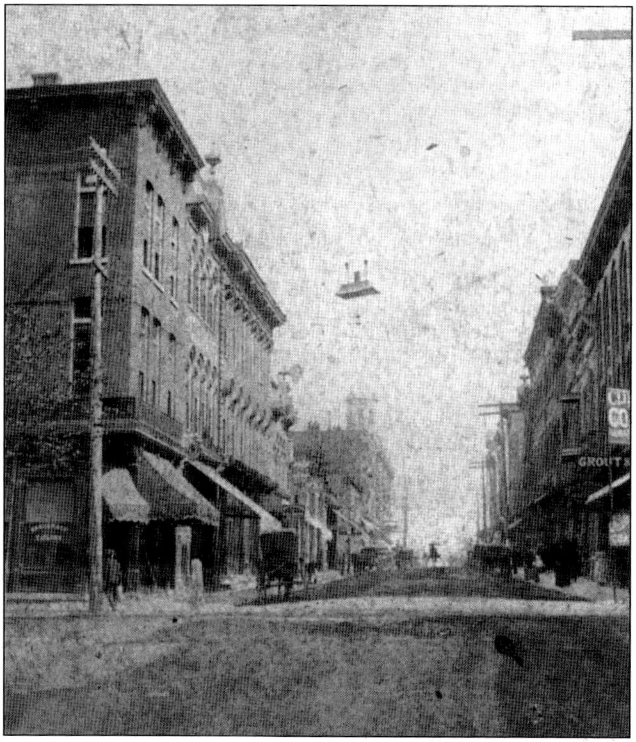

This is a view of Summer Street, looking south from Union. The corner tower on the now former First Presbyterian Church is visible in the center. Osborn & Co., tailors, are on the corner of Summer (Fifth) and Union. Across Summer Street is the Clifton Coal Co.

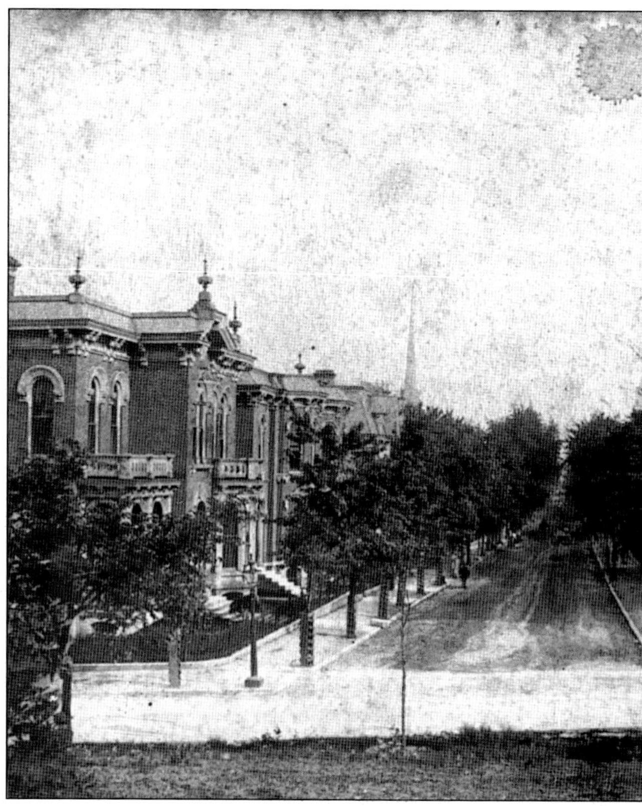

This is a photograph showing High Street (Sixth) looking south from Cedar (Charlotte). The church steeple is that of McKendree Methodist Church. This is the 1879–1905 building occupied by that congregation. Also visible, in the distance to the right, is the tower on the Watkins Institute. The third house back from the corner was the home of Gates P. Thruston.

This is the 81 North High Street residence of General Gates P. Thruston, president of the Tennessee Historical Society, president of State Insurance Co., and father of Tennessee archaeology. His collection can be found at the Tennessee State Museum. Today, the Rachel Jackson State Office Building is located upon the site.

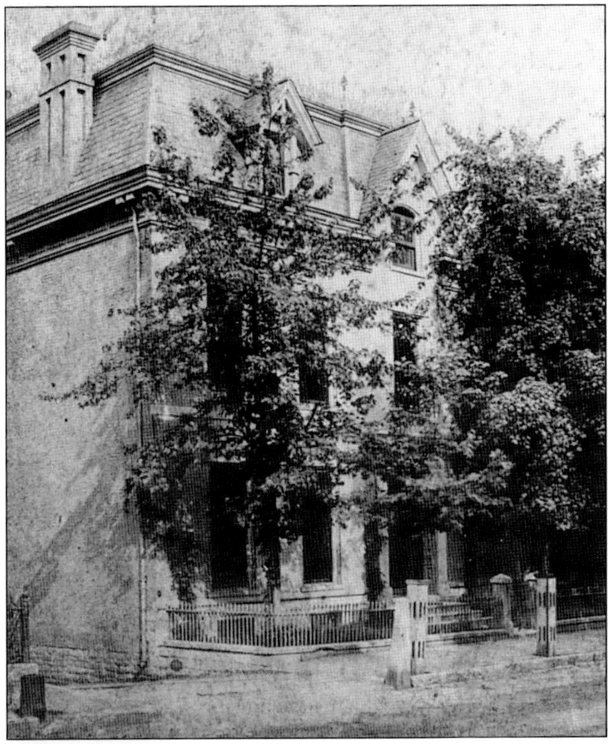

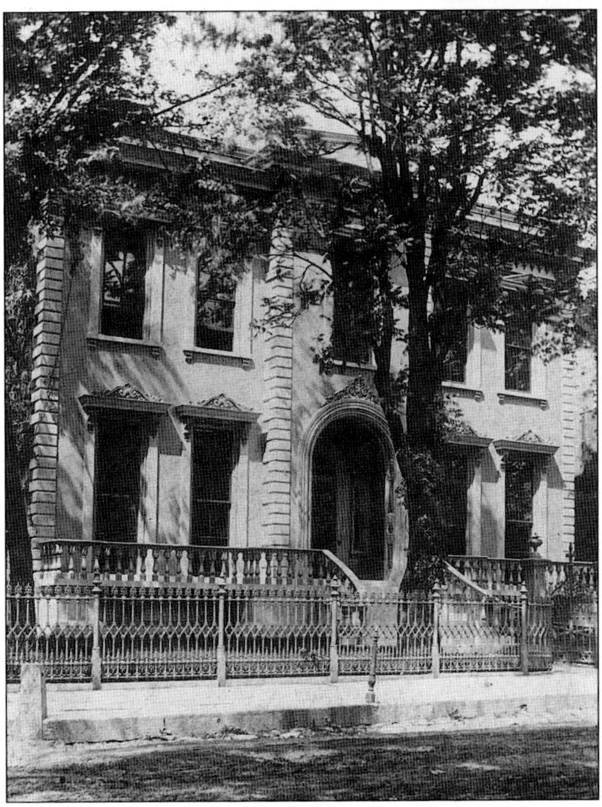

Seen here is the former home of George W. Cunningham, which is located on High Street (Sixth), where the Capitol Boulevard Building now stands. Mr. Cunningham was a Confederate Army major in the Quartermaster's Corps. His wife and family went south when the Civil War broke out. When Nashville was conquered and occupied in 1862, the U.S. Army seized this house. Generals Don Carlos Buell, William Rosecrans, Ulysses S. Grant, William T. Sherman, and George H. Thomas all used it. Rosecrans's chief of staff, James A. Garfield, also worked there. From there, Rosecrans left for the Battle of Stones River/Murfreesboro, and Thomas planned the Battle of Nashville. Following the war, the Cunninghams sold the house, which had been constructed in 1858. It then served as the Hermitage Club until 1934 and was later torn down for a surface parking lot.

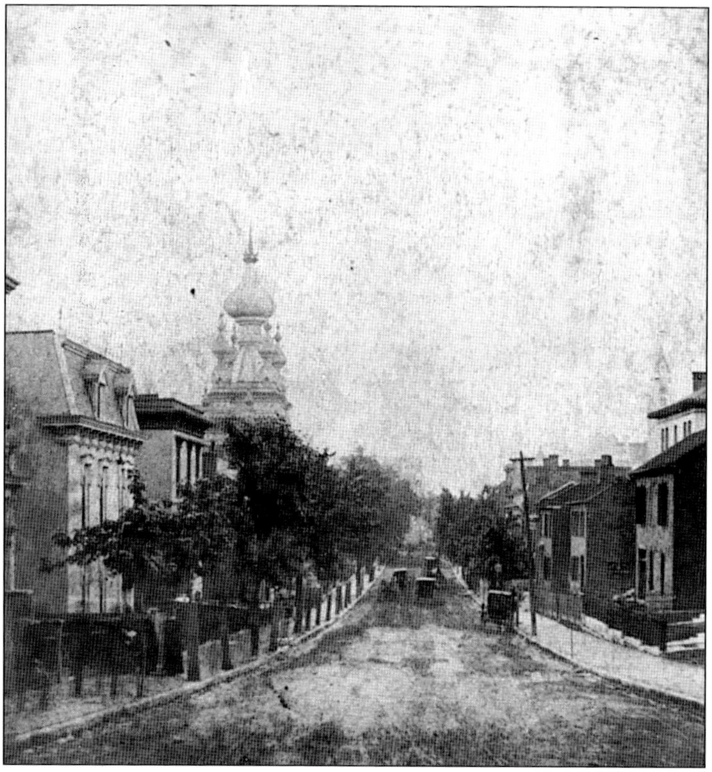

This is an image of Vine Street (Seventh) looking south from Church. The Vine Street Temple, 1876–1955, is the structure with the nine onion domes on its facade. The tower of the U.S. Customs House is seen to the right.

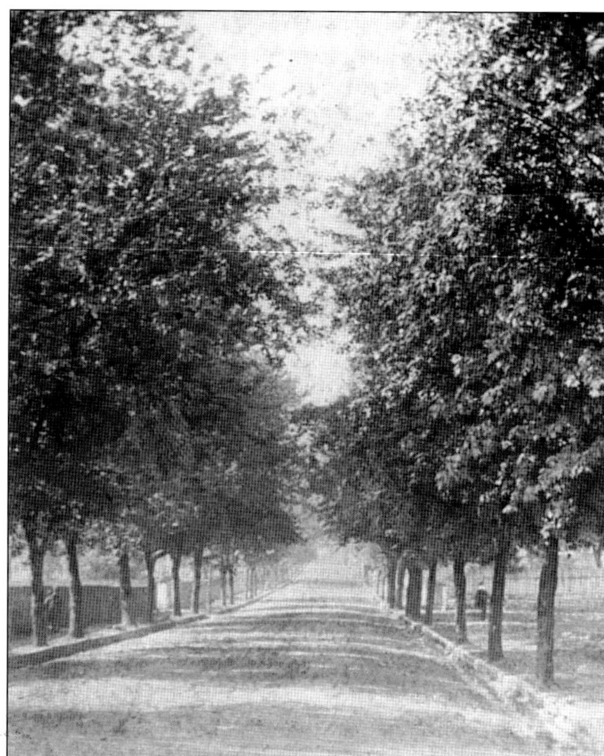

Stevenson Avenue, a residential area at the time, is shown here. It ran roughly where Seventh Avenue is today in South Nashville, from Lee Avenue to St. Cloud Hill.

This photograph shows Spruce Street (Eighth) looking south from Church Street, along the west side of the street. Note the man on the scaffolding on the third floor of the building to the right. The building just beyond is the Ward's Seminary for Young Ladies. Beside it, behind the trees, is the Savage-Zerfoss house, which still stands at Eighth Avenue North, as the Towne House Tea Room and Gas Lite Lounge.

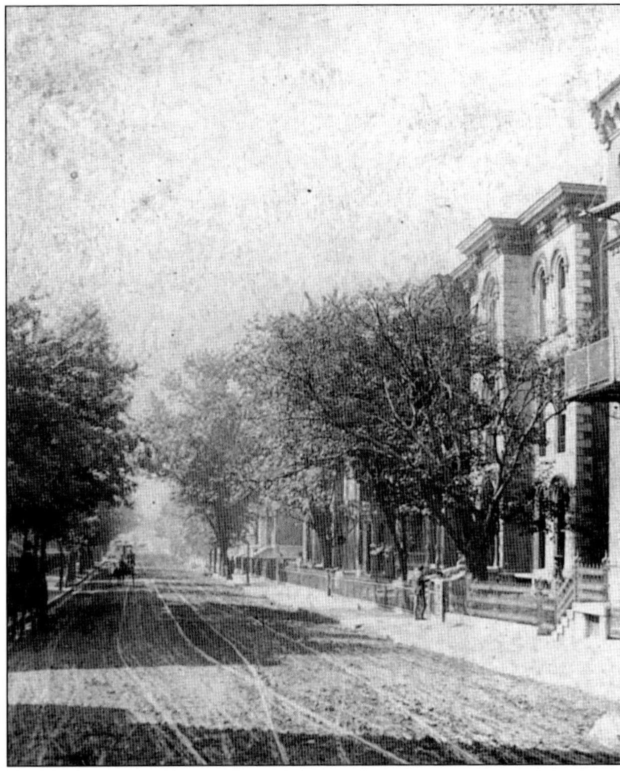

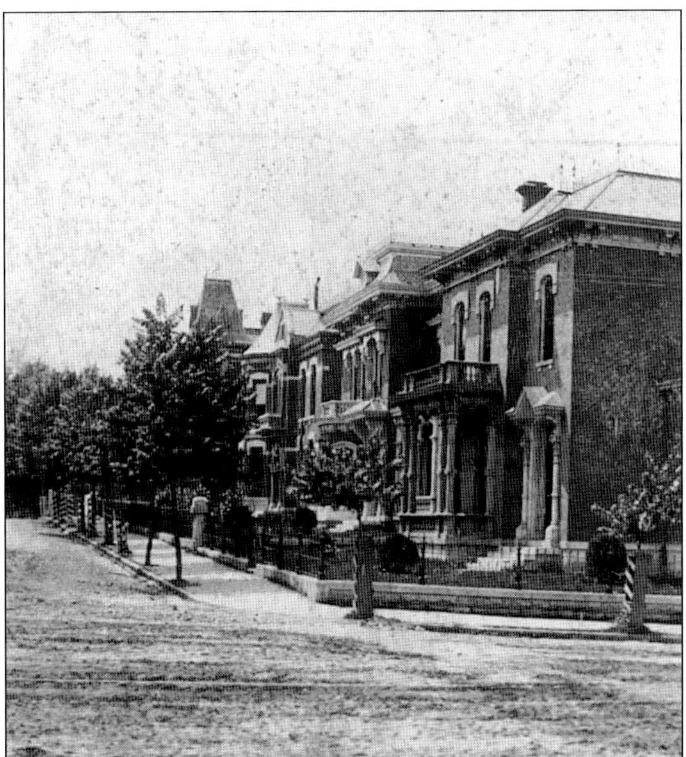

This is Vauxhall Street looking south from Broad, along the west side, where the former post office building, housing the Frist Center, is now.

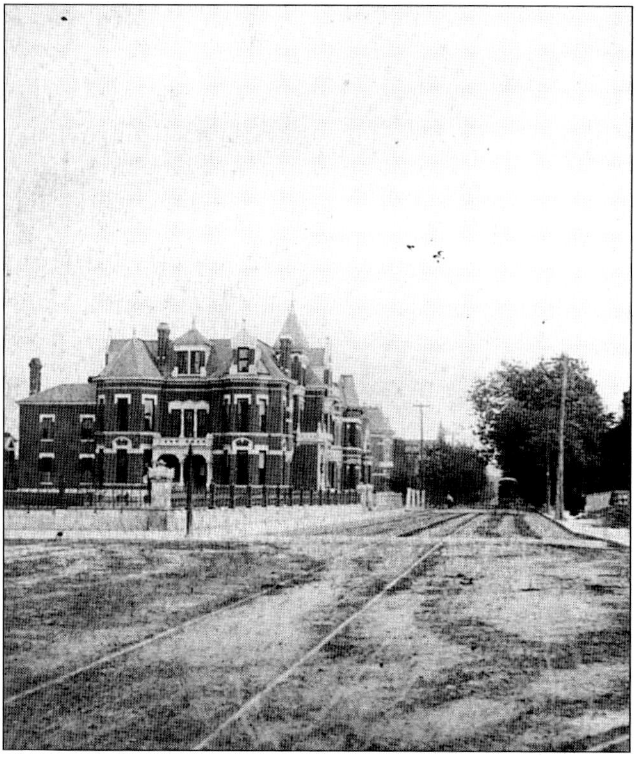

This is Spruce Street (Eighth) looking south from Broad. The stone and cast-iron fence borders the grounds to the U.S. Customs House. Richard Douglas, physician and surgeon, bought the large house seen here in 1889. It was at 10 South Spruce. A tire store is there now.

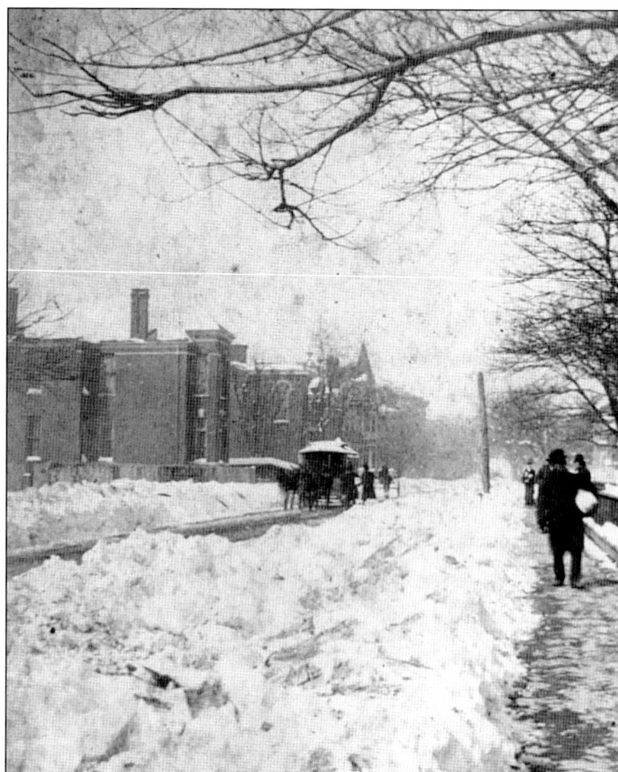

This view shows a scene during the Great Snow of 1884–1885. The location is unknown, but note the mule-drawn streetcar.

This is the Luck Block on Church Street, just east of McKendree Methodist Church. Charlton & Adamson, wholesalers and retailers of confectioneries and fancy groceries, was located here at 218 Church. The sign of A. Setliff, books and stationery, is seen at 212 Church. John Luck sold toys and fancy goods at 216 Church.

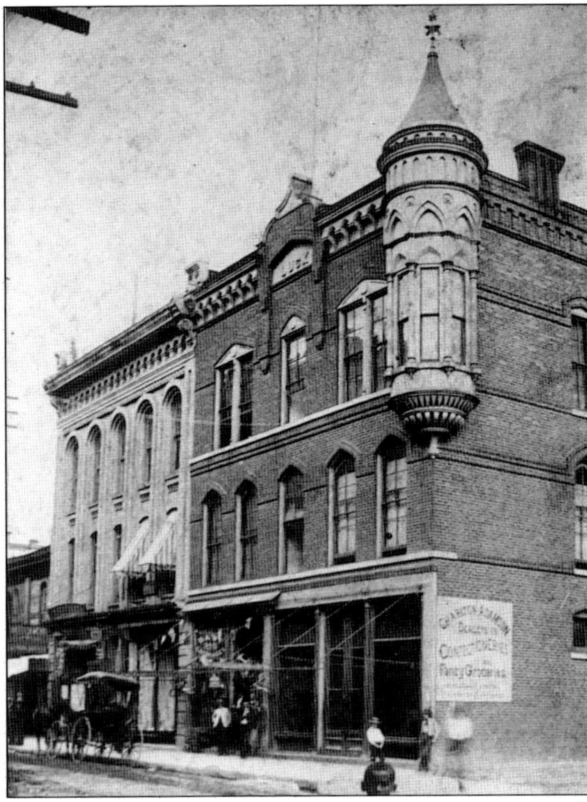

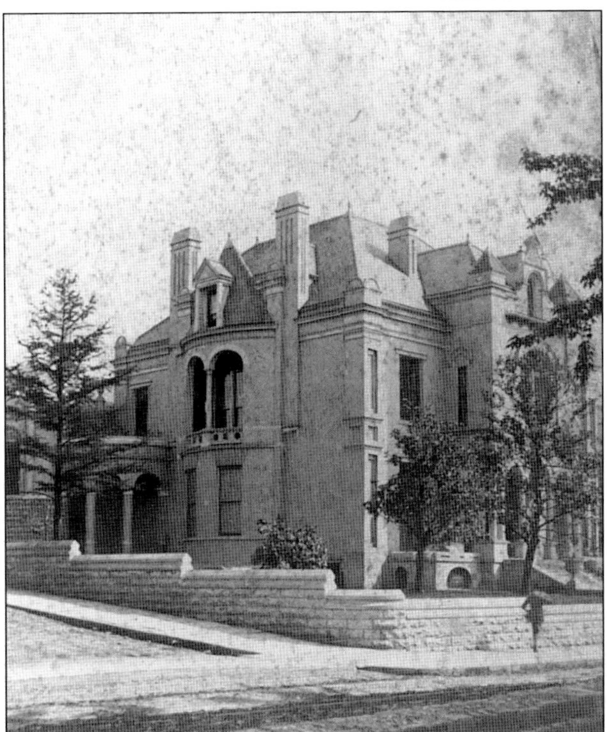

This is a view of the residence of Colonel E.W. Cole, located at the corner of Church Street and Polk Avenue. The street going uphill is Polk and leads to Polk Place, home of Mrs. James K. Polk.

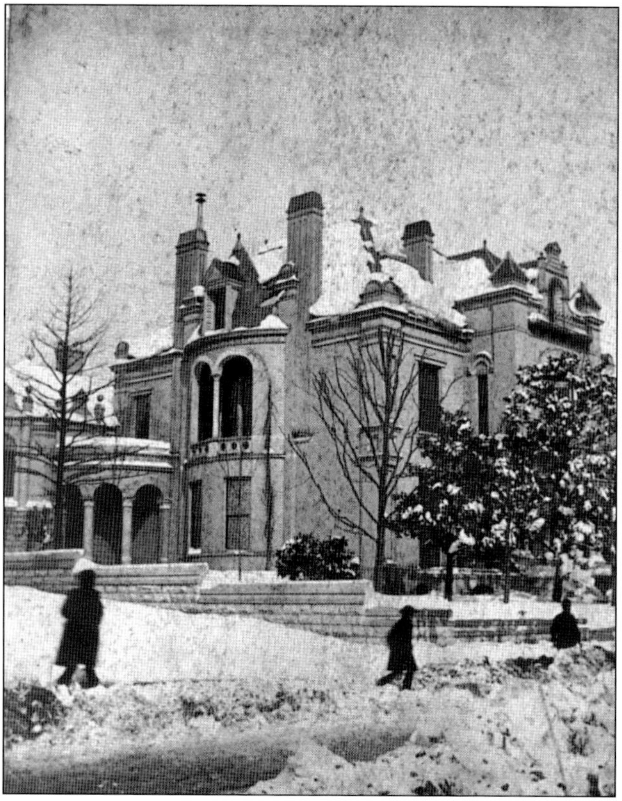

In this photograph of the Great Snow of 1884–1885, the residence of Colonel E.W. Cole, president of the Nashville, Chattanooga & St. Louis Railroad, is visible. When he retired in 1889, he built Colemere, his country estate on Murfreesboro Pike. This house stood at 305 Church, between Vine (Seventh) and Polk, on the north side. Willy Betty Newman's portrait of Mrs. Edmund W. Cole, which shows her wearing a heliotrope dress with a very high lace collar, hangs in Kirkland Hall at Vanderbilt University. The Coles were benefactors of the school.

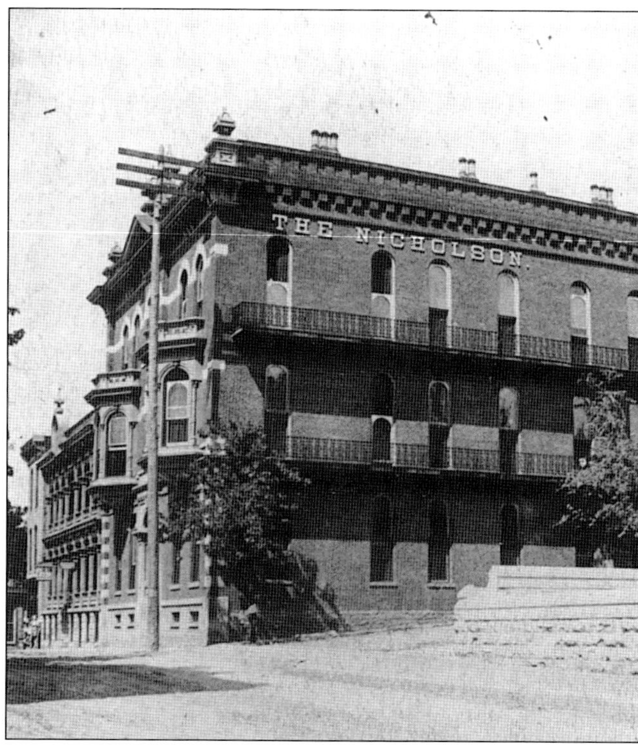

The Nicholson House Hotel, located between Polk Avenue and Spruce (Eighth), stood across from the Cole residence.

This is a view of the Spruce Street side of the Nicholson House Hotel. The Tulane Hotel was later built here, and the site is now a surface parking lot down from the Ben West Library.

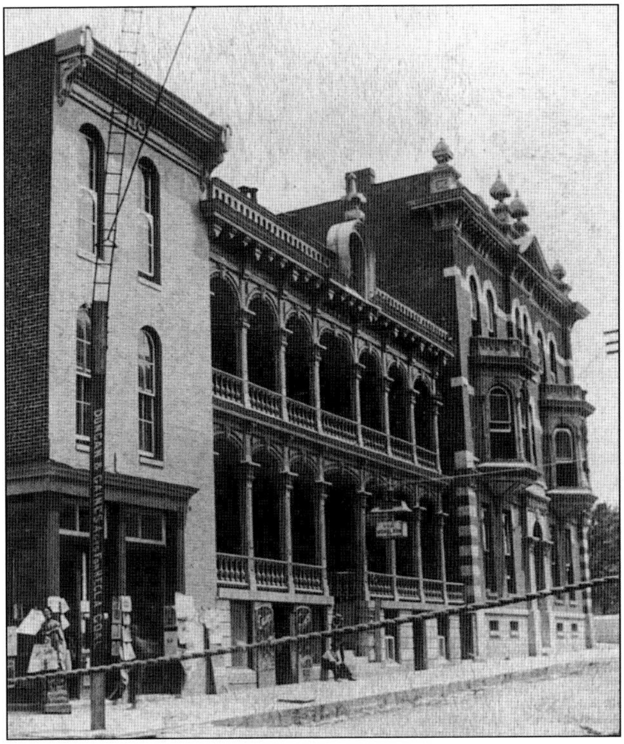

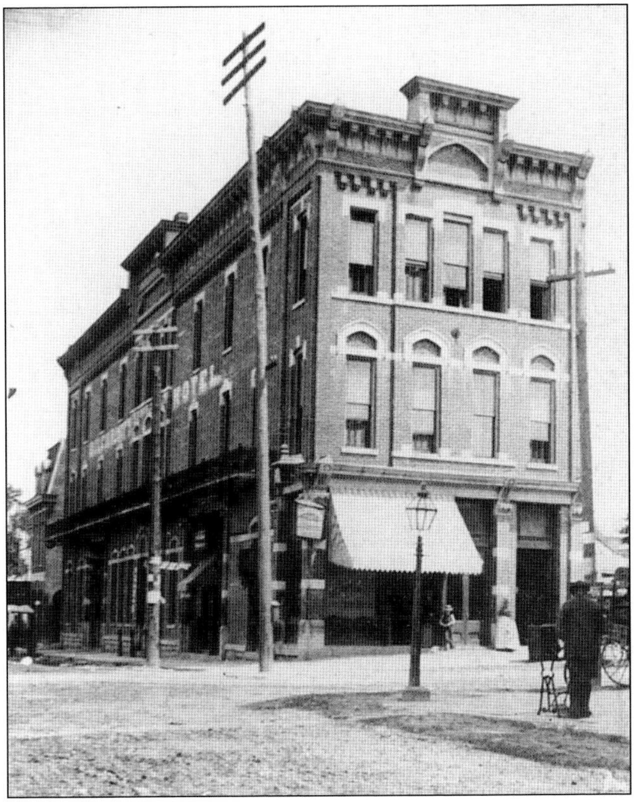

Gilchrist's Hotel is seen here at the northeast corner of Church and Walnut (Tenth) Streets.

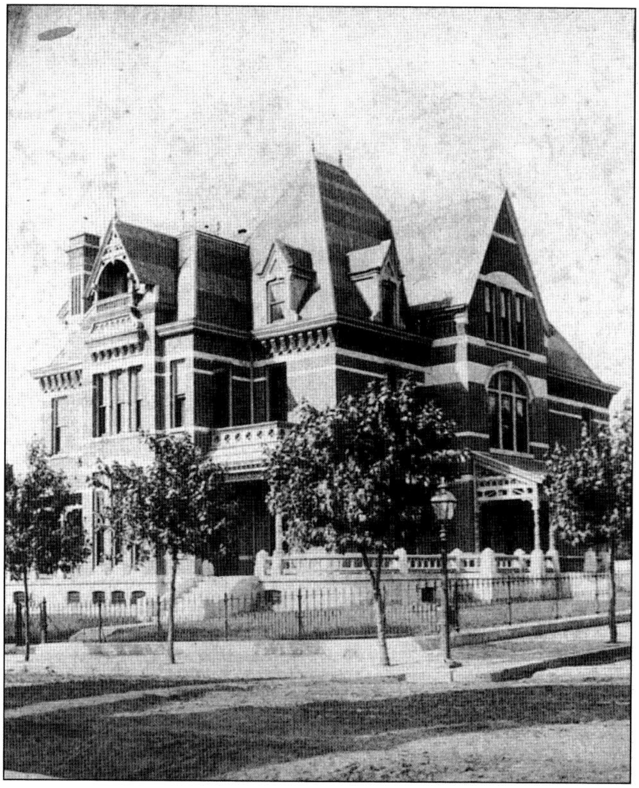

The residence of William H. Cherry was located at the southwest corner of Demonbreun and Spruce. Cherry was the partner of William Morrow in leasing convicts from the Tennessee State Penitentiary to work at their Tennessee Wagon Works.

This is a view of the William Duncan residence, located at 622 Broad, to the east of First Baptist Church. Duncan was a partner in Duncan & Gaines Coal and also served as the president of Brush Electric Light & Power Company.

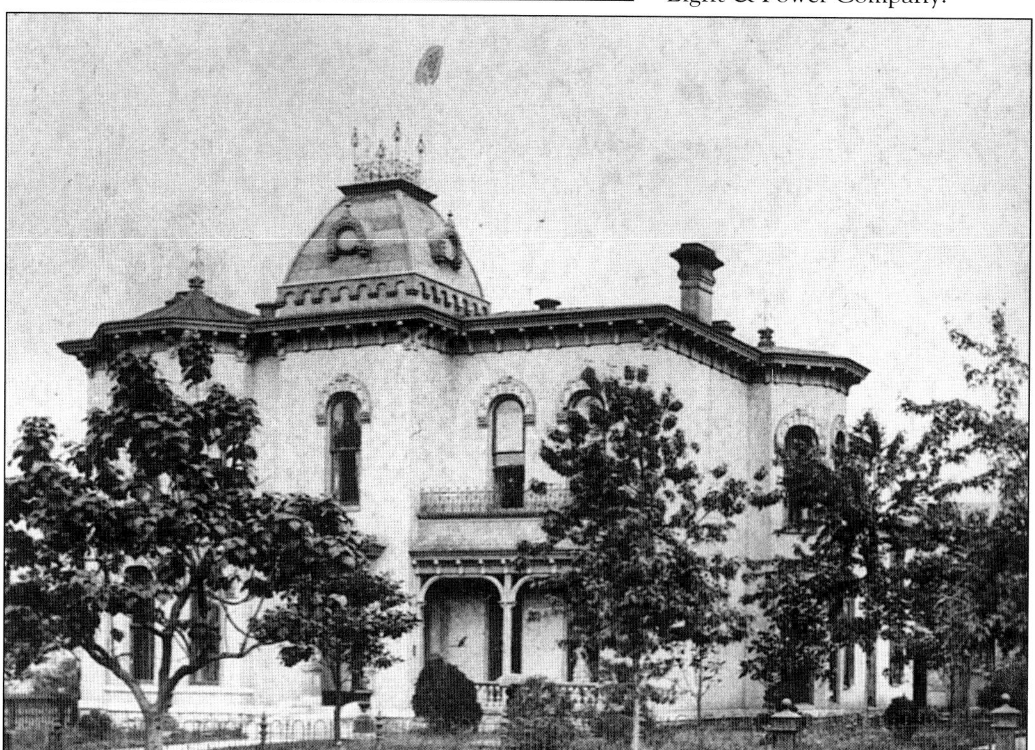

Four

Seat of State Government

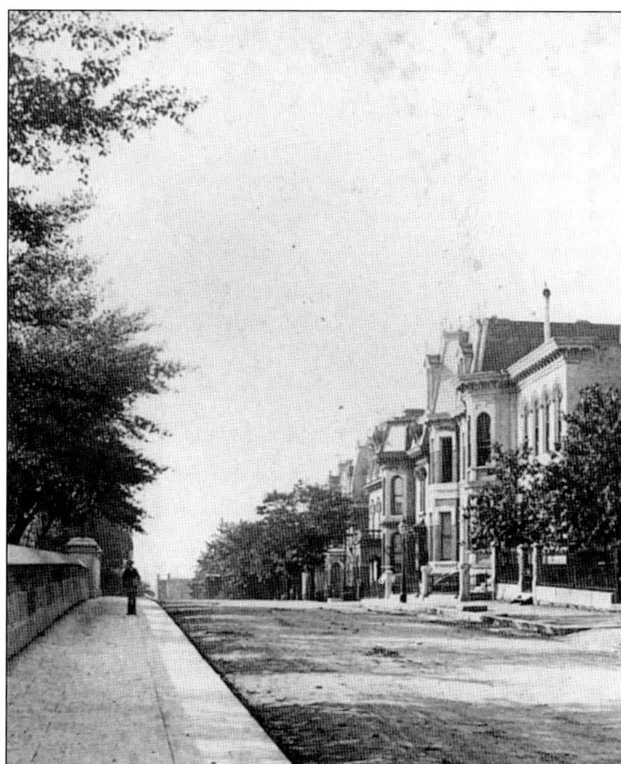

Park Street, seen here, was opposite the carriage entrance to the Tennessee State Capitol grounds. Fine Victorian row houses faced the front of the Capitol from the east side of the street.

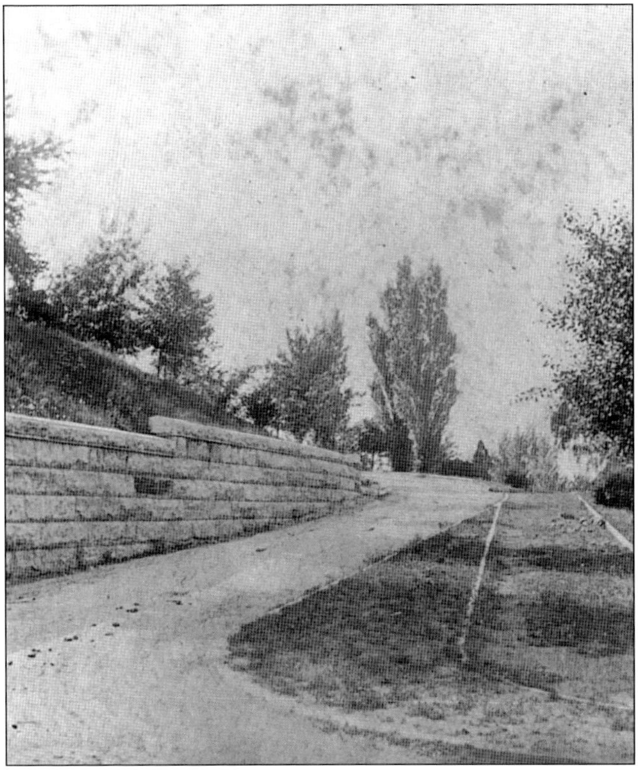

This is a view of the carriage drive up the hill to the Capitol. This approach was used for 100 years; then, in the 1950s, it was removed, and cars were made to approach the Capitol from the rear.

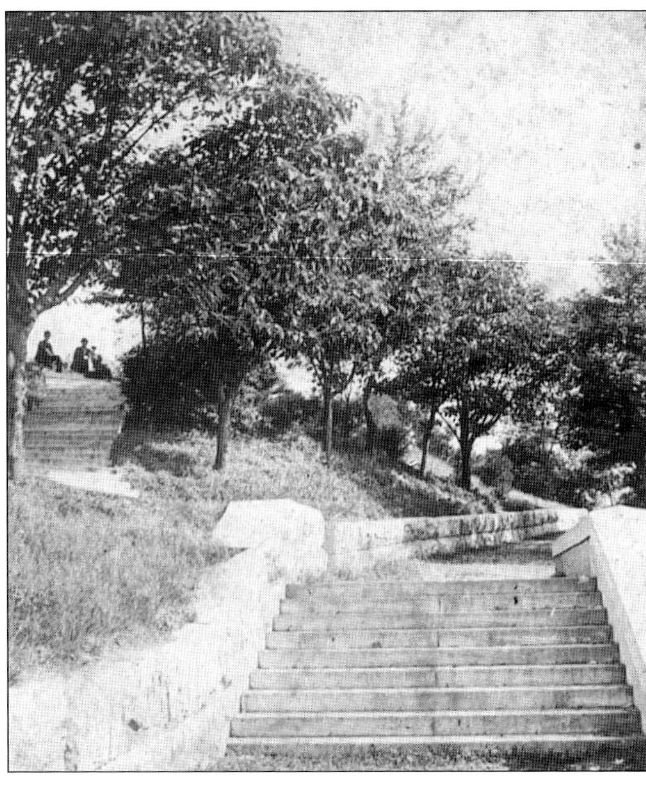

The grounds to the Capitol served as a public park. Winding pathways wound their way around the hill. At one time, a greenhouse and an artificial lake were also on the north slope to the hill.

The chief monument on the grounds is an equestrian statue of General Andrew Jackson, by Clark Mills. Two other castings also exist. One is located in Lafayette Square in Washington, and the other is in Jackson Square in New Orleans.

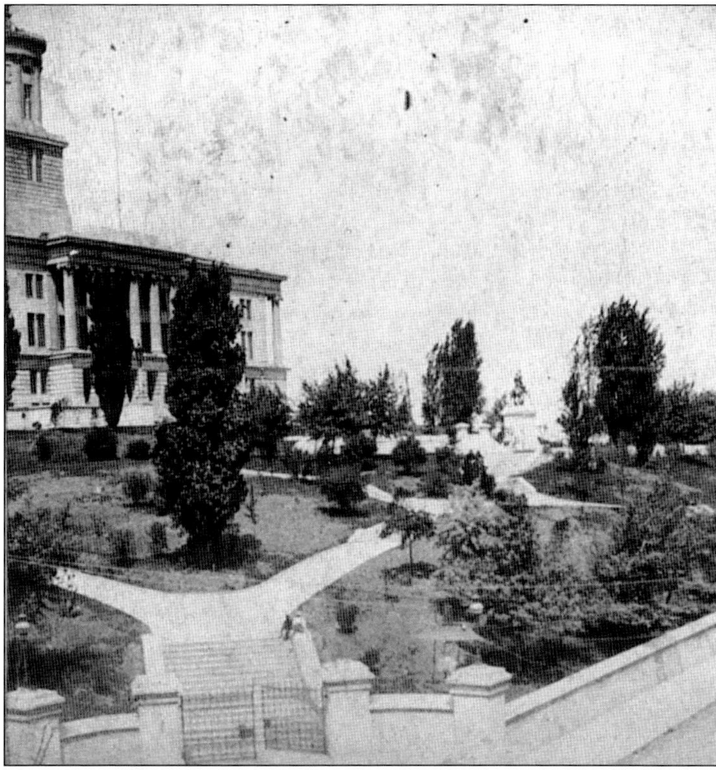

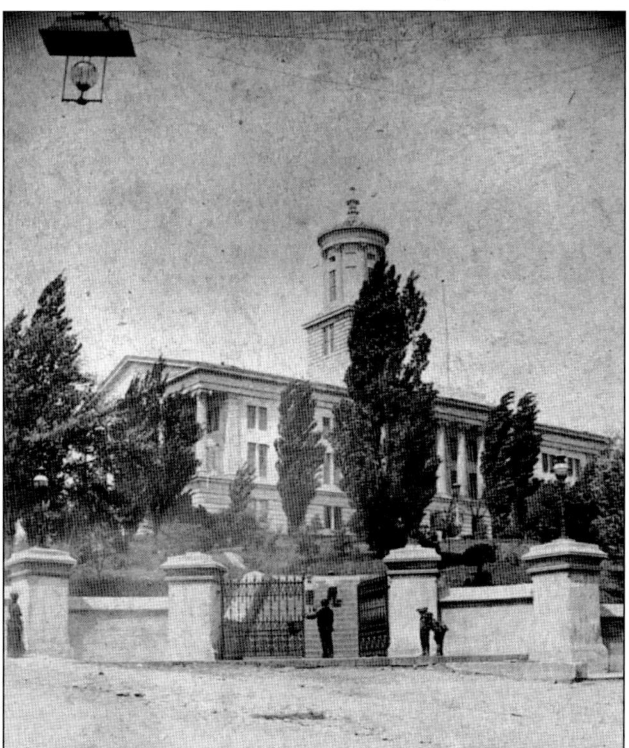

Gas lamps illuminated the approaches to the Capitol grounds and gates, from the entrance piers.

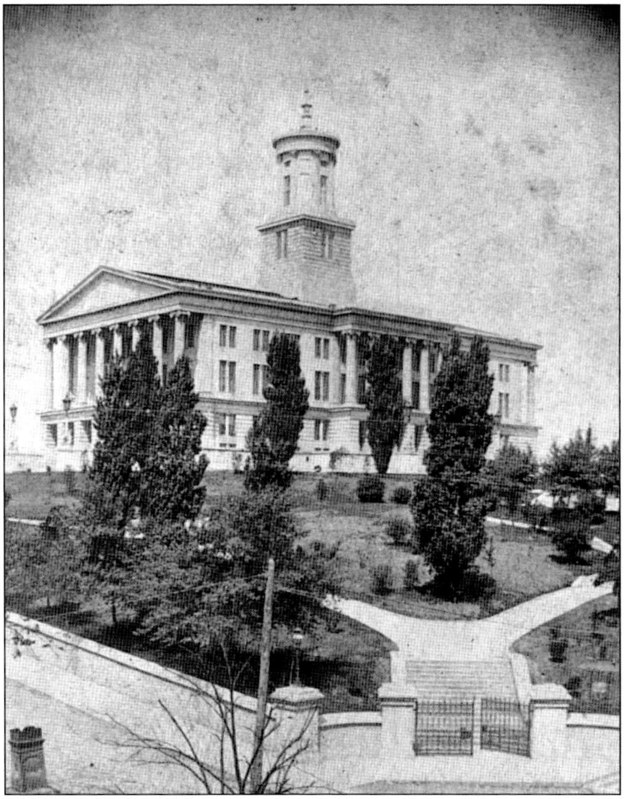

Lombardy poplars blow in the wind on the front lawn to the Capitol.

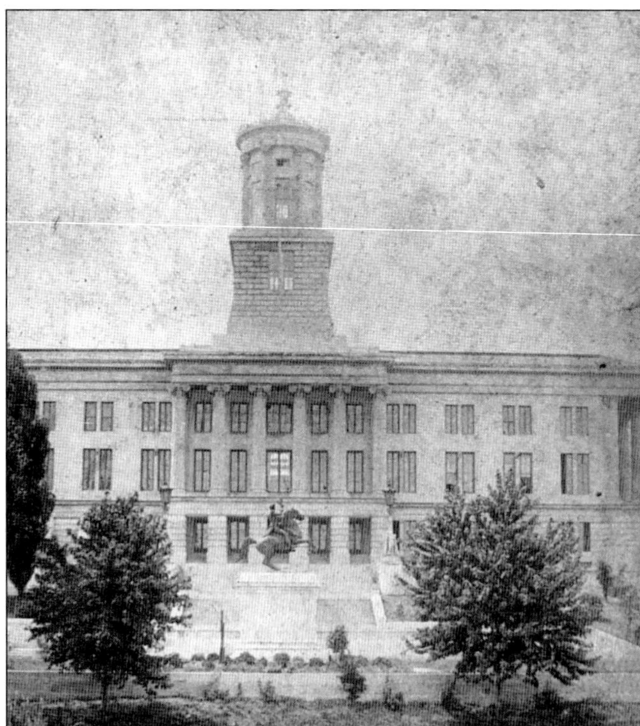

William Strickland, of Philadelphia, was the architect of the Tennessee State Capitol. He worked on it from 1845 until 1854, when he died. His son, Francis, then served as supervising architect until 1857. He was then dismissed by chairman of the Capitol building commission, Samuel Dold Morgan, in order to save money. In 1858 the commission hired Harvey Akeroyd to complete the State Library chamber in the Capitol. Both William Strickland and Samuel Morgan are buried within the walls of the north and south porticoes, respectively.

When Clark Mills cast this equestrian bronze, it was the first such American statue. The Tennessee Historical Society gave the statue to the state in 1880, on the centennial of Nashville's founding.

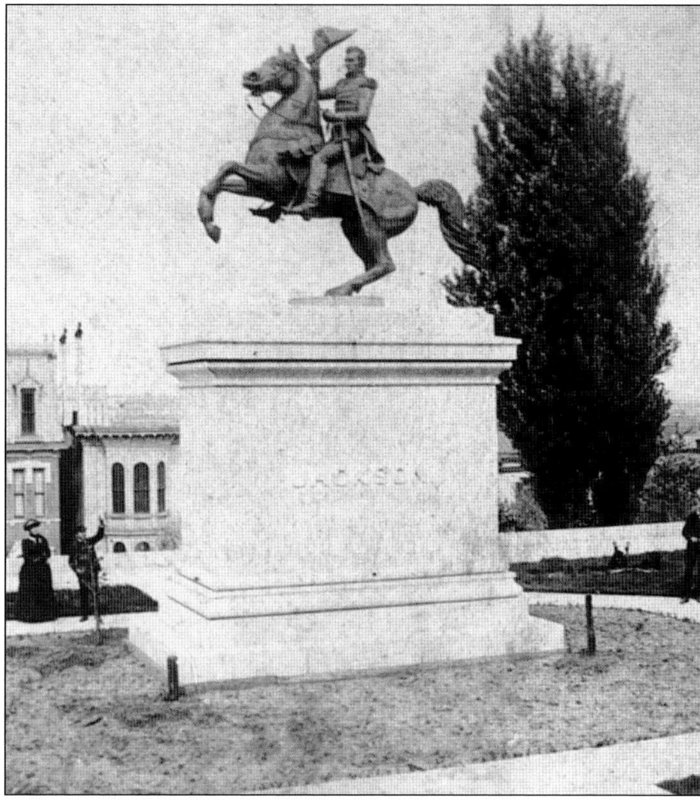

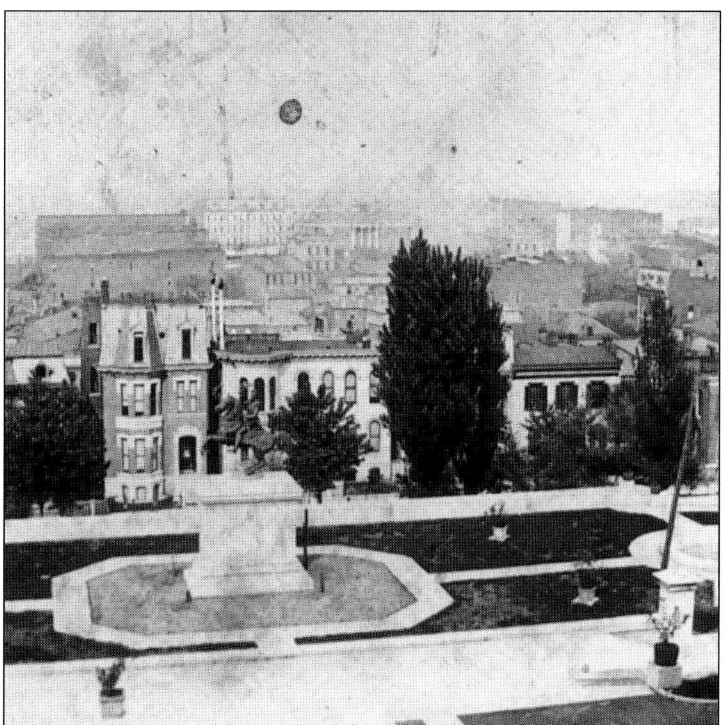

The front lawn to the Tennessee State Capitol is highlighted by the Jackson statue and two round stone-lined fountains. About 110 years later, they were restored after having been used as planters during most of their existence. The Public Square is visible to the east.

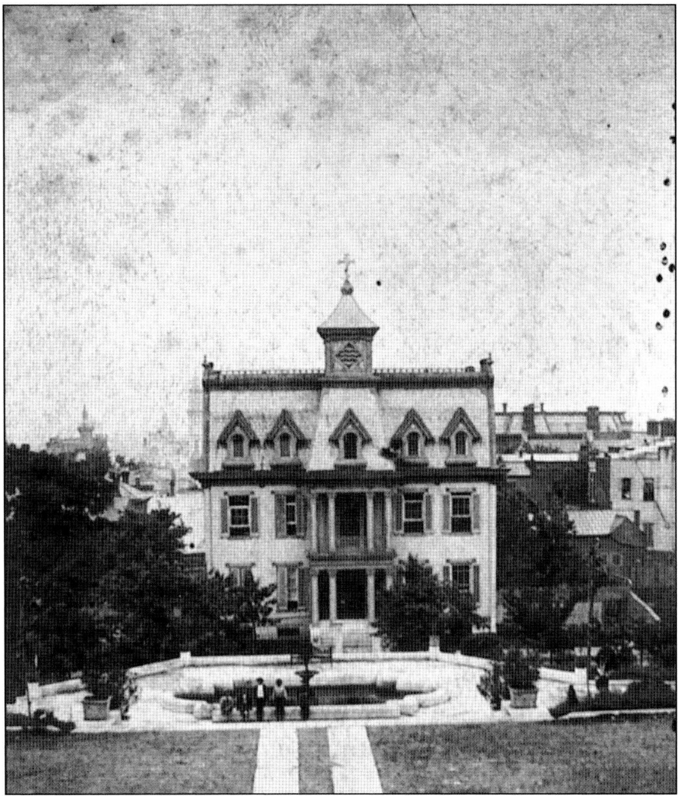

This view is looking south from the side entrance to the Capitol on Cedar (Charlotte). The house was the one George Washington Campbell built after he sold his frame house atop Capitol Hill in 1843 to Nashville as a site for the Capitol building. This house had gardens running between High (Sixth) and Vine (Seventh). During the Civil War, military governor Andrew Johnson lived in the house, and he was succeeded there by Reconstruction governor William G. Brownlow. In 1868 the Catholic Diocese purchased the house and added a third floor and tower. Later, St. Bernard's Convent occupied it as a school. The fountain basin in the foreground is now the base to the Edward Ward Carmack statue.

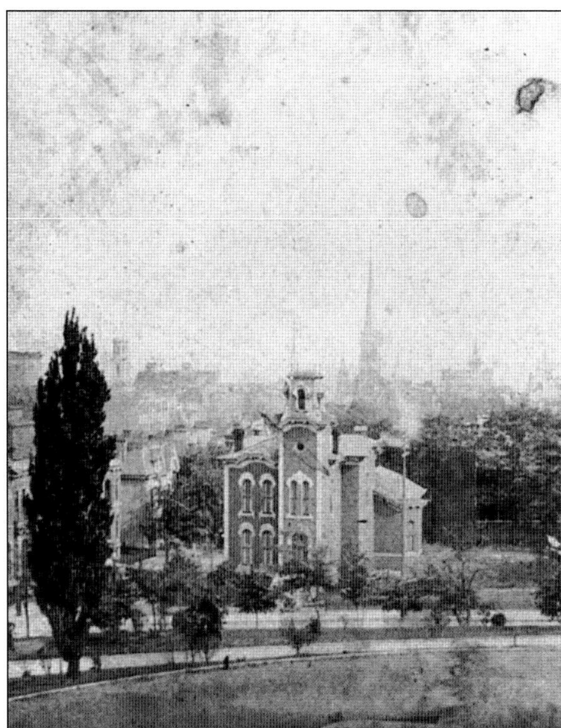

This view is looking south from the Capitol, along High Street (Sixth). The First Presbyterian Church, McKendree Methodist Church, Watkins Institute, and the Customs House make Nashville a city of towers.

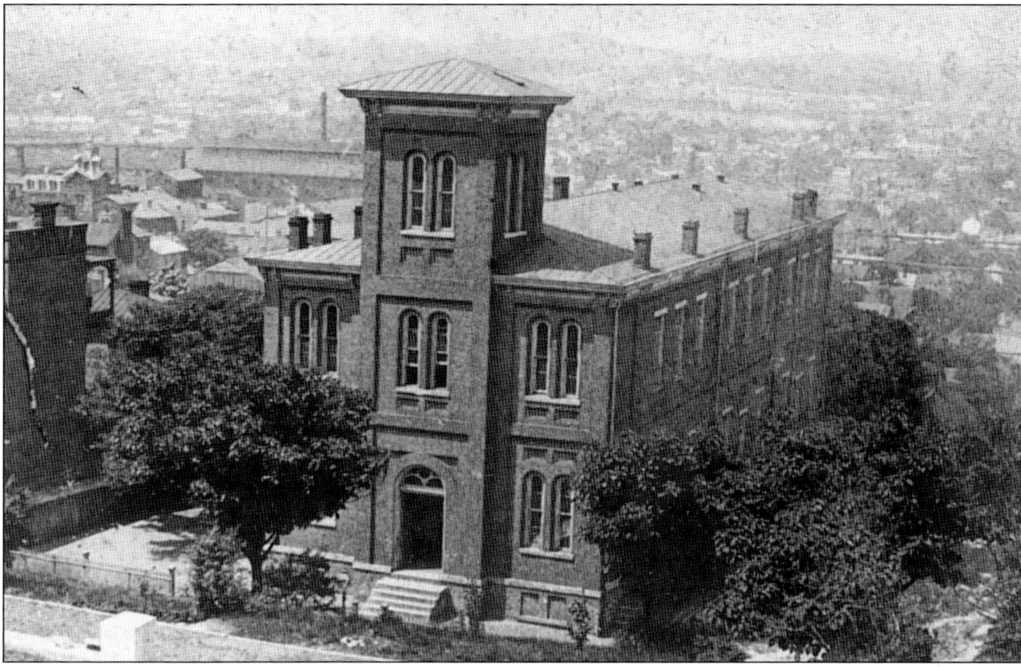

The view west from the Capitol shows St. Mary's Roman Catholic School standing where the Tennessee State Supreme Court building is now. The railyards are visible down the hill.

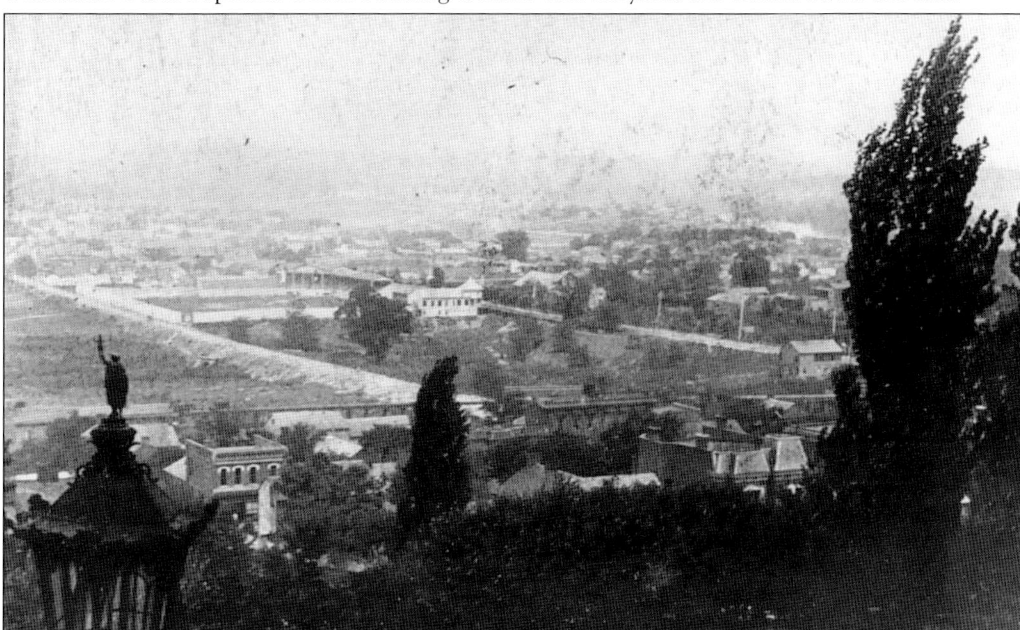

The view north from the Capitol shows the rail line in the same location as today. To the north of the railroad is the Sulpher Dell Ball Field. Baseball was played on that site from the 1860s to the 1960s. The Tennessee Bicentennial Mall and Sulpher Dell Greenway are located there today. Note as well the gas lamp in the lower left. A pair of these flanked all four staircases leading up the exterior terraces to the Capitol. They too survived 100 years, only to be thrown away by the state architect in the 1950s. One statue from them is known to remain.

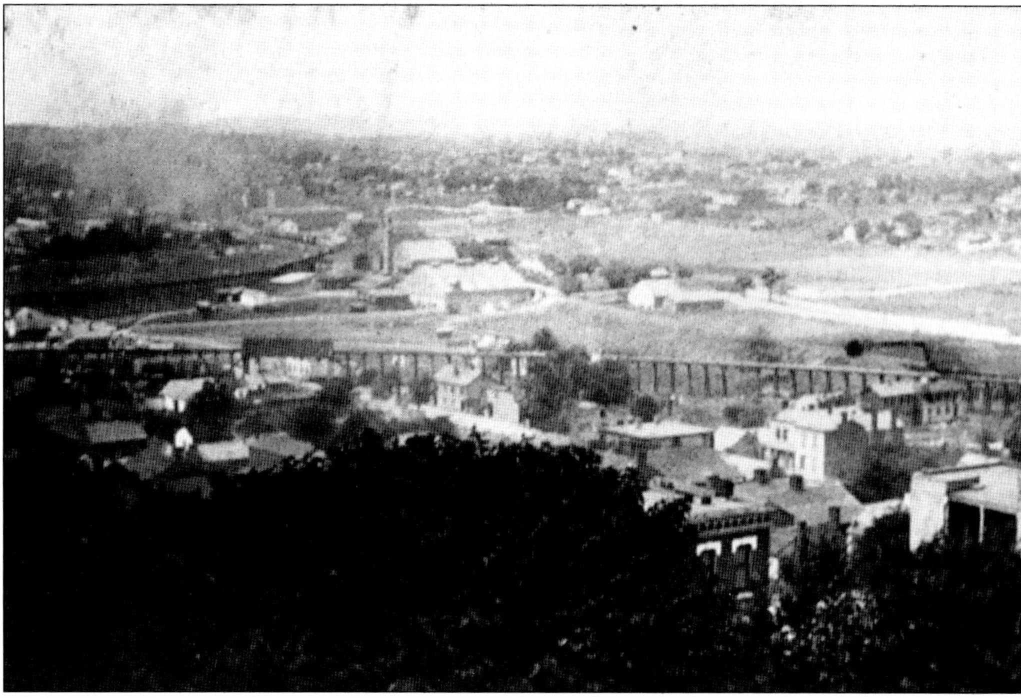

Looking northwest from Capitol Hill, we see the rail trestle that was built to keep the rails above periodic flooding. Also visible are the tannery works along Line Street and Belleville (Tenth).

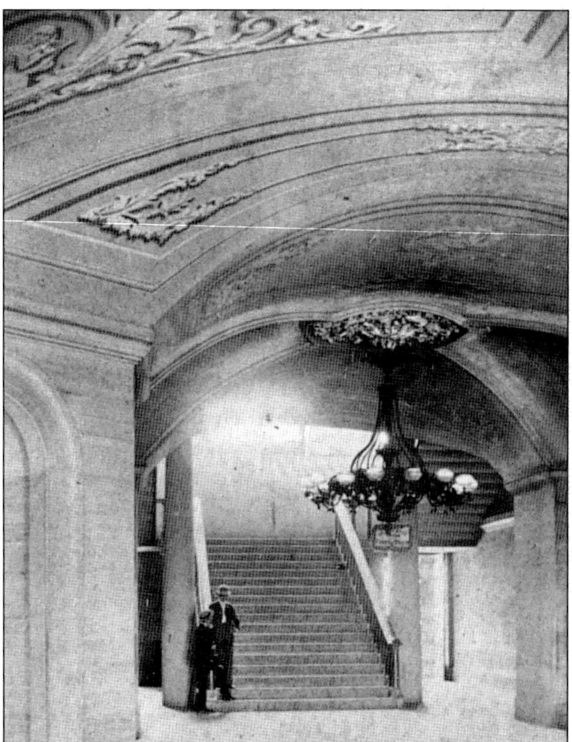

One of the most important pieces of documentation that Otto Giers gave the community is a series of interior views of the Tennessee State Capitol. They are the earliest known interiors of the building. This view is of the entrance. Knowing of these since 1979, I was allowed to use them by Sarah Marks for the restoration of the Capitol in the late 1980s. This view shows the basement hall, or the executive and courtroom floor, in the Capitol. Also of use to us in the restoration was this image of a now missing original gasolier. From this and the next image, the Capitol Restoration Commission was able to recreate the three missing hall gasoliers on this floor. The ceiling restoration was also aided by this image. Theo Knoch and John Schleicher did the decorative frescoes in 1857. In 1882 they frescoed the other Strickland building in Nashville, the present Downtown Presbyterian Church.

Looking the length of the basement, or executive and courtroom floor, we again see a now missing original gasolier. Also, this view confirms Therese Yelverton's account in *Teresina in America* of her visit to the Capitol in 1875. In tones rather like Thackeray and Dickens used in describing American manners, she said that tobacco juice was much in evidence here. In this photograph, Giers shows spittoons at intervals all through the center hallway. Also a hand-lettered sign reads "DO NOT SPIT on the FLOOR OR STEPS."

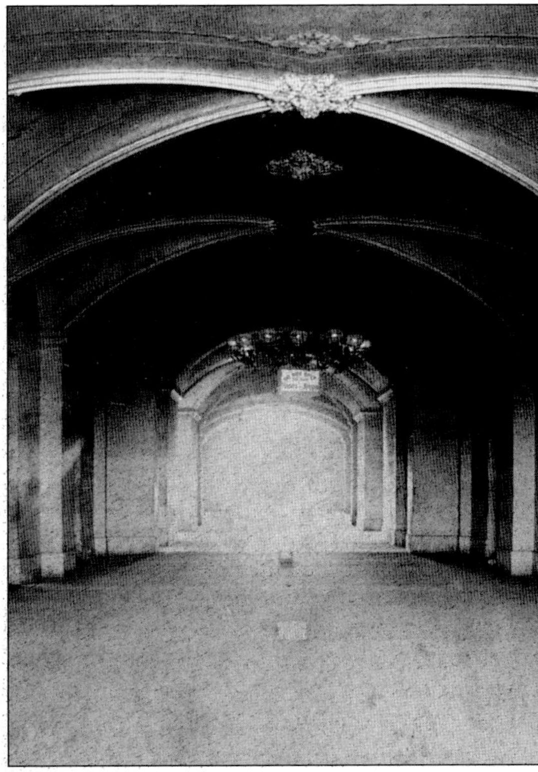

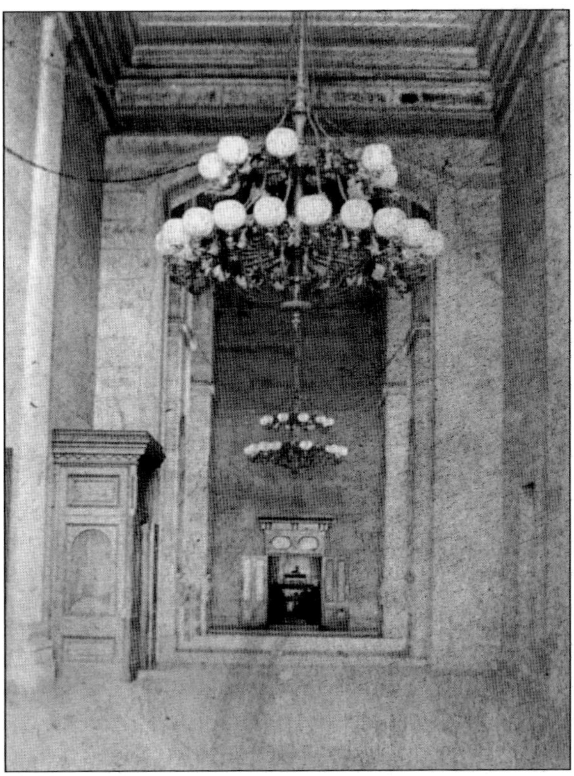

On the first, or legislative, floor to the Capitol, we see the original gasoliers, which are still in place today fortunately. Then, they had decorative stabilization chains attached to them. The purpose for the chains was to prevent the lights from swinging too much when the windows and doors were opened to cool to building. The air locks on the doors are also a seasonal necessity. In fall and winter, when the legislature was in session, they helped to retain what little heat could be produced in a space with a 42-foot ceiling. Note the spittoons again on this floor. I remember spittoons beside members' desks in the 1970s.

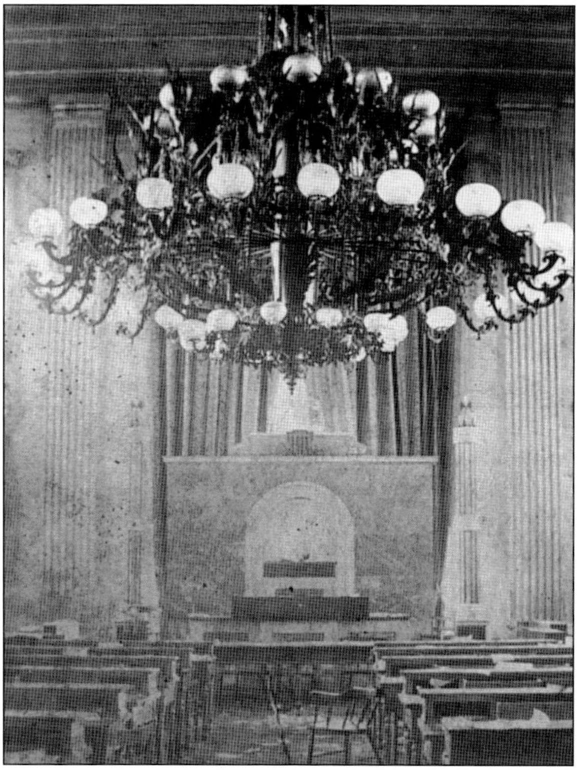

The Tennessee House of Representatives chamber contained the finest ornament of the Capitol, a unique creation. It was a 48-burner gasolier. It had three levels of gas burners encircling it, and it hung from an ornate ceiling medallion in the center of the chamber. Between the center and top rings of gas burners were arranged cast-metal figures of Native Americans and corn plants, with ears formed on their stalks. Cotton blossoms hung about in cast metal as well. Above the top circle of gas lights was a circle of six buffalos. Above that were tobacco plants in blossom and a circle of bald eagles. The Speaker's rostrum and the Clerk's well were made of East Tennessee red and white marble. The screen behind the speaker was red and white marble as well.

In 1889 the gasolier was removed at the urging of a Shelby County representative, who sat beneath it and was unnerved by it when it moved in the wind. What had been hailed by the press in Philadelphia, where the Cornelius and Baker firm had made it, was destroyed in one generation. Cornelius and Baker had received the contract to illuminate the building and placed over 30 fixtures in it; of those, only four survive. All of the others were destroyed over the years. During the partial restoration from 1984 to 1988, we were able to reproduce the hall lights on the basement level and to locate four period gasoliers for the restored supreme court chamber and the comptroller's lobby. These two images by Otto Giers are our only source for seeing what this gasolier looked like; they were 21 feet high and 45 feet in circumference.

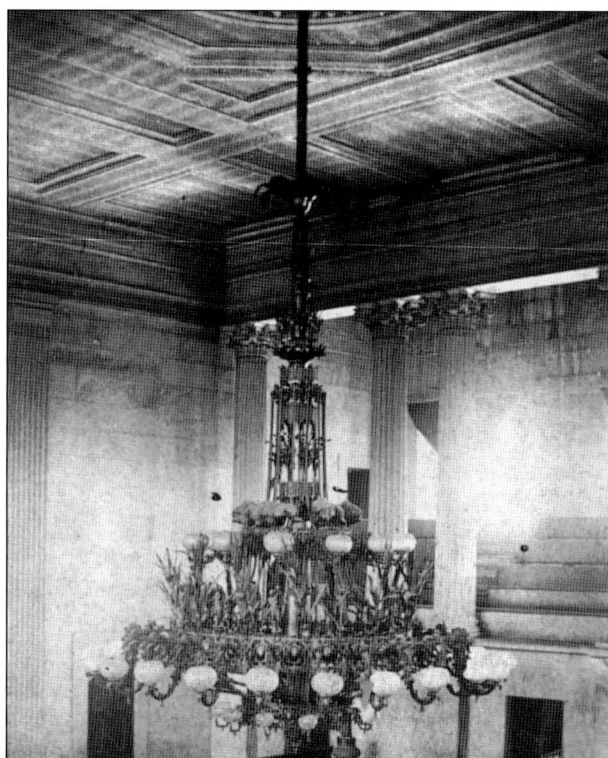

In 1969 the original marble Speaker's rostrum and Clerk's well were removed from the house and senate chambers. This view shows the original configuration. The original drapery cornices were also destroyed in 1969.

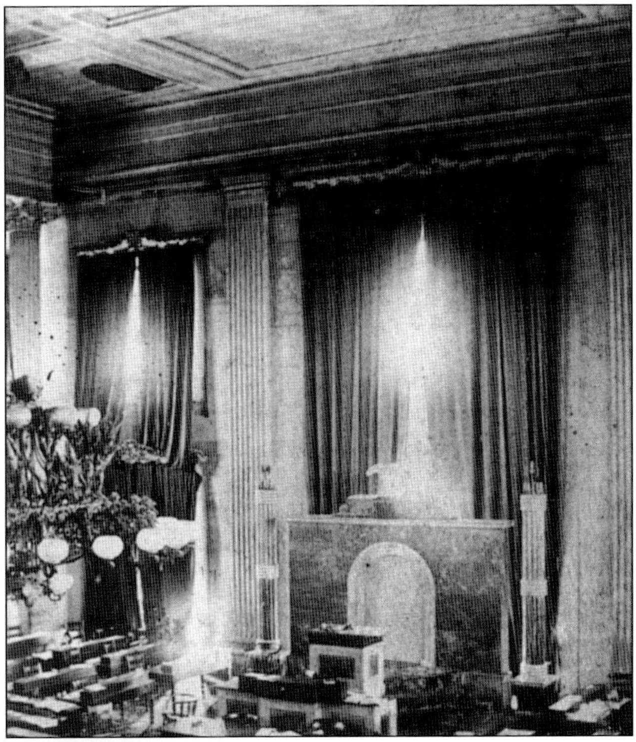

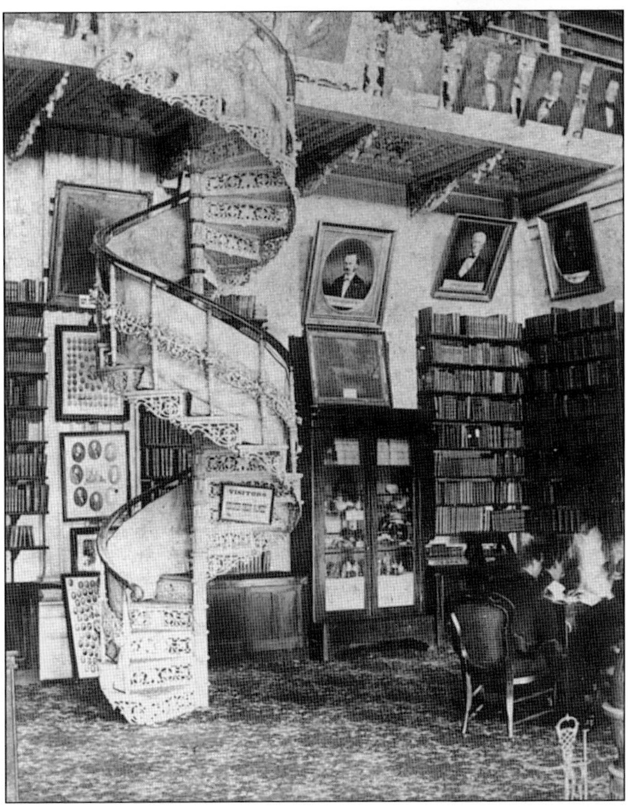

The Tennessee State Library was housed on the first, or legislative, floor of the Capitol from 1853 to 1952. From 1853 to 1885, the Tennessee Historical Society (THS) also used this space, as is evident from this photograph. The THS collection of portraits hangs from the walls, as well as the railings. Artifacts in cases even block one of the doors into the room. A cast-iron stove to heat the room was to the right, as evidenced by the fire set. A modesty curtain hangs on the spiral staircase railing to shield the librarians ankles from prying eyes.

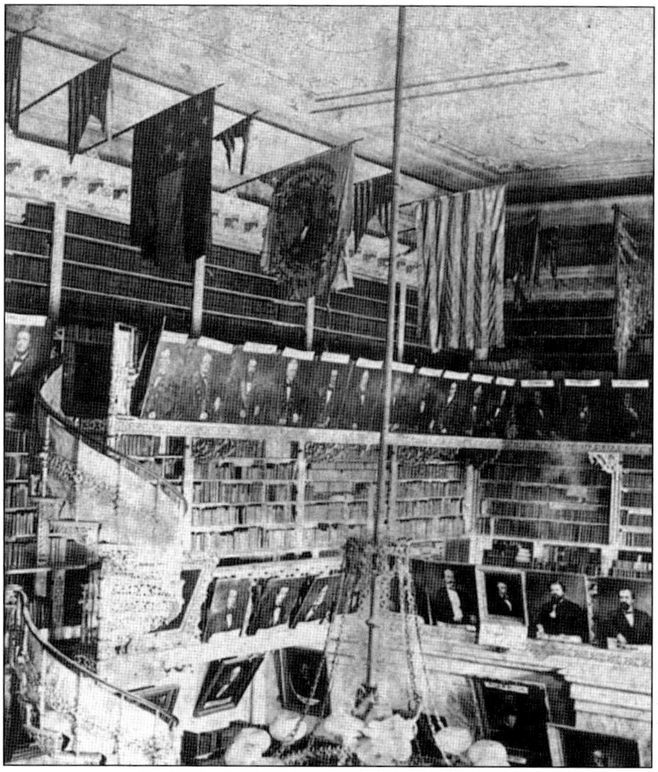

The balcony to the State Library contained the Grand Masonic Lodge of Tennessee's Grand Master's portraits, historical flags, and banners.

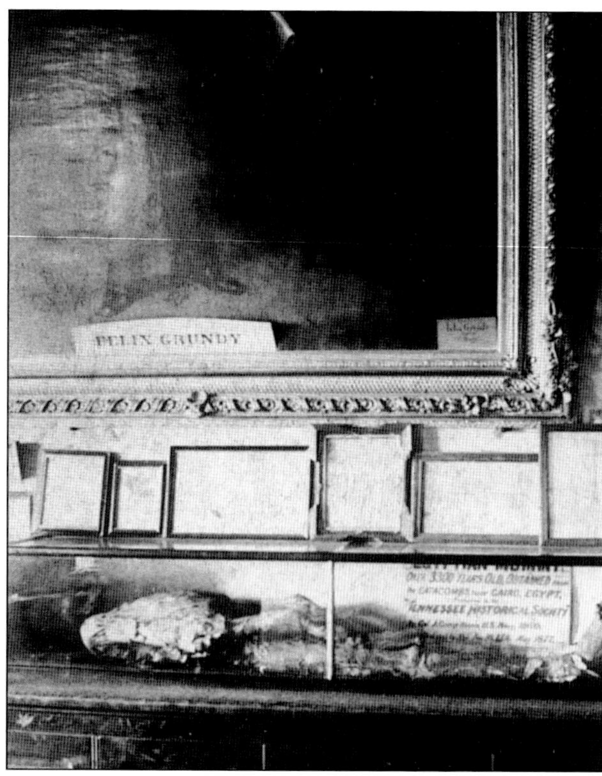

Egyptian human and cat mummies, 3,300 years old, lie in a case in the State Library chamber. They are part of the Tennessee Historical Society collection, now housed at the State Museum.

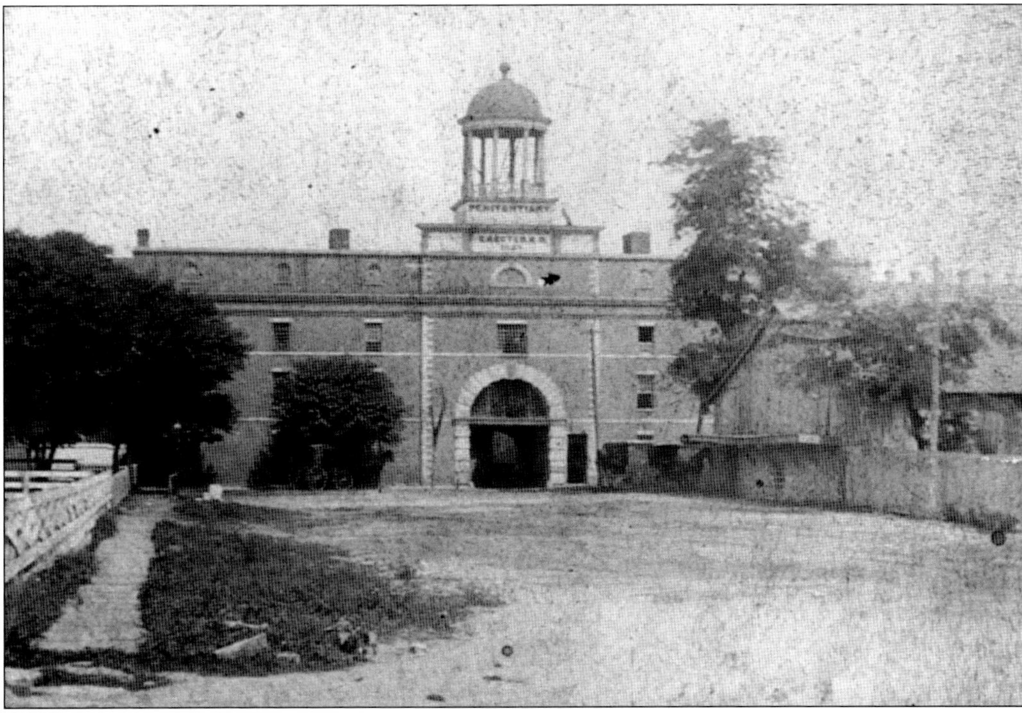

The Tennessee State Penitentiary, located on Church Street at Stonewall Avenue (McMillin), is seen here. Built between 1828 and 1830, it was replaced by the Cockerill Bend Tennessee State Penitentiary in 1898. Part of this complex still stands on McMillin. David Morrison was the architect. A menopteron, or pavilion above the gate, is what he also used at the Hermitage as the tomb for Rachel Jackson.

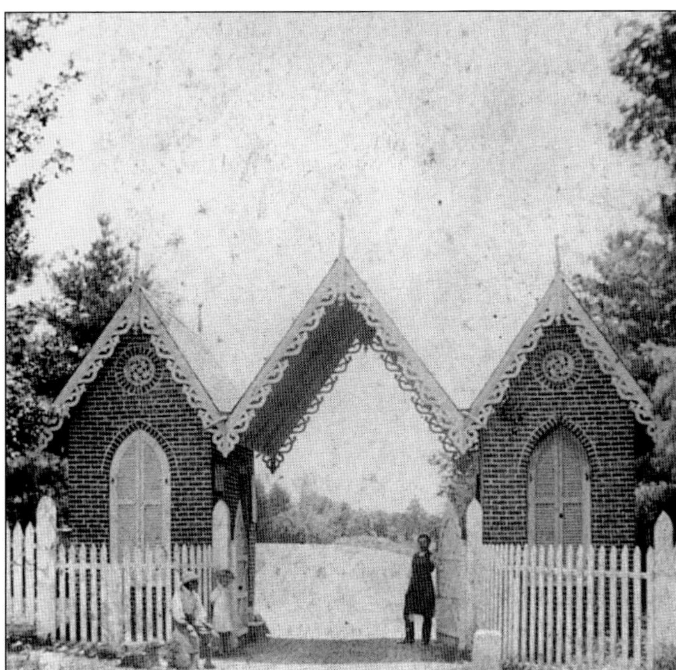

This is the entrance to the Tennessee Insane Asylum on the Murfreesboro Pike. It stood on today's Dell Computer complex site.

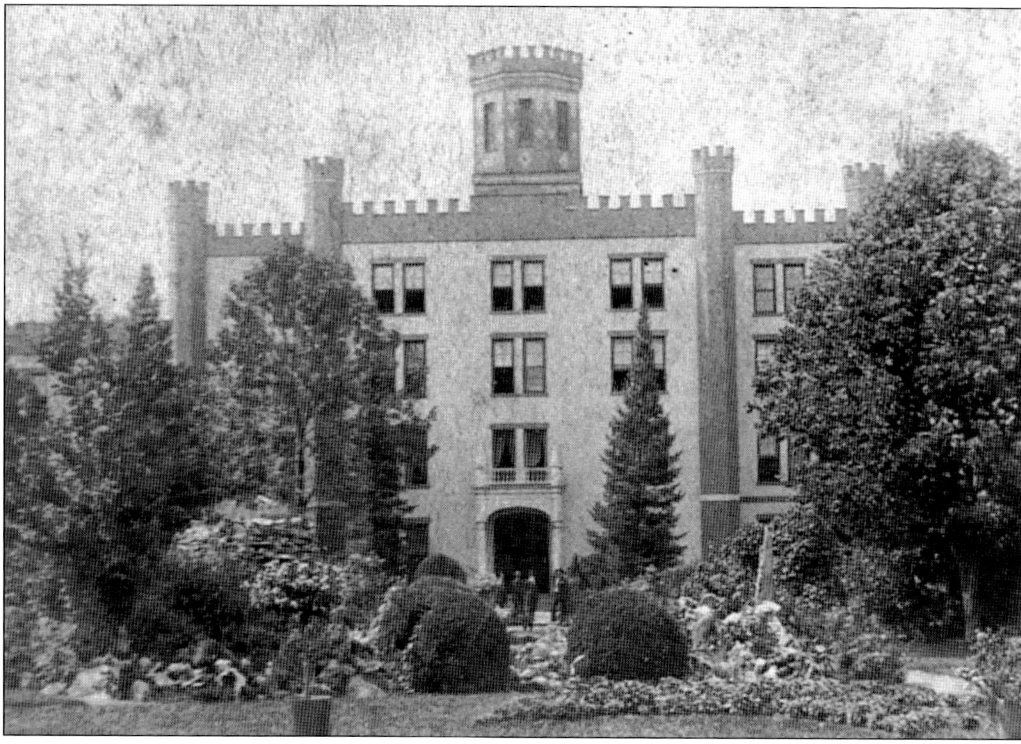

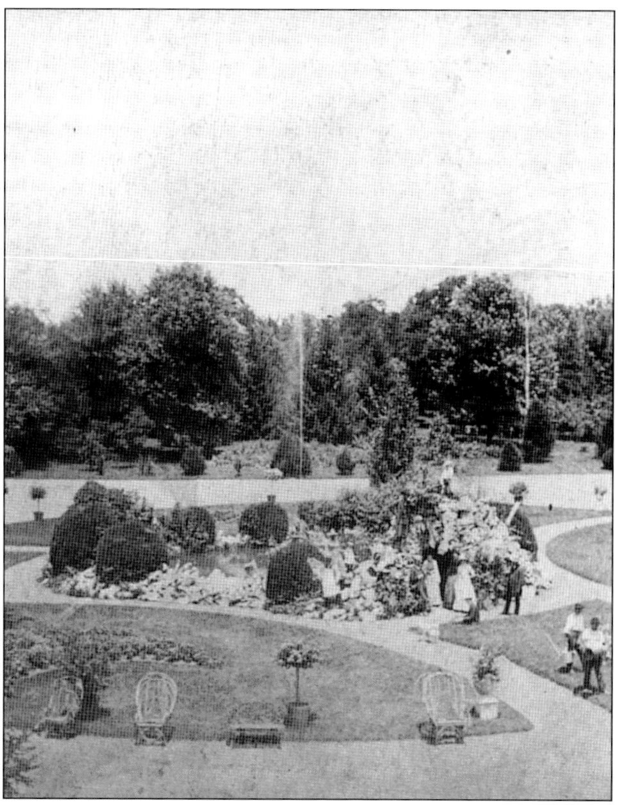

The Tennessee Insane Asylum was designed by Adolphus Heiman and constructed in stages between 1849 and 1857. The central block, seen here, was built first, and it later had a pitched roof and larger towers put on it. The asylum was built in the country, as this was seen as a healthful place. Nearby were the Weaver home, Kingsley (also probably designed by Heiman), and Colemere, the home of Colonel Edmund W. Cole.

Gardens were considered to be therapeutic, so the Tennessee Insane Asylum had large Victorian gardens and outdoor chairs for the patients to enjoy the air.

A lake also graced the grounds of the Tennessee Insane Asylum.

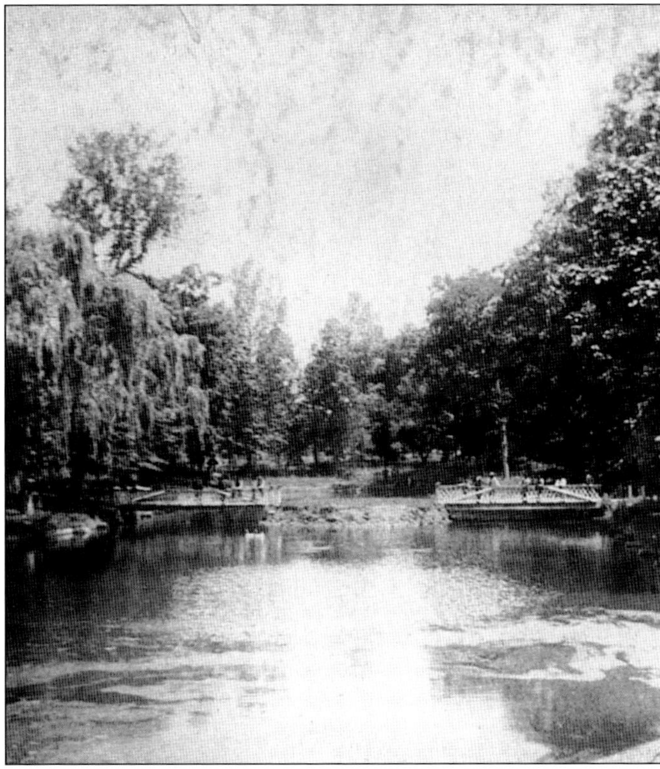

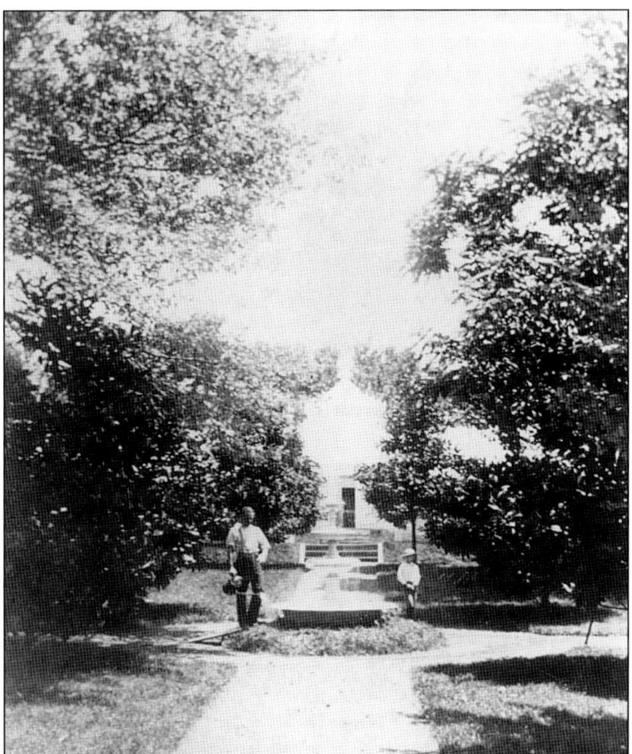

This fountain was outside the Conservatory and the Main Building at the Tennessee Insane Asylum.

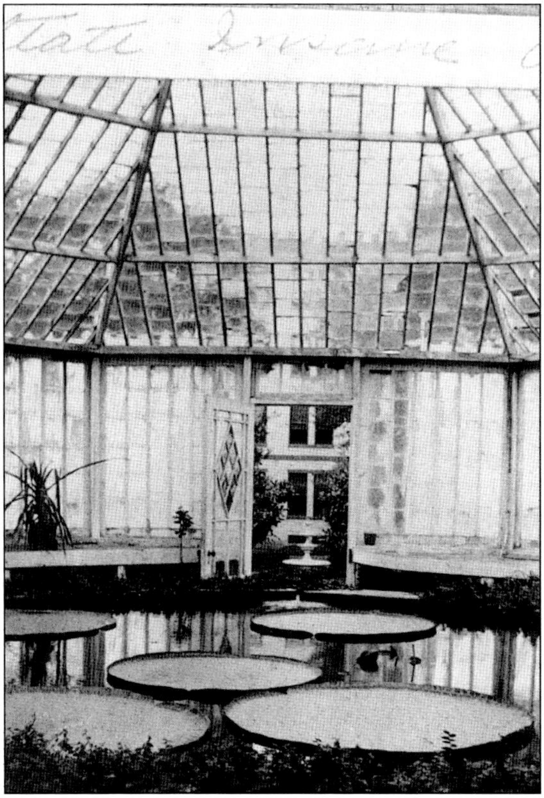

The fountain seen in the previous photograph is viewed from inside the Conservatory. The large water lilies are from the Amazon.

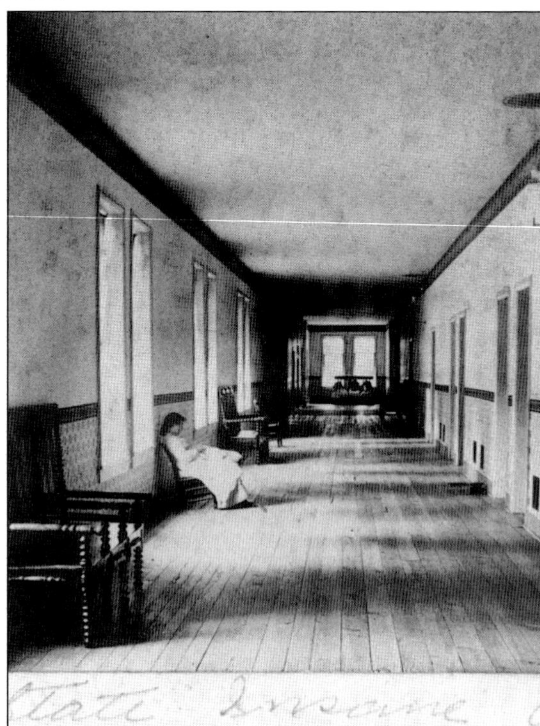

This photograph shows a hallway in the wards at the Tennessee Insane Asylum.

This is the Colored Department, or the segregated African-American ward, of the Tennessee Insane Asylum.

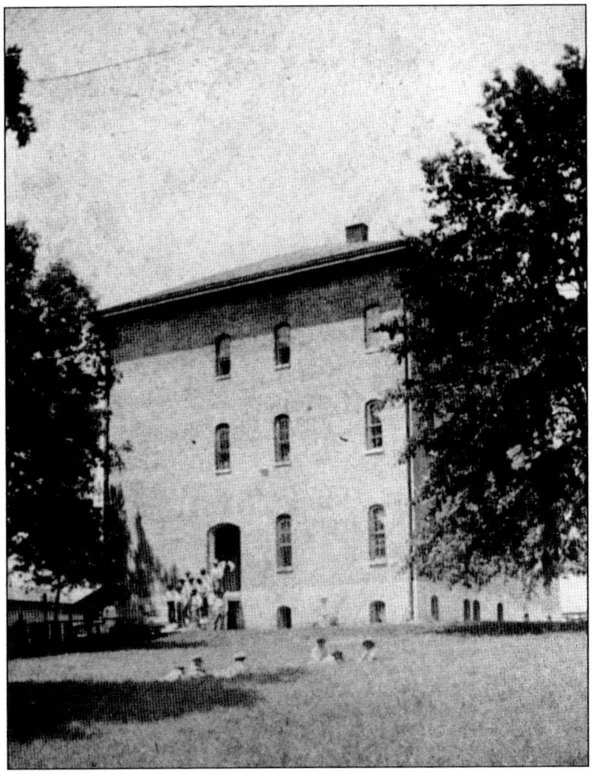

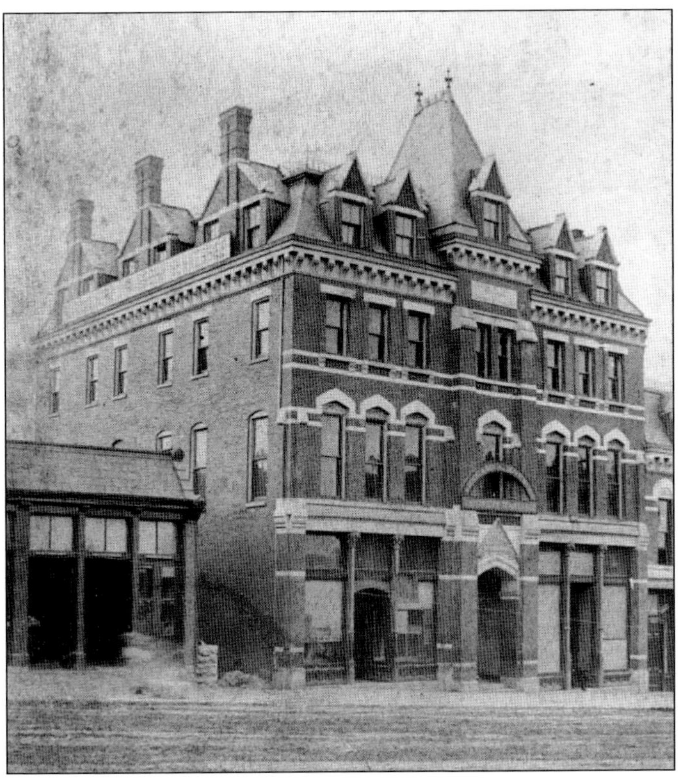

The University of Tennessee Medical and Dental Department was located on the north side of Broad, between High (Sixth) and Vine (Seventh). It was at the center of the block on the alley.

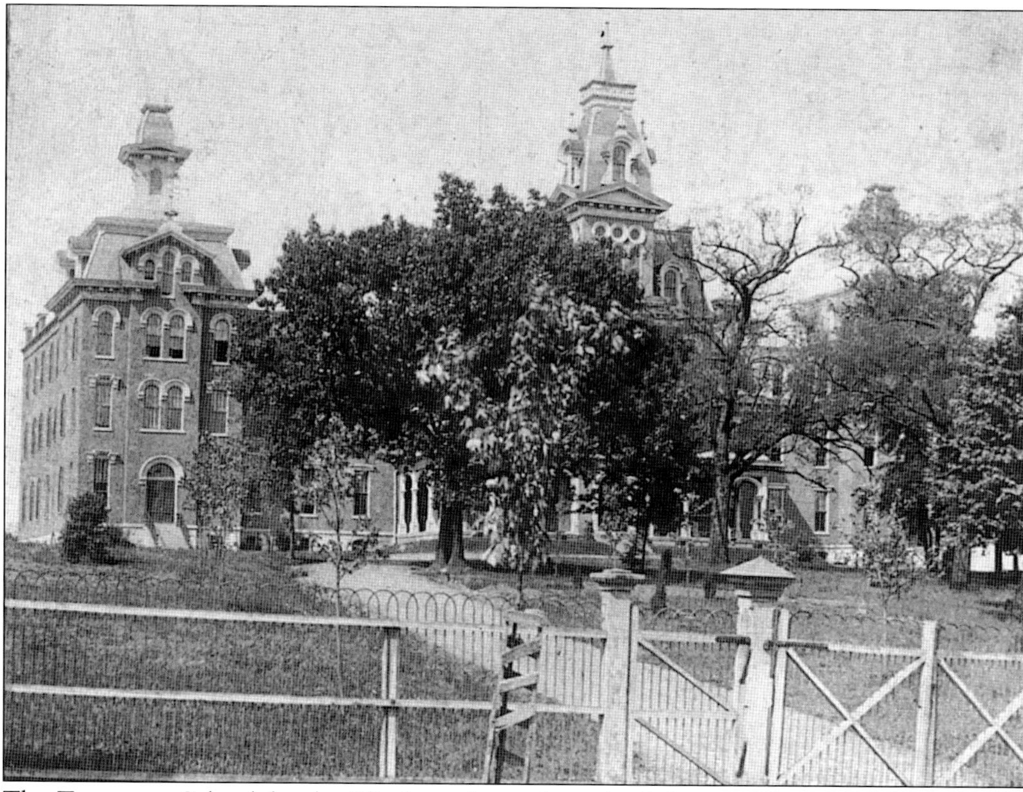

The Tennessee School for the Blind was located on the Lebanon Pike in South Nashville. The former General Hospital was to its north. The stone wall, still along the road today, was for this school.

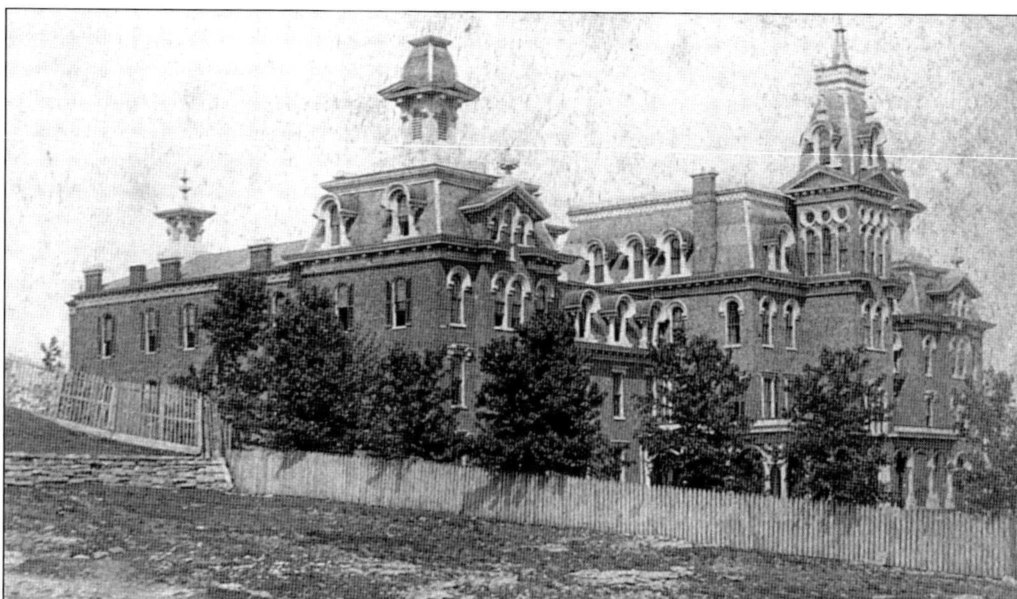

This is another view of the Tennessee School for the Blind, designed by P.J. Williamson in 1874.

Five

The Athens of the South

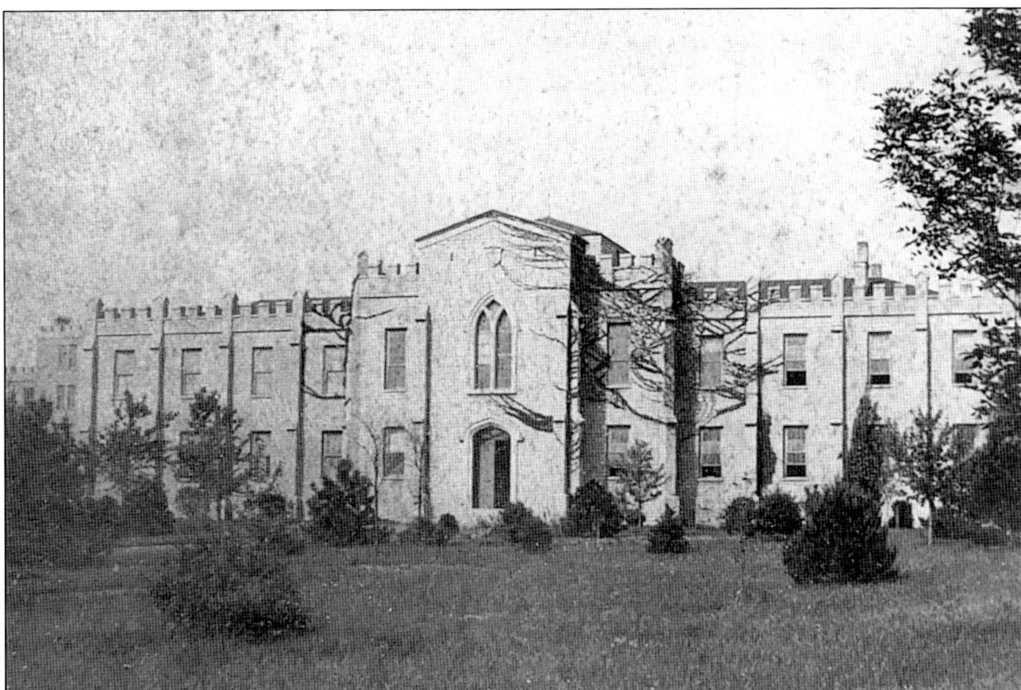

Priding itself on being a center for education, the city had numerous schools. By 1884, when Otto Giers made these photographs, the former University of Nashville had become the State Normal School. This building, which still stands, was built by Adolphus Heiman between 1853 and 1854, for $45,000. It was the main academic building. To its left, in the background, is the dormitory, Lindsley Hall, which was also Heiman's design.

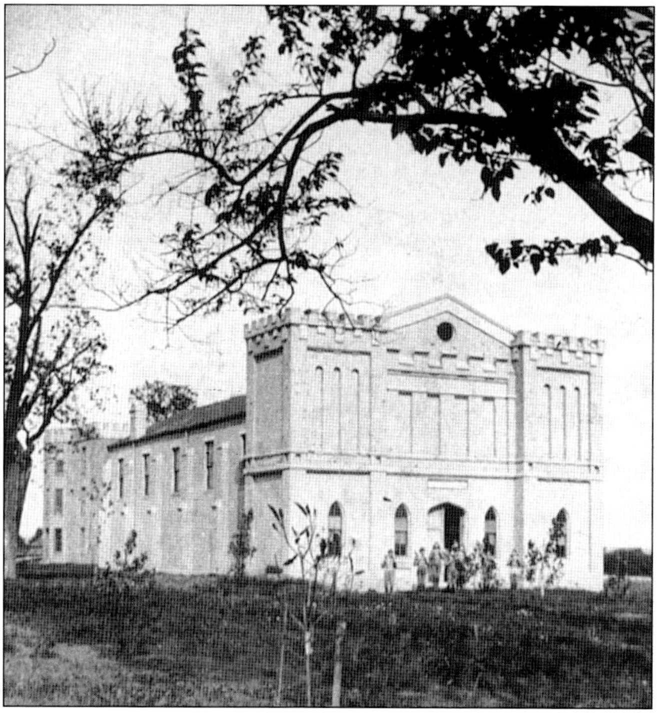

A band poses in front of the State Normal School Gymnasium, which stood north of the academic building.

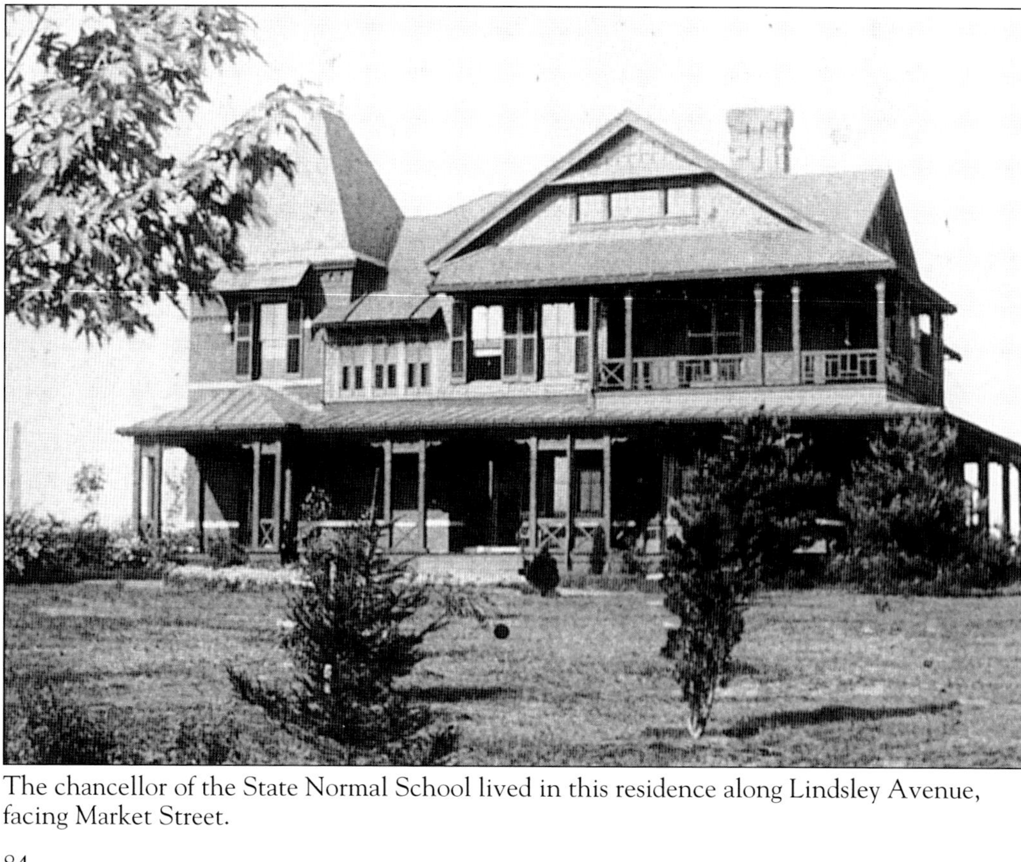

The chancellor of the State Normal School lived in this residence along Lindsley Avenue, facing Market Street.

A prep school for boys, Montgomery Bell Academy, was also on Lindsley Avenue, behind the State Normal School. Today it is located on Harding Road.

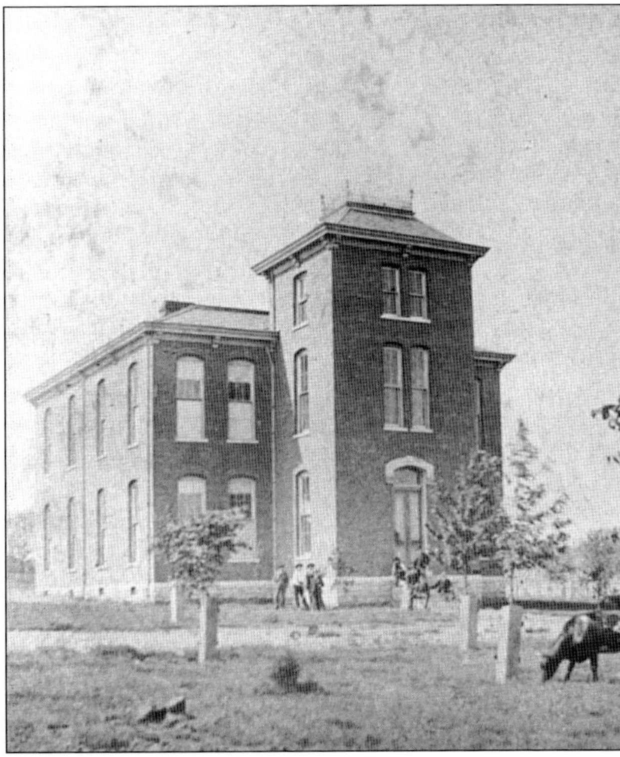

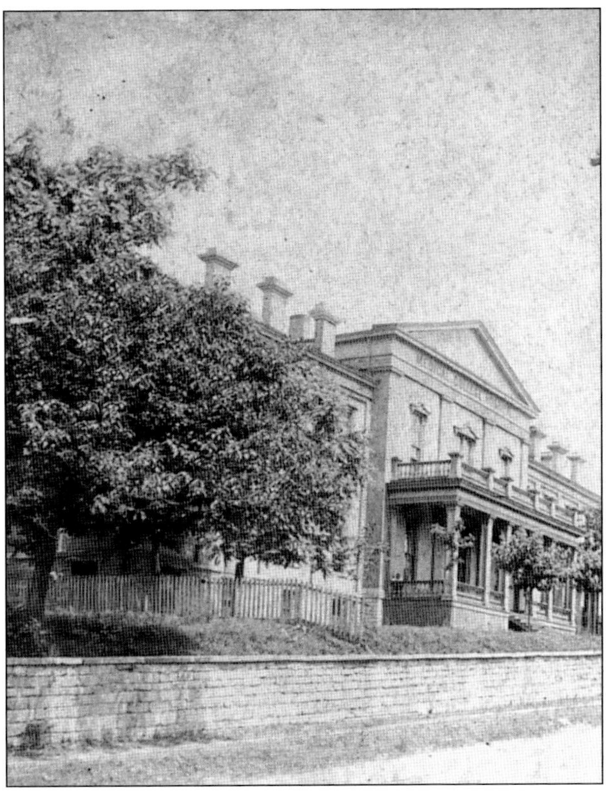

Seen in a side view, the University of Nashville Medical College and Hospital, built by Adolphus Heiman between 1851 and 1854, was on College Street South, between Franklin and Peabody.

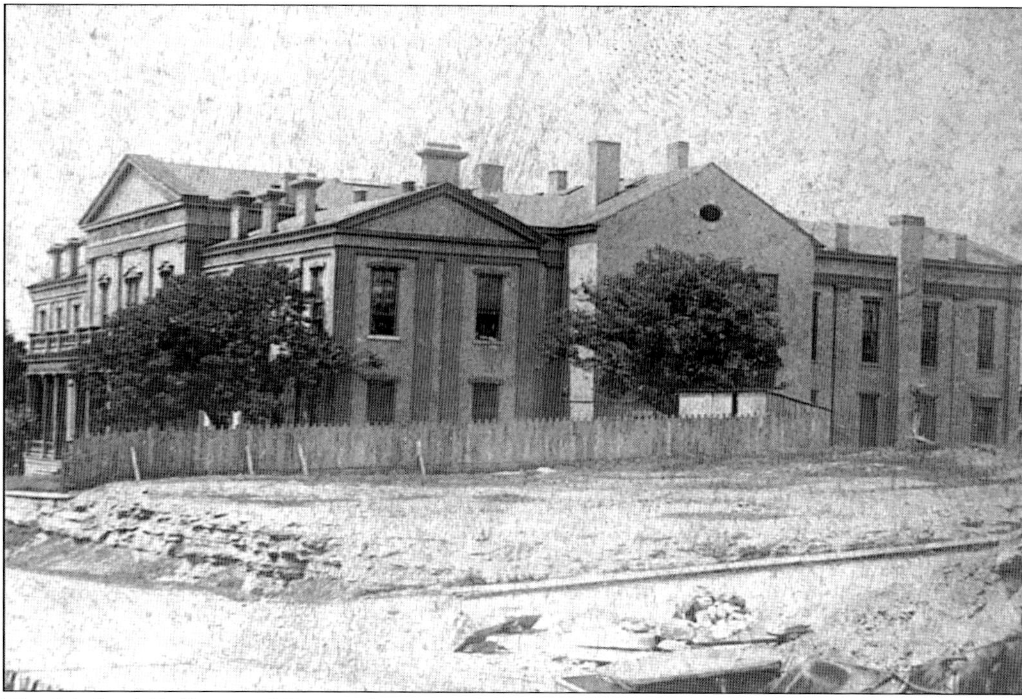

The Medical College and Hospital are seen here from the rear.

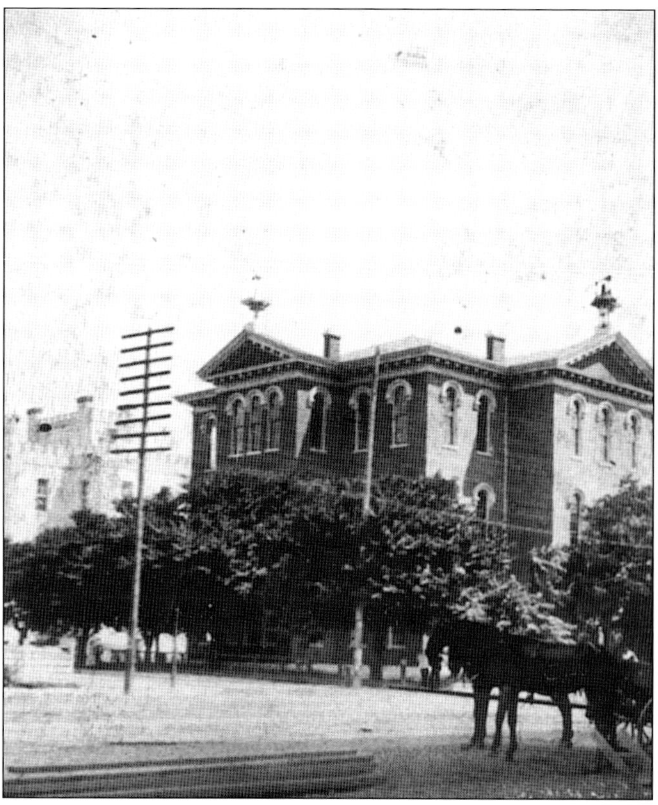

Nashville's first public school, Hume School (seen here to the left), was designed by Adolphus Heiman in 1855 in the Gothic style. Fogg School (seen here to the right) was built in 1874 as the first separate high school in Nashville. Both were torn down in 1910 for Hume-Fogg High School.

Fogg School stood at the northeast corner of Broad and Spruce (Eighth) Streets.

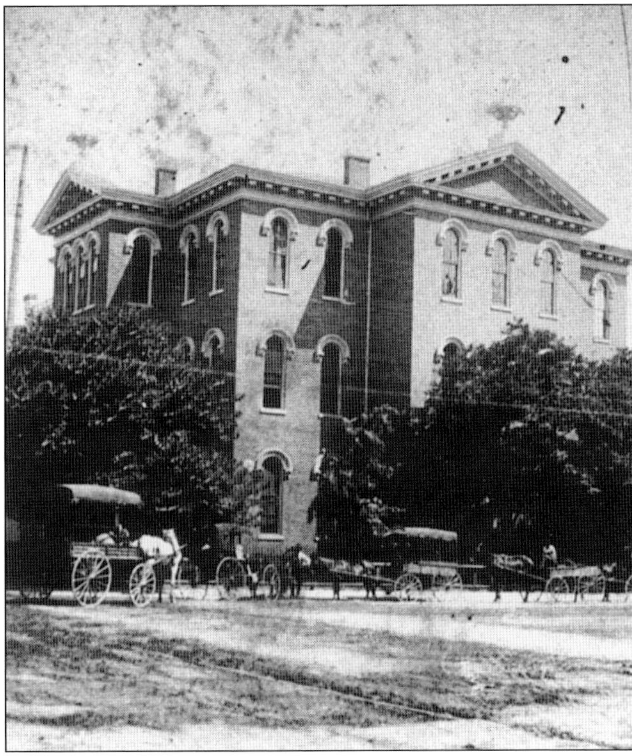

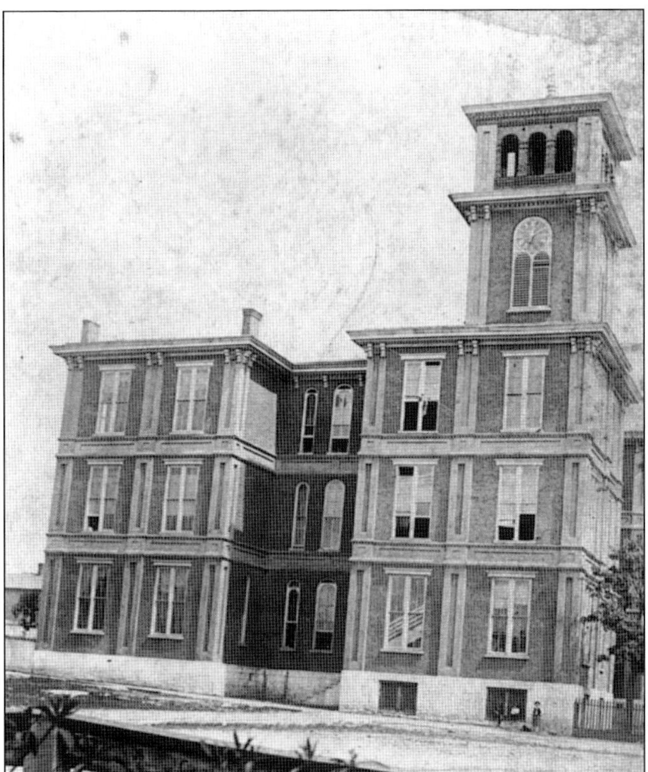

Its northwest corner visible in this photograph, Howard School stood on College Hill on College (Third) at Highland. It was designed in 1860 by Harvey Akeroyd.

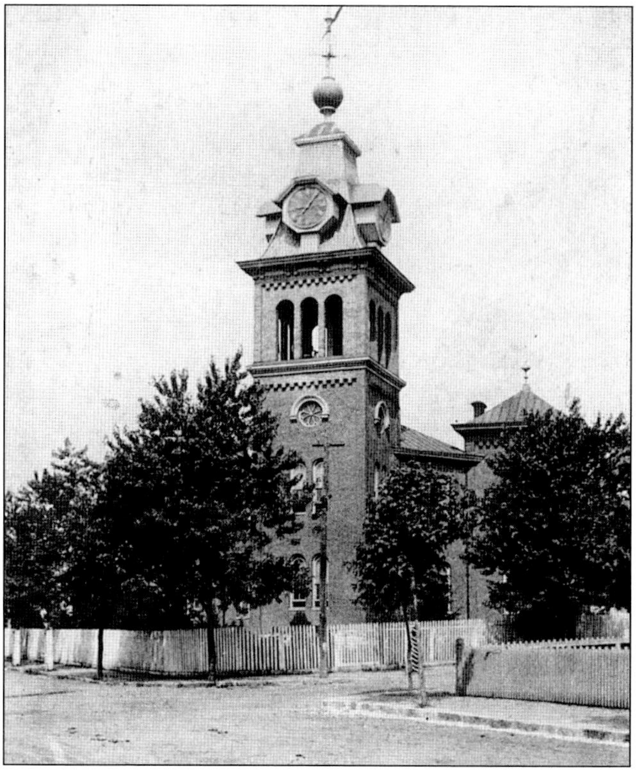

The Ninth Ward School stood at the northwest corner of High (Sixth) and Jefferson Streets. The building which housed the former Elliott School is there now.

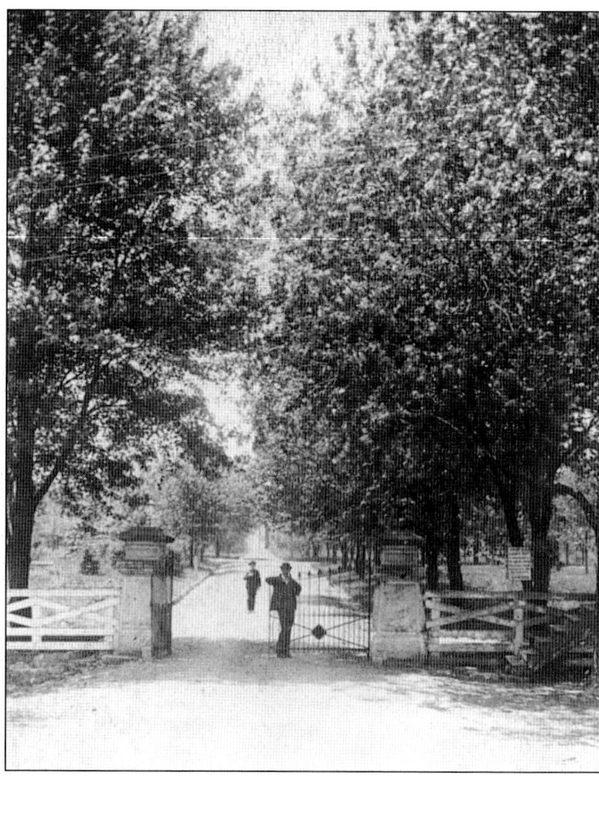

Founded in 1873 by the Methodist Episcopal Church South through a gift of cash from Commodore Cornelius Vanderbilt, Vanderbilt University is one of the leading university's in the South. This was the main gate into the university. The sign to the right reads as follows: "Know All * * * Leroy Day is employed and he alone to keep the Gate at main entrance to this University."

This is the drive leading from the former main gate at present-day Broadway and Twenty-First Avenue, South, to the Main Building. On April 28, 1874, the cornerstone was laid to this building.

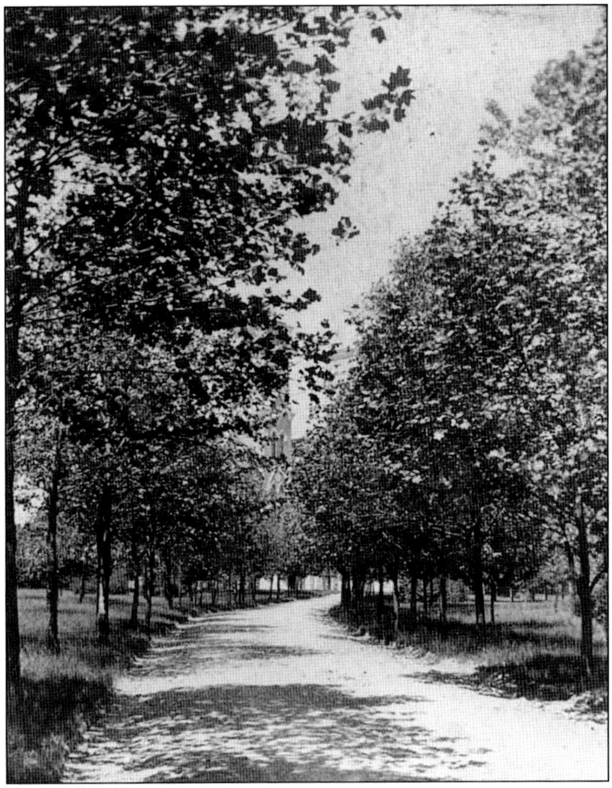

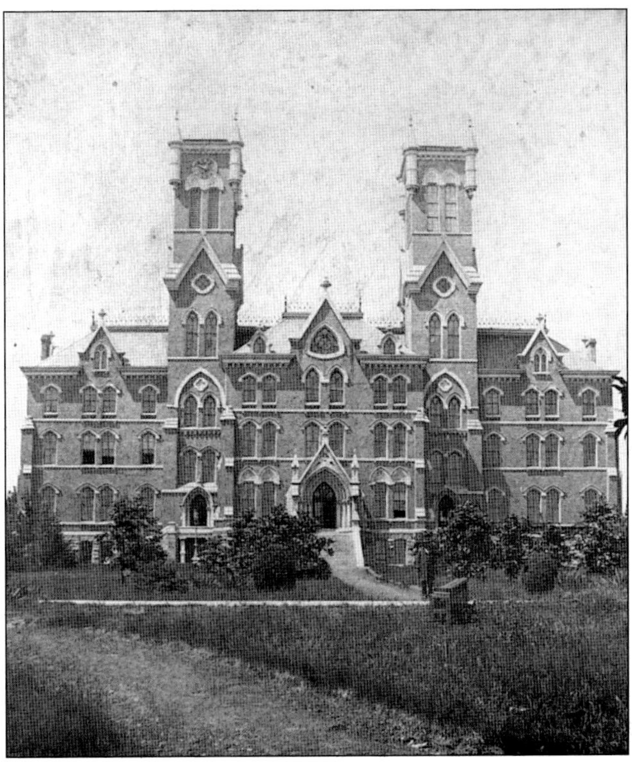

The Main Building, now called Kirkland Hall, opened for classes in October 1875. The towers soon leaked, and their mansard roofs had been taken down by 1884, when Otto Giers made this photograph. On April 20, 1905, the building was gutted by fire, and the right tower was demolished. The remaining tower was remodeled after a Siennese example.

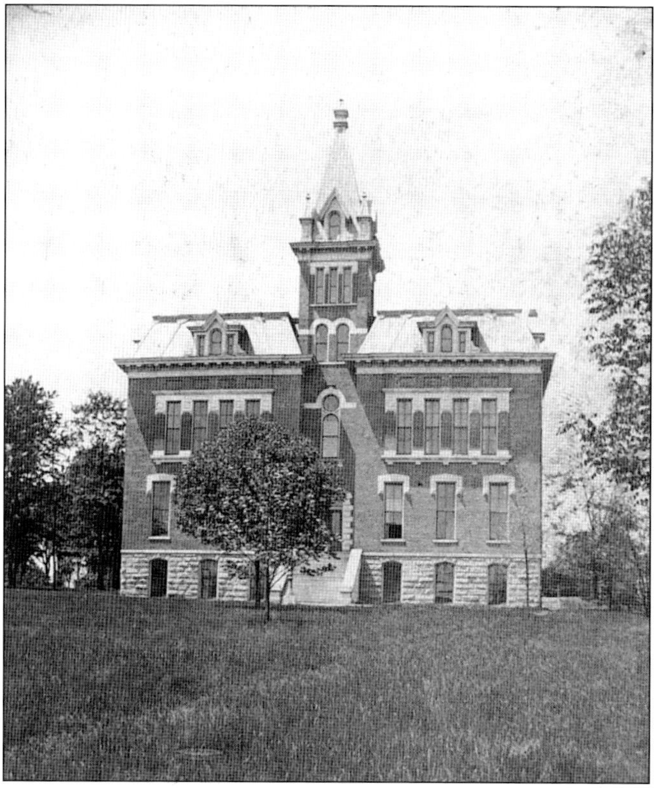

Still standing today, Science Hall, at Vanderbilt University, was opened in 1880.

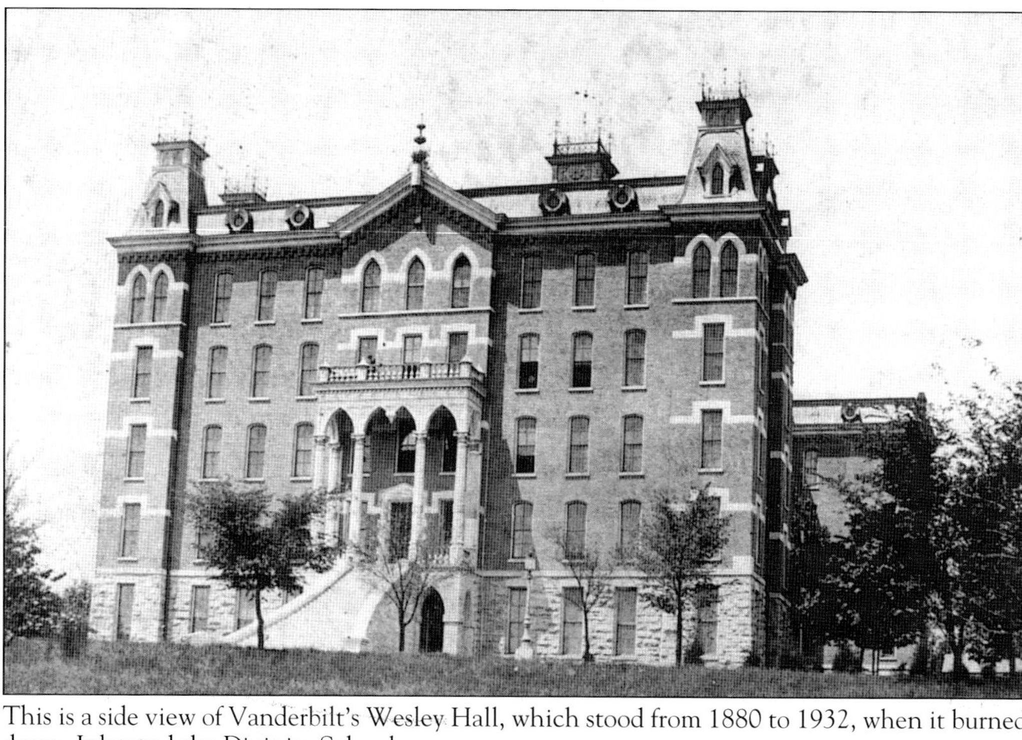

This is a side view of Vanderbilt's Wesley Hall, which stood from 1880 to 1932, when it burned down. It housed the Divinity School.

This is a view of Wesley Hall showing its front elevation and side.

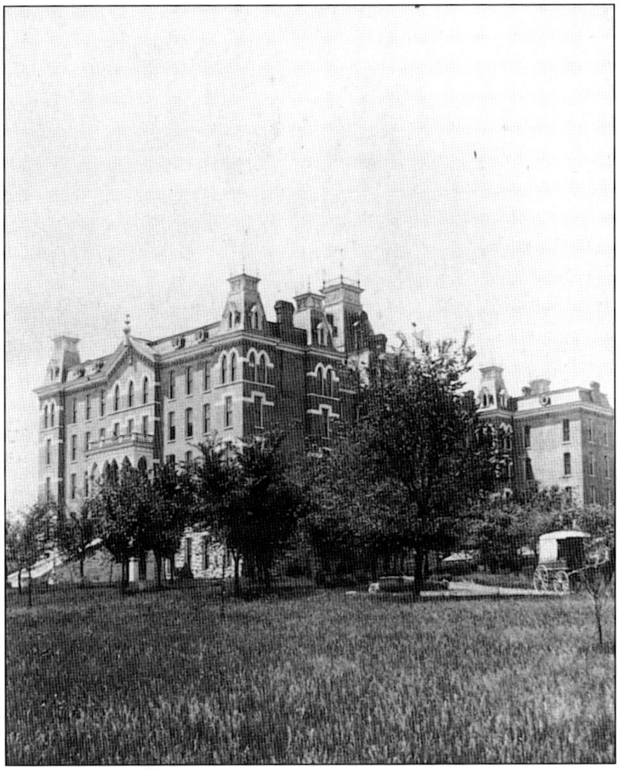

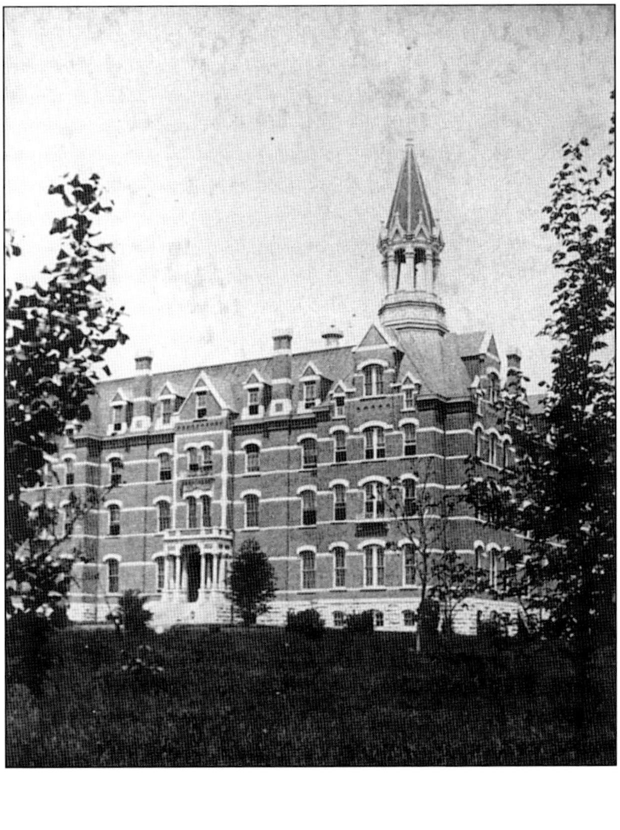

Fisk University was founded in 1866 to educate the newly freed slaves. Jubilee Hall (built from 1873 to 1876), seen here, was the first permanent building on the campus. It is still in use and stands on Jefferson Street. The Jubilee Singers gave their name to the building. A student choral group, they toured giving concerts, and thus raised the money to build this structure—their lasting monument.

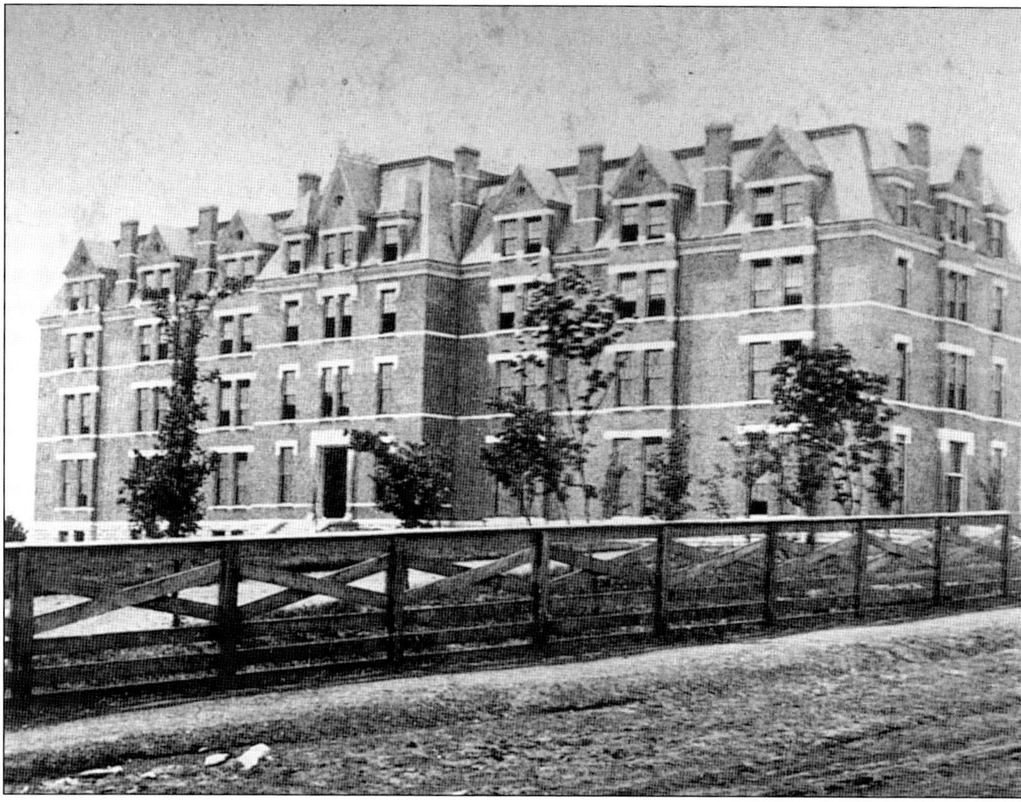

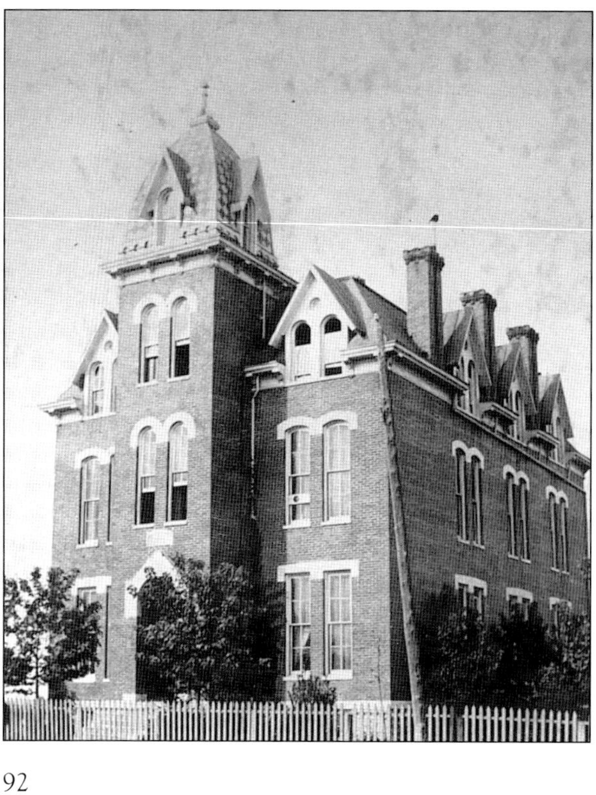

Livingstone Hall was built in 1882 and burned down in May 1970. It served as both an academic and a residential building. It was bounded by Robertson Street to the front and Salem Street to the rear; Jackson Street was to the north and Hamilton Street to the south.

Established in 1865, Central Tennessee College was located on Maple Street, south of Lafayette. It closed in the late 1920s. It was an African-American school.

The Main Building to Central Tennessee College burned in 1903, killing several students.

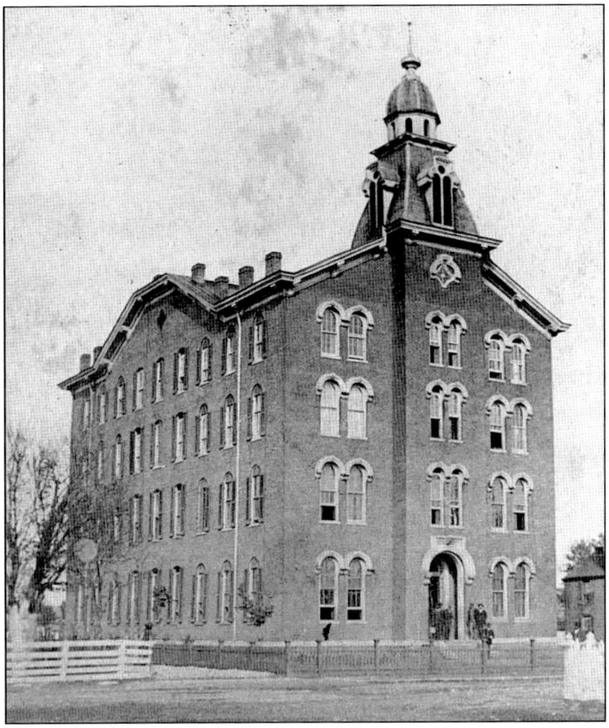

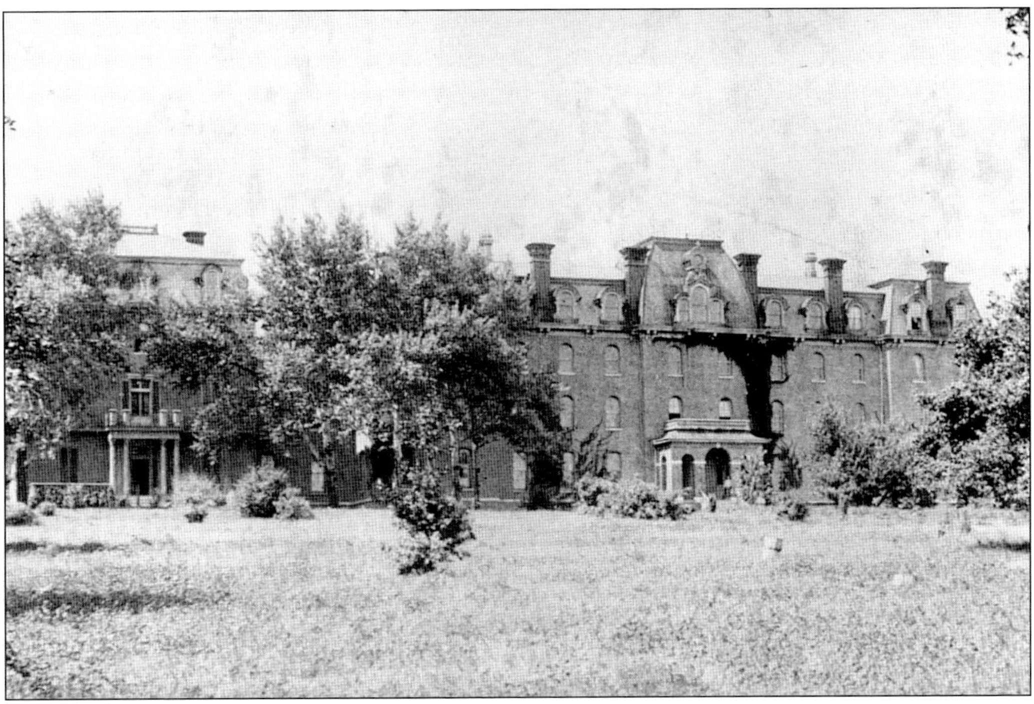

The Nashville Normal and Theological Institute was founded in 1867 by the American Baptist Home Mission Society and was incorporated as Roger Williams University on February 13, 1883. In 1876 Centennial Hall was built at this African-American university. It included most of the structure seen here, except for Mansion House to the left. It burned on January 24, 1905.

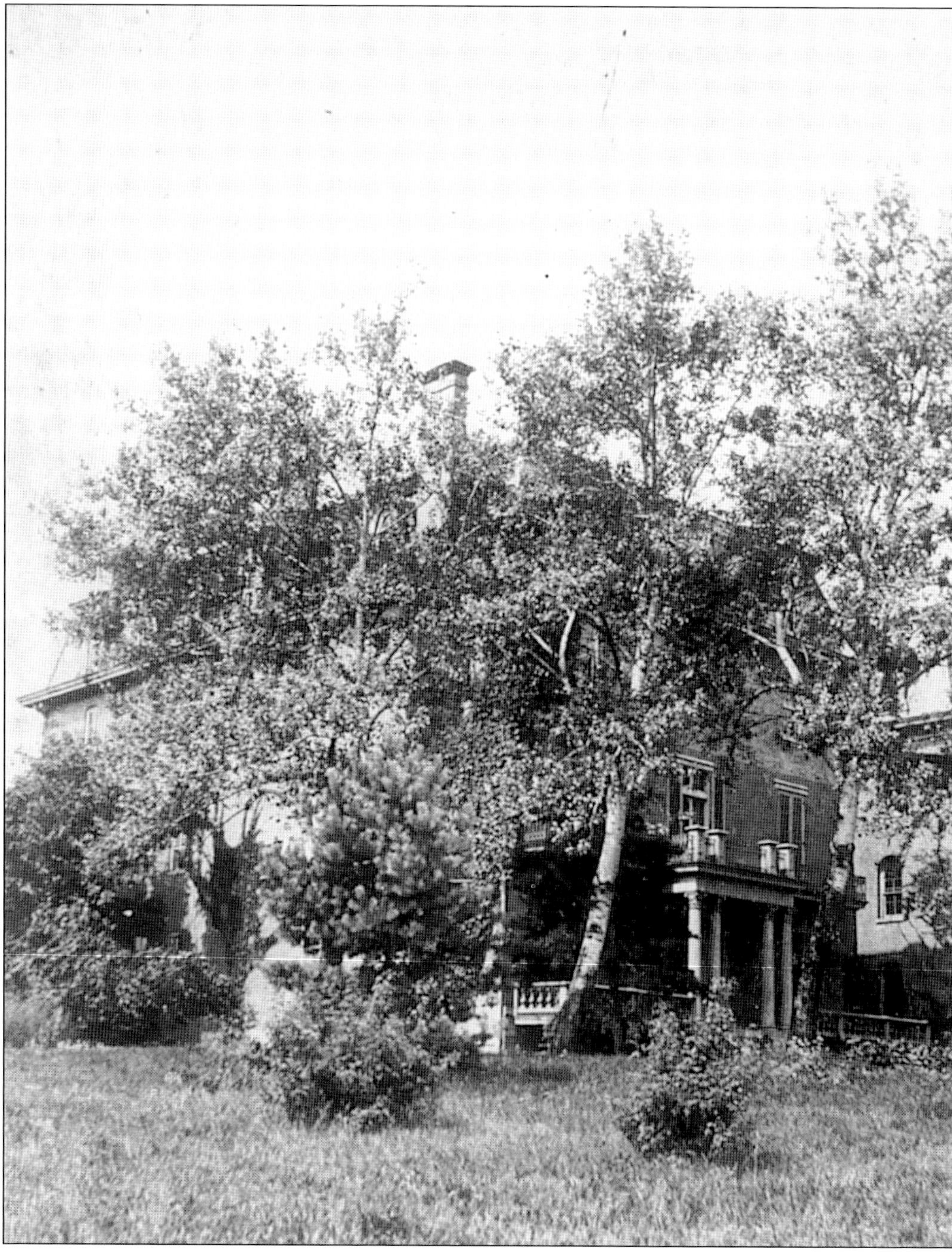

The Mansion House of William H. Gordon was purchased along with 30 acres of land on which the present campus of George Peabody College for Teachers at Vanderbilt University and part of Hillsboro Village are located today. It stood where the Social and Religious Building is now. Built in the 1850s, a third story with a mansard roof was added in 1875, when the school moved to this new location. It burned on May 22, 1905. In 1908 the school relocated to White's Creek Pike. In 1910 part of the property was purchased for Peabody College.

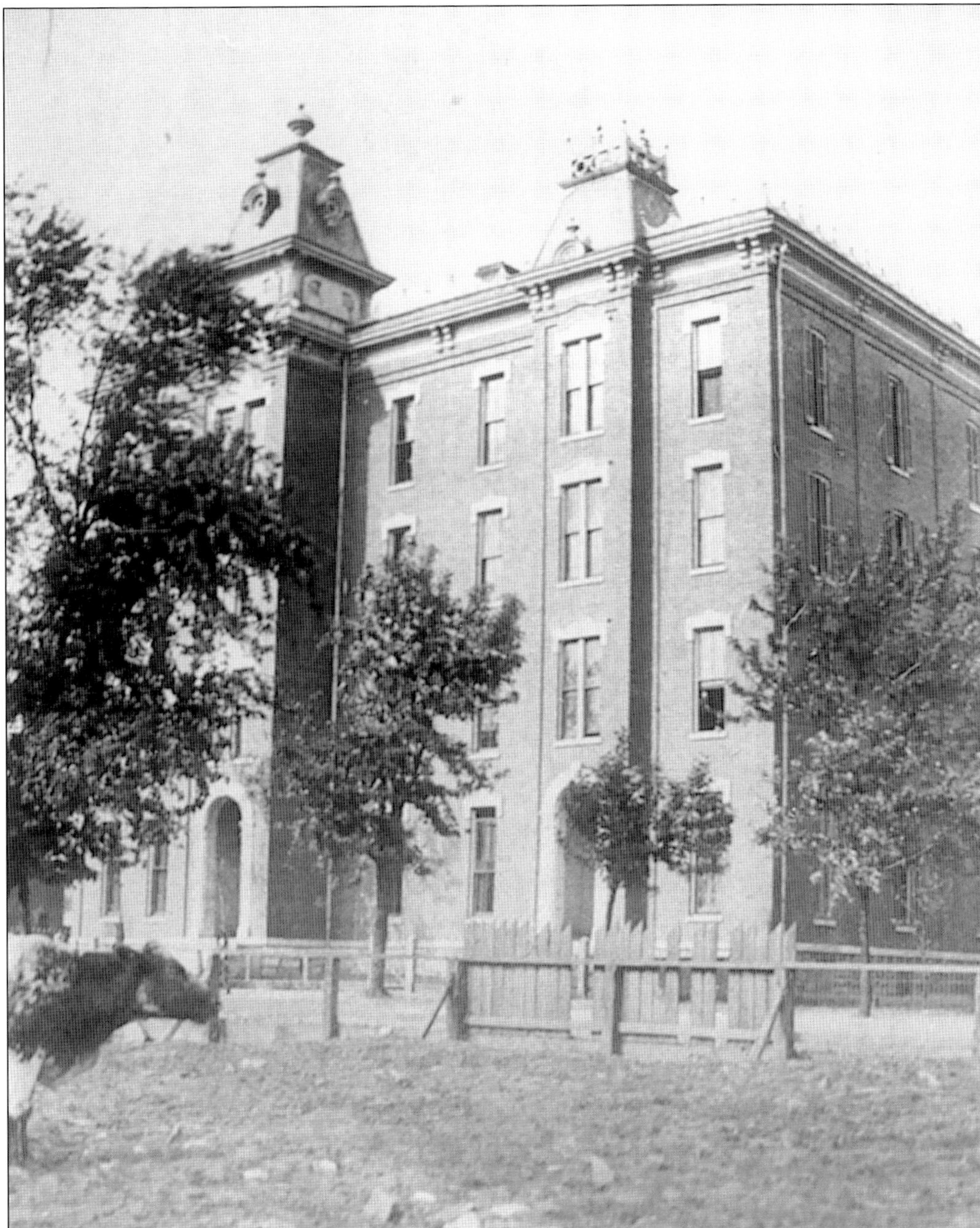

George W.F. Price operated the Nashville College for Young Ladies from this building at 6 Vauxhall Street. The Federal Courthouse is there today. Apparently, they had fresh milk.

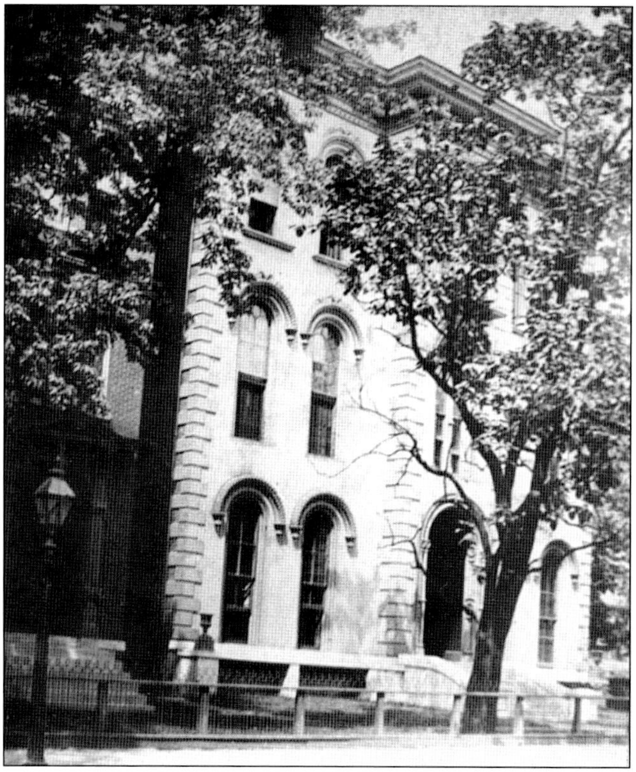

Ward's Seminary was a Presbyterian girls' school on Spruce (Eighth) Street near Church Street, on the west side. The Savage-Zerfoss house, at 165 Eighth Avenue North, is the building to the left.

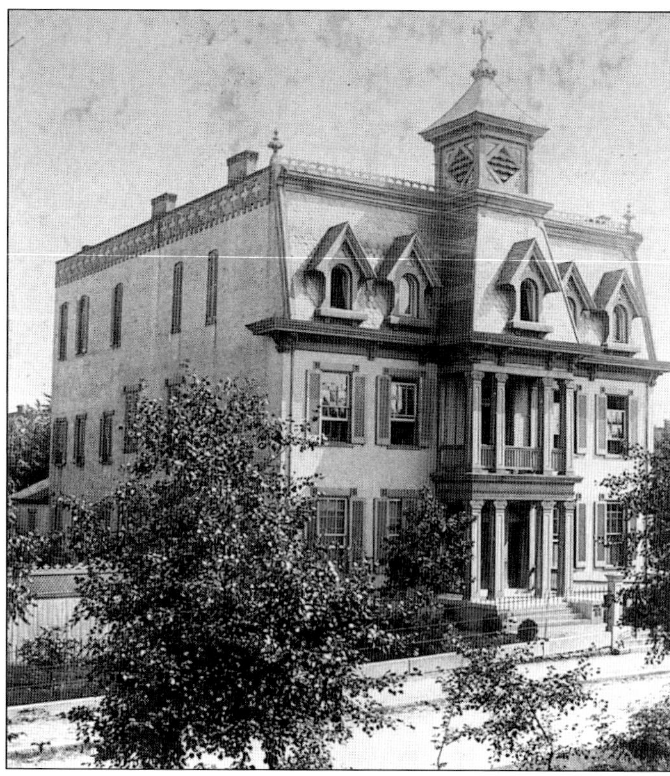

St. Bernard Academy was housed in the former home of George Washington Campbell, on Cedar Street, across from the south entrance to the Capitol.

Six

THE BUCKLE OF THE BIBLE BELT

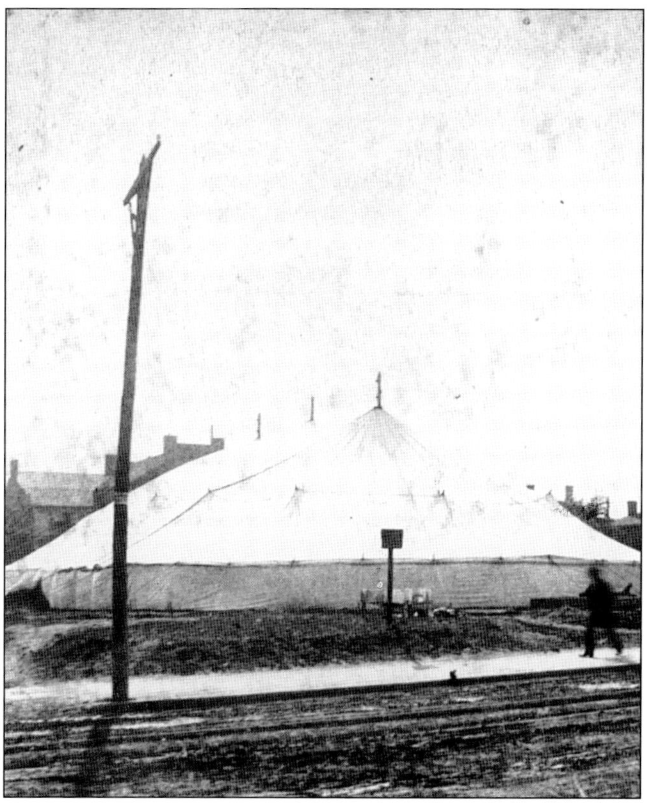

On May 10, 1885, evangelist Sam Jones held a revival in this tent at Spruce (Eighth) and Broad. Tom Ryman and some other riverboatmen attended. They had intended to beat up the preacher, but instead, they were won over. Attendance reached 10,000 people, one fifth of the city population, and 2,500 were turned away. Ryman led a campaign to build a Union Gospel Tabernacle for revivals to be held in. It was built on Summer (Fifth) Street, and Jones preached in it when it opened. After Ryman's death in 1904, its name was changed to the Ryman Auditorium, and Sam Jones preached to 4,000 people at the funeral.

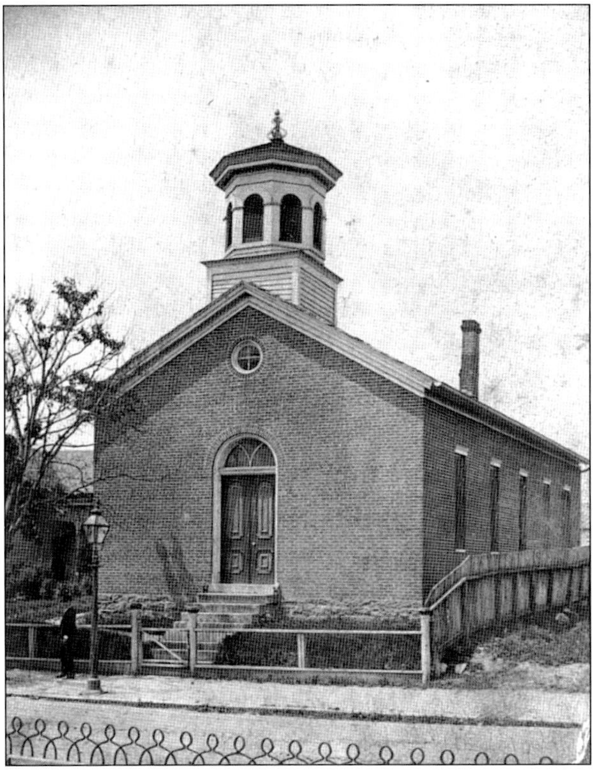

This is an unidentified Nashville church.

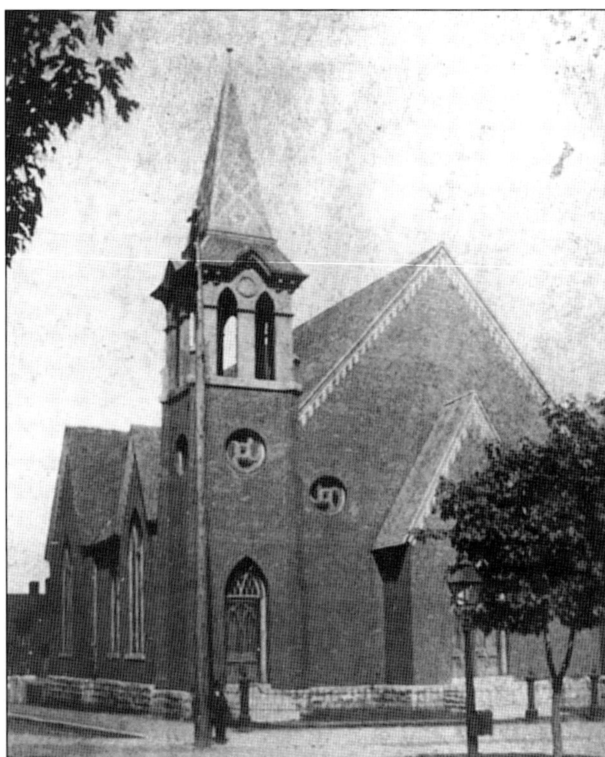

This is another unidentified Nashville church.

St. Ann's Episcopal Church, on Woodland Street, was located between Fourth Street and Fifth Street and was destroyed by the April 16, 1998 Nashville tornado. Bishop Charles Quintard laid the cornerstone in 1882, and the church was consecrated on June 10, 1885. It had a signed Tiffany glass panel in the door leading from the nave to the Parish Hall.

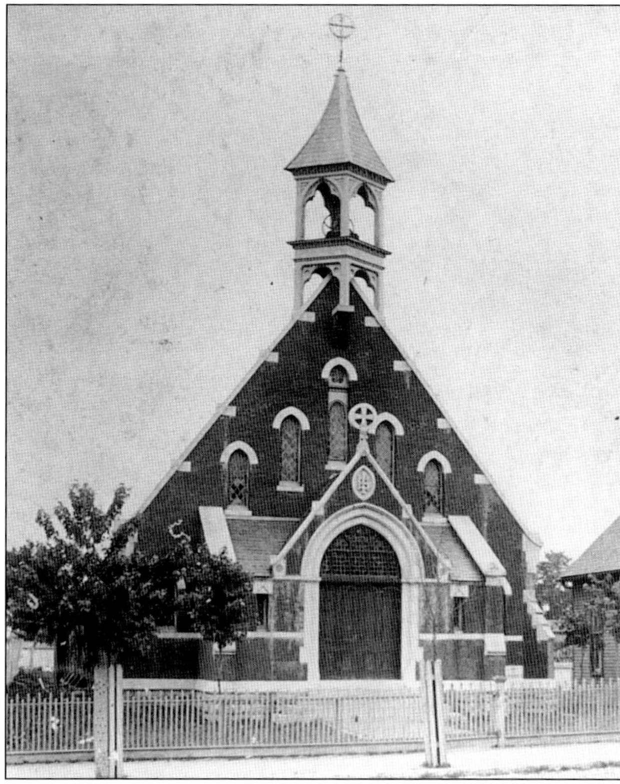

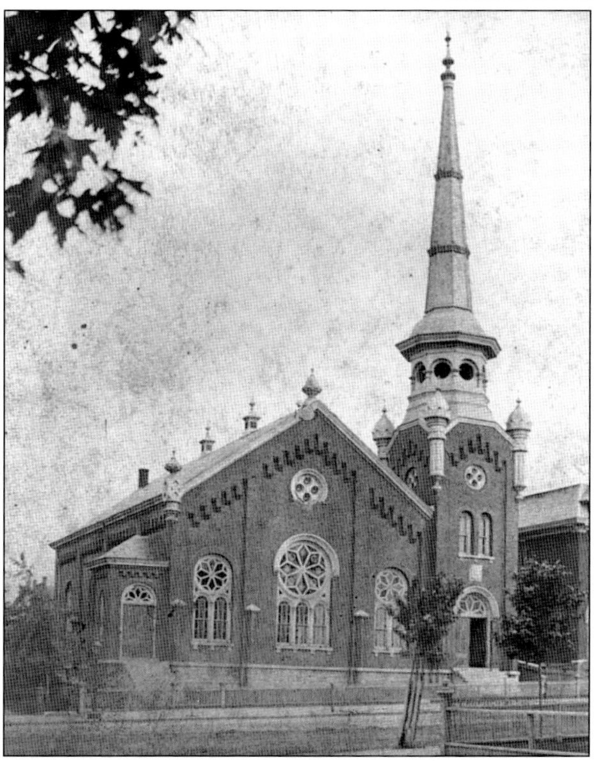

Moore Memorial Presbyterian Church was begun in 1872 and was designed by W.K. Dobson. It stood on Broadway, prior to the fork in the road, on the north side near Stonewall Avenue.

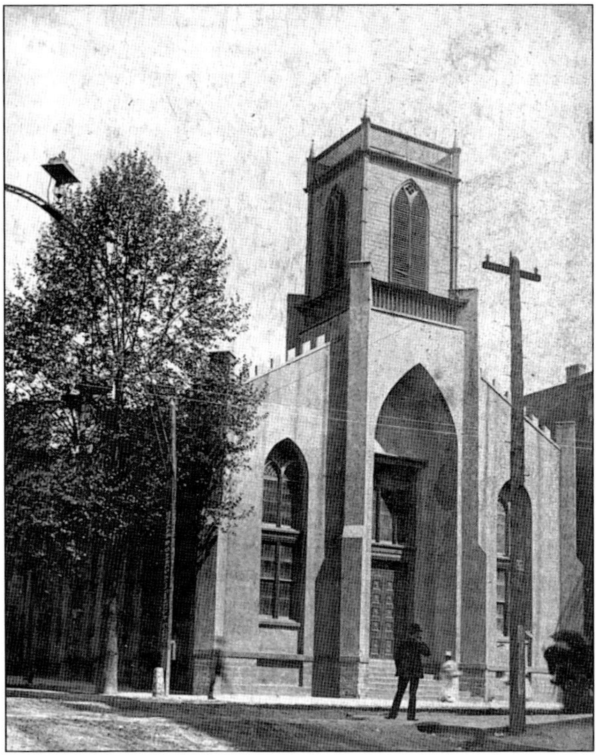

Christ Episcopal Church stood on Church Street at the northeast corner of High (Sixth) Street. It was designed around 1830 by Hugh Roland and was one of the earliest Gothic Revival buildings erected in Tennessee. The congregation moved to Broad and McLemore (Ninth) in 1890.

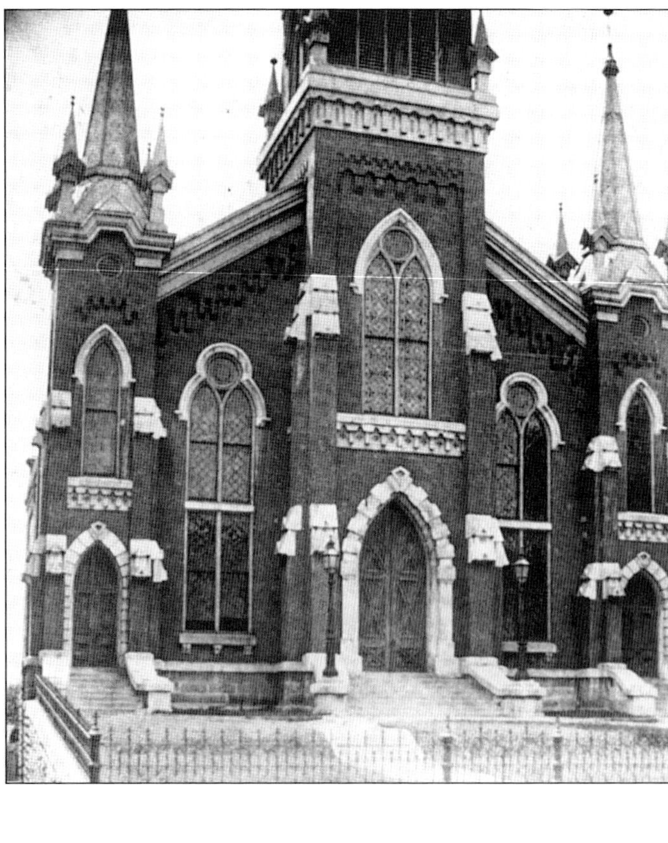

McKendree Methodist Church, designed by Hugh C. Thompson, opened in 1879. It stood where the present building is on Church Street, between Summer (Fifth) and High (Sixth). It burned in 1905. McKendree is the oldest congregation in Nashville.

First Presbyterian Church of Nashville, designed by William Strickland in an Egyptian Revival style, opened in 1851. The congregation divided in 1954, and most of them moved to the city of Oak Hill, Tennessee. Since then, this has been The Downtown Presbyterian Church. It stands at the southeast corner of Summer (Fifth) and Church Streets. When this photograph was made *c.* 1885, the windows were still clear glass. Stained glass was installed in 1887. Note the staircase visible in the tower. Also note that the tower has a decorative grillwork in it.

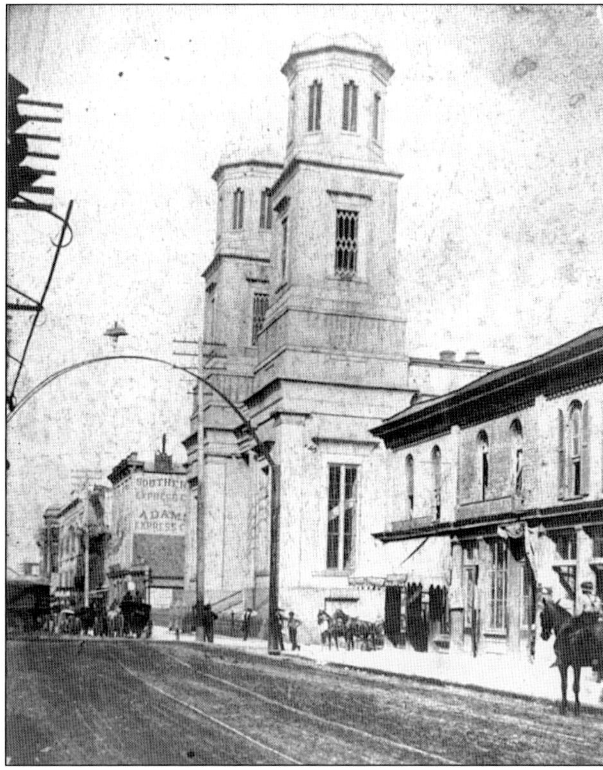

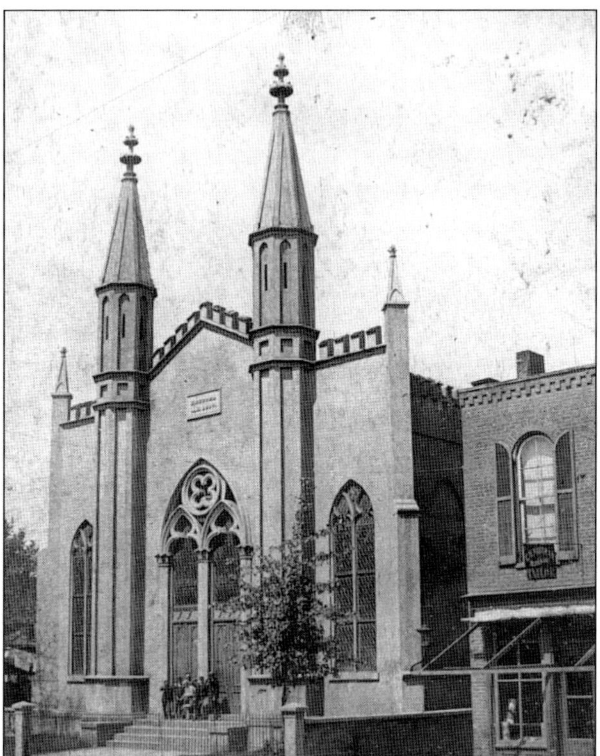

Built from 1839 to 1841, this building, designed by Adolphus Heiman, was originally the First Baptist Church of Nashville. The Baptists worshiped here until 1884. When Otto Giers photographed it that year, it had just become the German Lutheran Church of Nashville and served First Lutheran until 1951, when it was demolished. It stood on Summer (Fifth) between Union and Deaderick, where the Bank of America has an office now. The Baptists had moved from here to Broad and Spruce (Eighth).

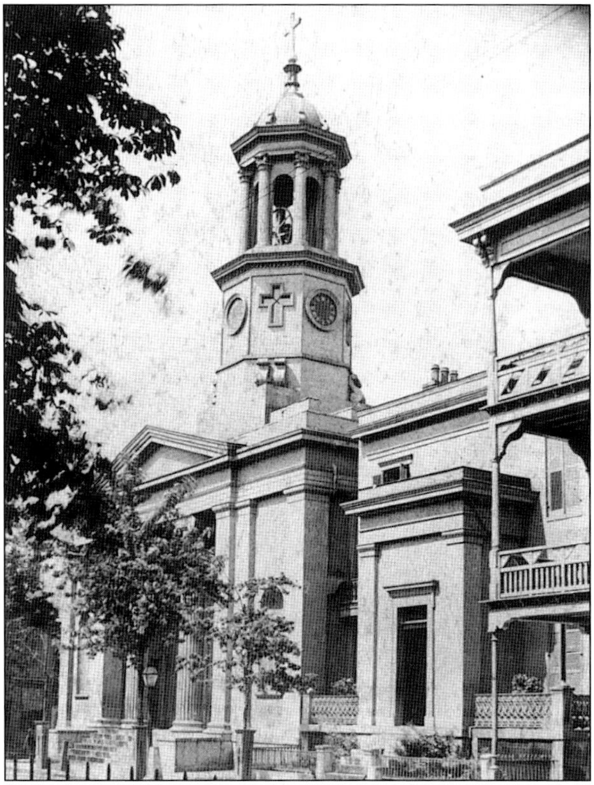

St. Mary's Cathedral was the Catholic center of Nashville. Its cornerstone was laid in 1844, and the structure was completed in 1847. Adolphus Heiman, whose home is seen here to the right of the church, was the architect. In 1926 the architectural firm of Asmus and Clark severely altered both the exterior and interior. The facade of brick was covered with limestone, and the wooden columns were replaced with stone. The volutes at the base and top to the tower were removed. The clocks were also removed, and the bell chamber was enclosed with louvers.

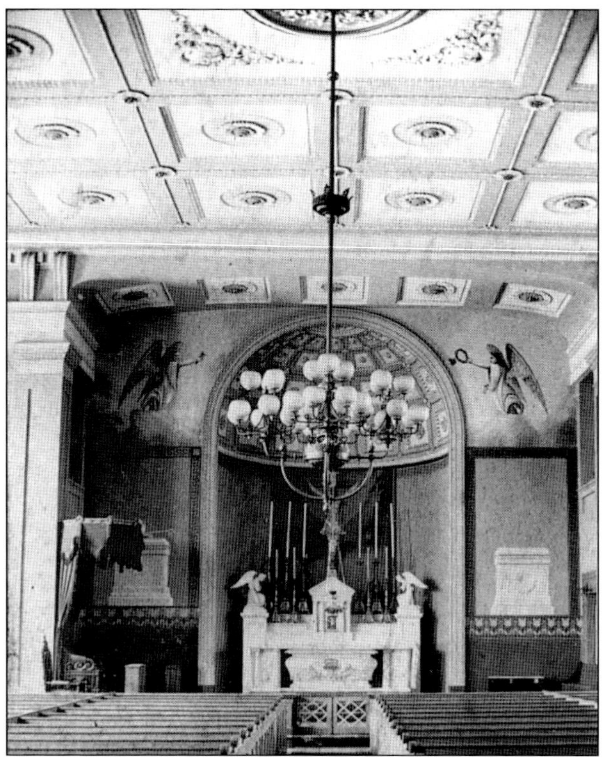

This is the original interior to St. Mary's, prior to the 1901 and 1926 remodelings. Bishop Byrne removed the gasolier and the ceiling, and he also removed the frescos. The one to the left is a representation of a cenotaph with Bishop Miles's miter and crozier resting upon it. Miles was the bishop who built the cathedral and was buried beneath the altar at that time. His coffin is now in the narthex.

This view is of St. Mary's Cathedral in 1884. The interior was severely altered in 1901 and 1926. The altar, ceiling, pews, frescos, and lighting have all been replaced.

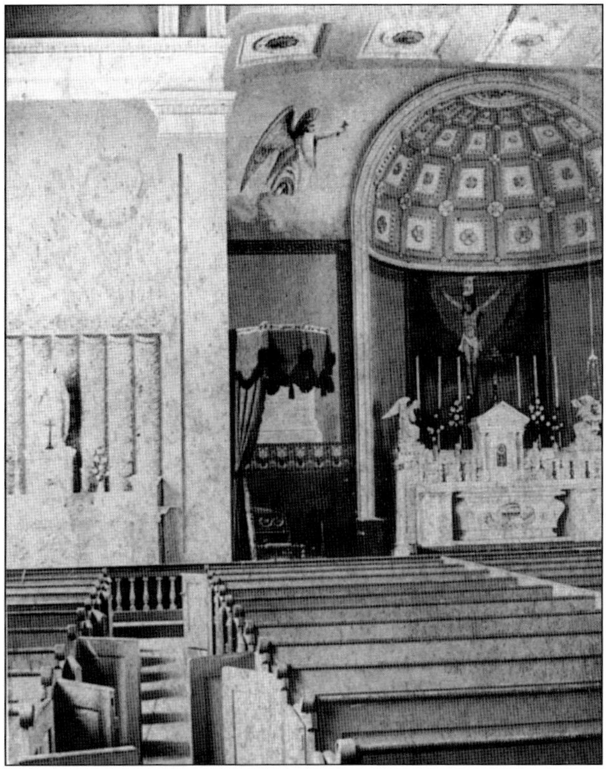

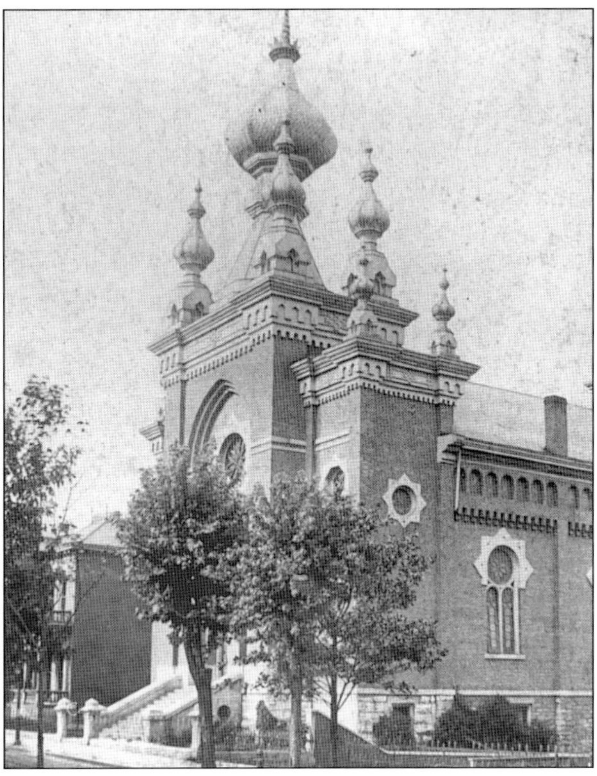

The cornerstone to congregation Ohavai Sholom's Vine Street Temple was laid in 1874. Former President Andrew Johnson attended the ceremony, led by Rabbi Isaac M. Wise. The building was dedicated in 1876 and continued in use until 1955. It stood on present-day Seventh Avenue, between Church and Commerce, on the east side. W.K. Dobson was the architect. Due to its nine Russian onion domes, it had a very interesting facade.

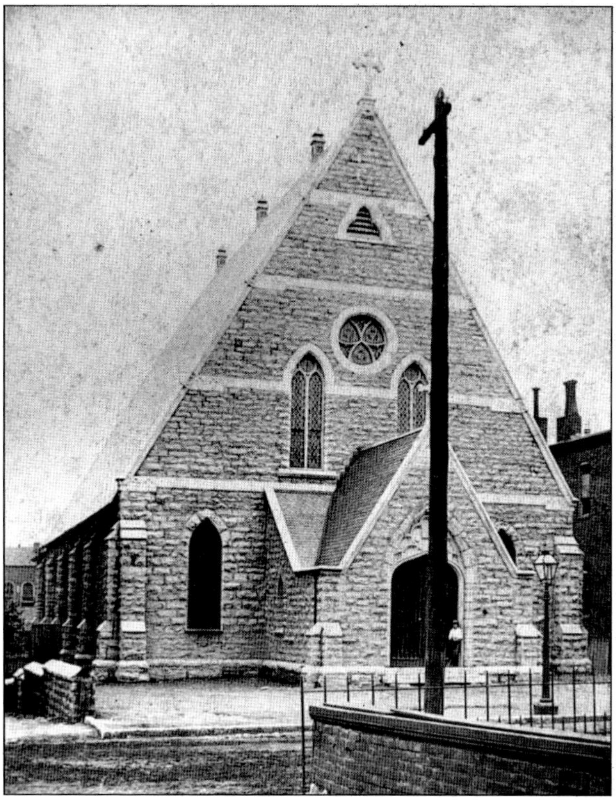

The Episcopal Church of the Advent stood on the corner of Vine (Seventh) Street and Cumberland Alley (Commerce Street), on the southeast corner. It was designed by Henry Dudley and was begun in 1859. The Civil War delayed its completion until 1870. Charles Tomes, the rector at Christ Episcopal, had resigned that congregation's leadership over their practice of renting pews. He saw this as a hindrance to the evangelization of the poor. He then founded the Church of the Advent but died within months of its founding. Charles Quintard succeeded him as rector. In 1910 they moved to Seventeenth Avenue South at Edgehill, and in 1972 they moved to Franklin Road. Each of those times they also moved four stained-glass windows and the stone cross above the door. The First Church of Christ Scientist used the building until 1955, when it was levelled.

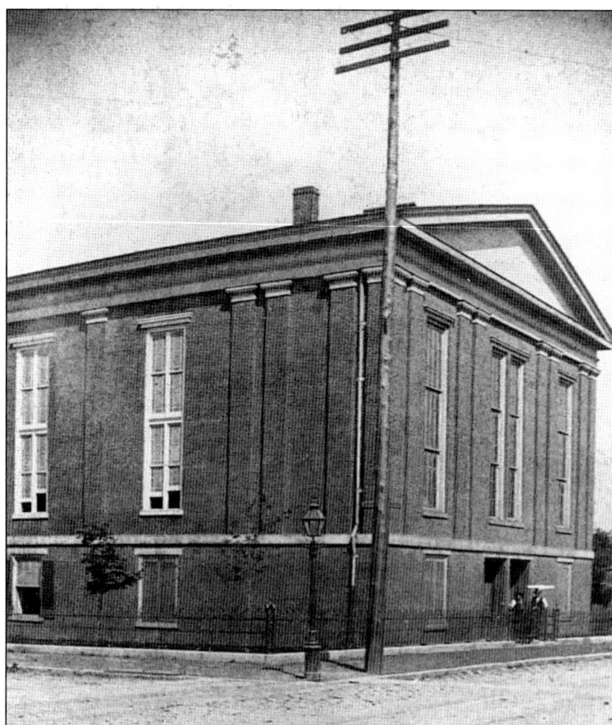

Measuring 58 by 92 feet, Central (or Cherry Street) Baptist Church was built from 1858 to 1859 at the southeast corner of Cherry (Fourth) and Elm Streets.

This is an interior view of Central Baptist Church in *c.* 1885. The ornamental stenciling on the baptismal walls and the gas lamps are of particular interest.

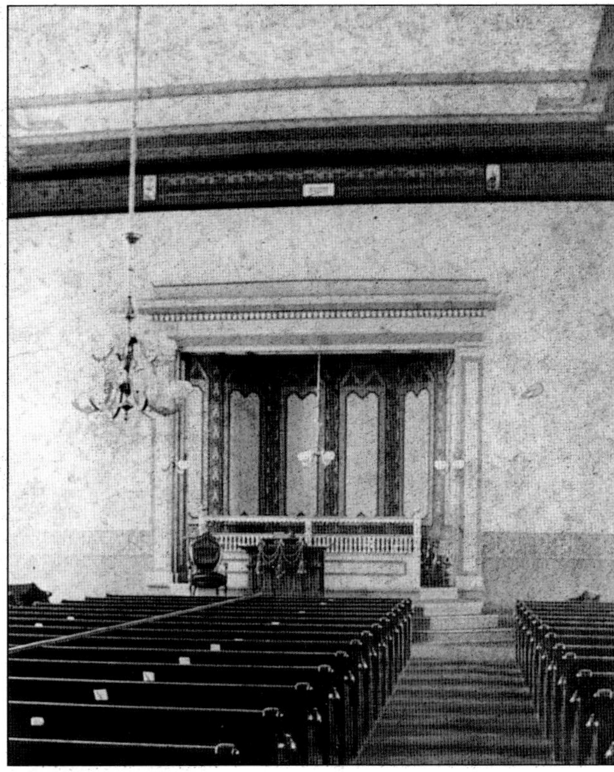

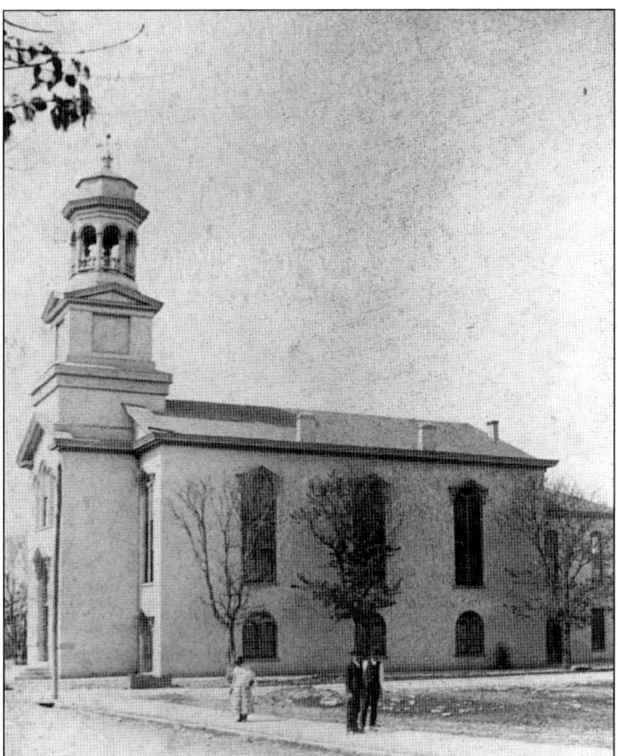

Elm Street Methodist Church, built in 1860, stood at the southeast corner of Summer (Fifth) and Elm Streets. Riverboat Captain Thomas Ryman joined the congregation in 1885, after attending a revival held by Sam Jones in a tent on Broad Street. The top of the steeple was lost between 1864 and 1885. The remaining half of the steeple, seen here, burned in 1925 and was not replaced. In 1971 the church closed, and the stained glass was sold to Friday's restaurant. It was converted into office space in 1987 for PMT Services, Inc., and Myles Maille was commissioned to paint two very large paintings of a church choir to hang on the front walls. In 1995 the architectural firm of Tuck Hinton moved into the building and remodeled the interior. The Maille paintings were given to the State Museum by the partners in PMT.

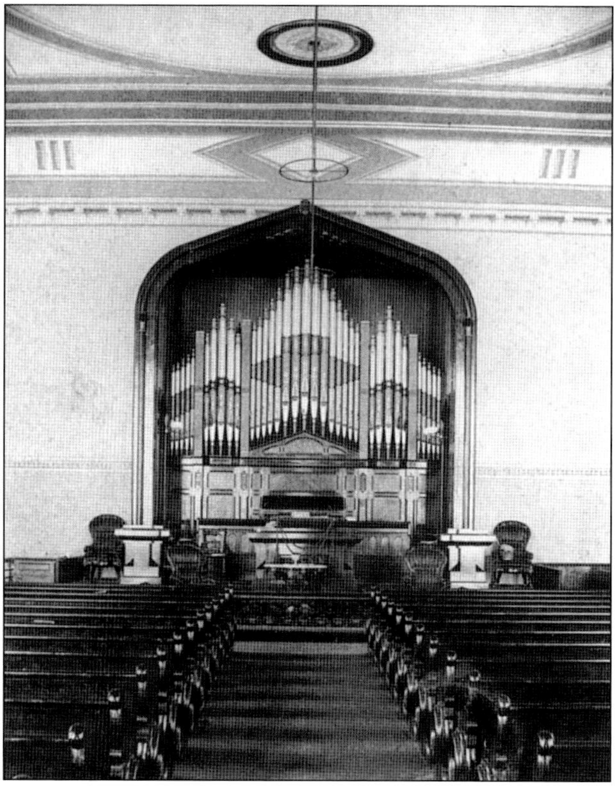

This is an interior view of Elm Street Methodist Church. The ceiling, walls, and organ pipes were all decoratively stenciled.

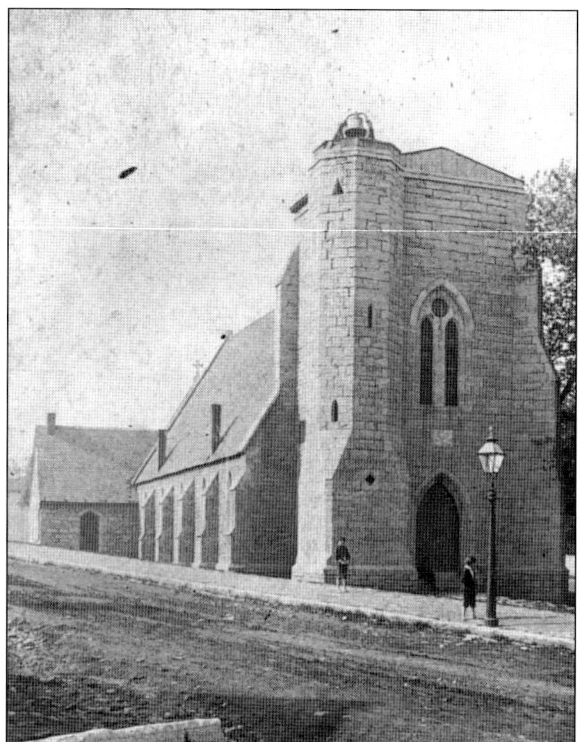

Holy Trinity Church's cornerstone was laid in 1852 by Charles Tomes, rector of Christ Church Episcopal. He had asked fellow Englishmen Wills and Dudley, architects of New York City, to design it. The tower was completed in 1887.

St. Peter's Episcopal Chapel stood on North McLemore (Ninth), between Scovel and Madison Streets, facing east. The Reverend M.C. Martin was the rector. This board and batten Gothic Revival chapel is reminiscent of Grace Episcopal Church in Spring Hill, which was designed by P.J. Williamson, so perhaps he designed this one as well.

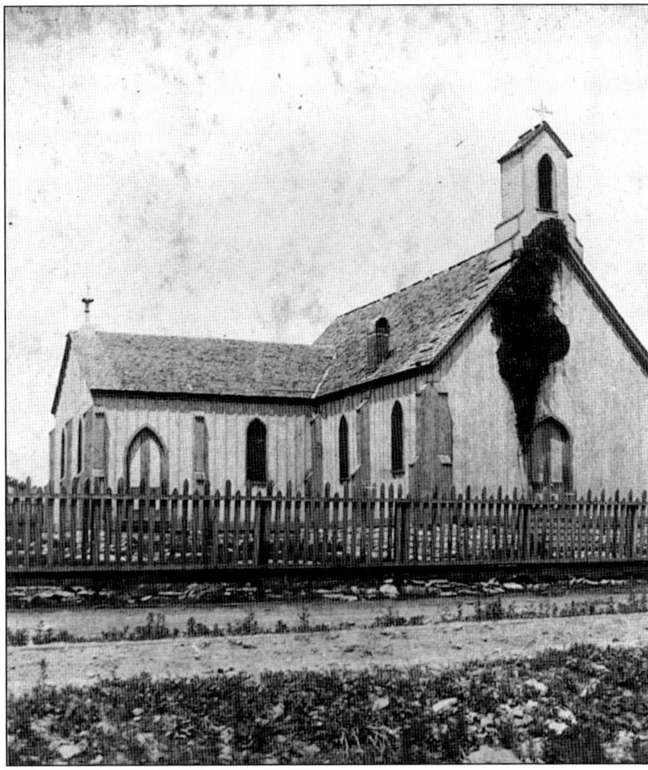

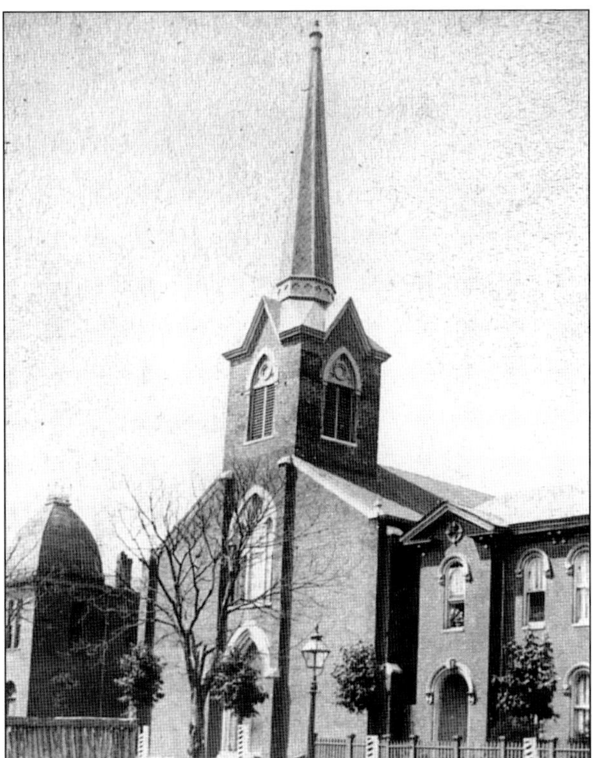

The Church of the Assumption of the Blessed Virgin Mary, built between 1856 and 1859, stands at the southwest corner of Vine (Seventh) and Monroe Streets.
The north wall is made from bricks from the first Roman Catholic Church in Nashville, Holy Rosary, which stood on Capitol Hill.

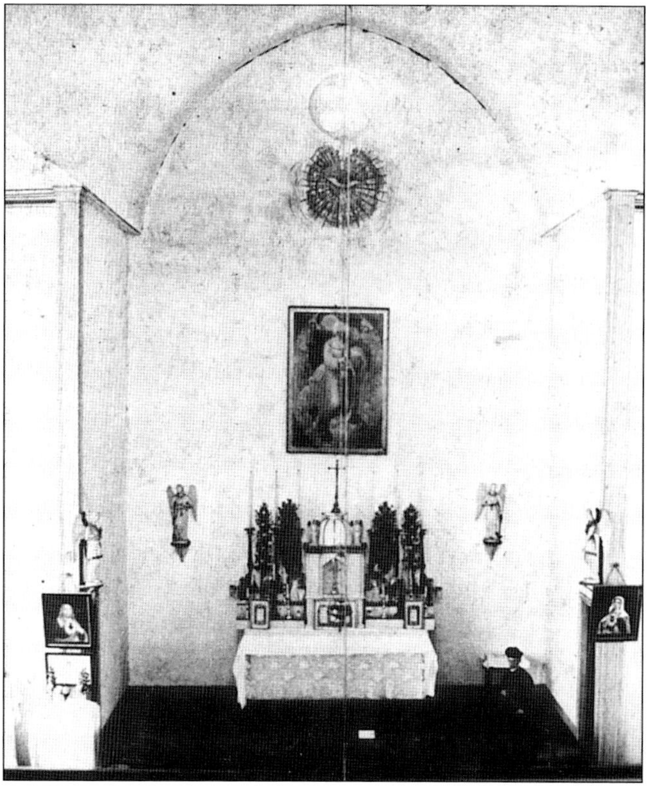

This is an interior view of Assumption c. 1885. In the next decade, this austere interior was heavily remodeled. Father John A. Vogel and Jacob Geiger are believed to have designed the original church.

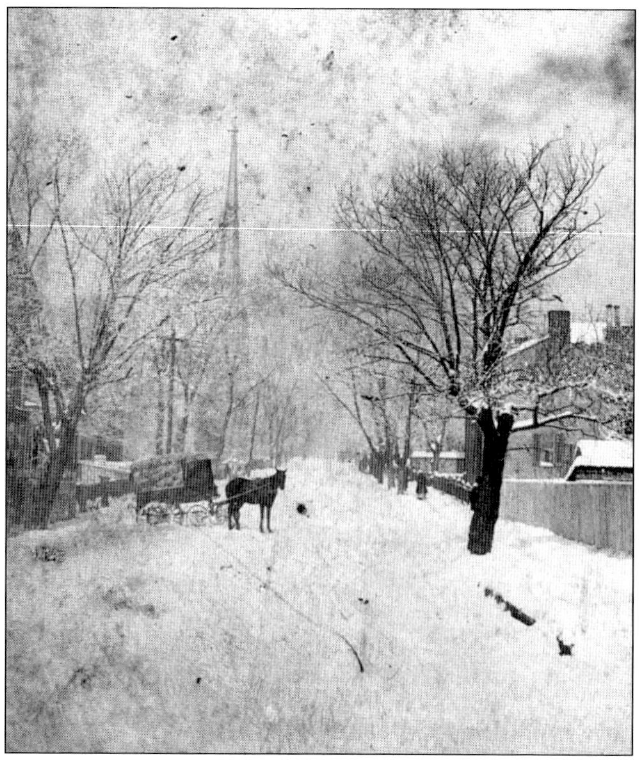

The Great Snow of 1884–1885 is seen here along Vine (Seventh) Street north near Monroe. The steeple on Assumption Church is seen on the left.

Advertising itself as open during the season from 4 a.m. to 9 p.m., the Nashville Sulphur Spring, with bathhouse attached, was at 276 North Cherry (Fourth) Street on the east side, about where Herman Street is now. Bath tickets were 30¢ or four for $1.

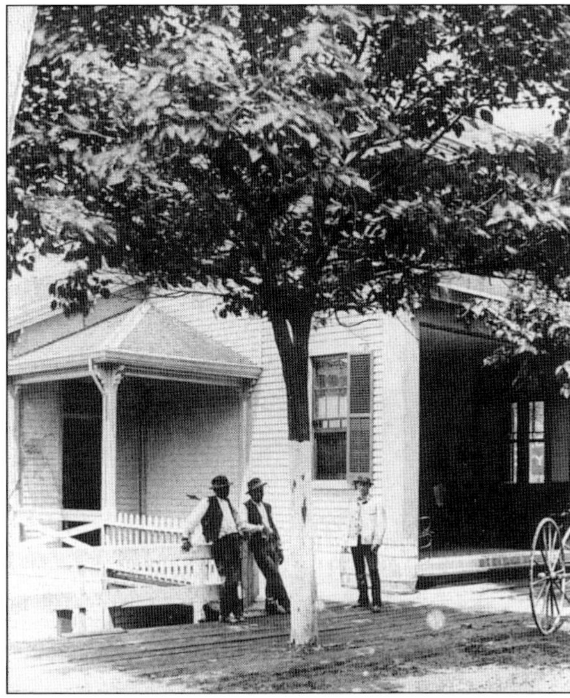

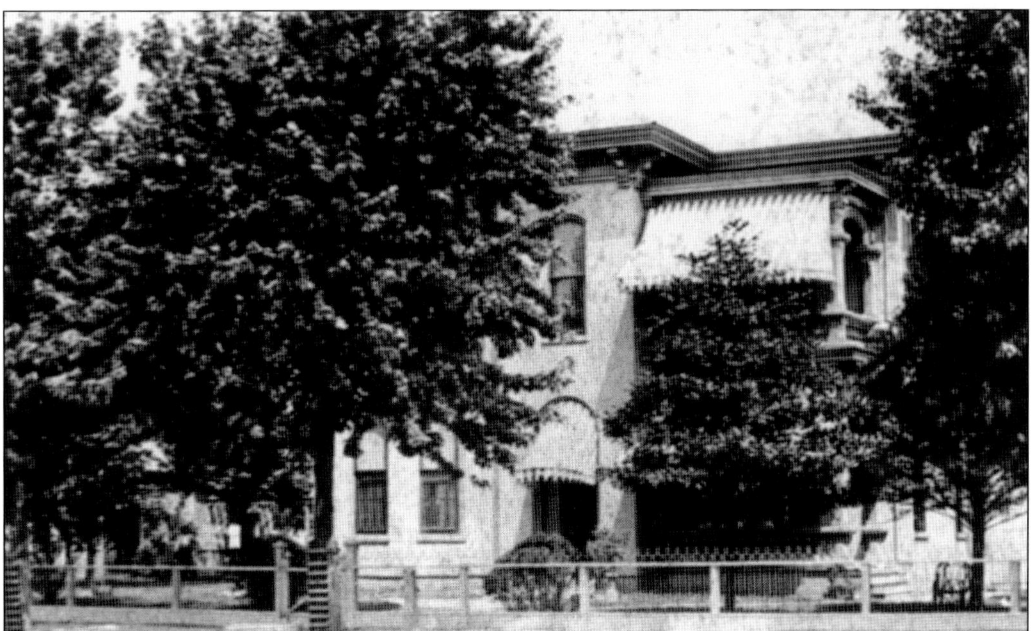

This is the residence of John Ruhm, editor of *The Tennessee Staats Zeitung* who campaigned editorially for the German neighborhood to be annexed to Nashville in 1865. After his work, it became the Ninth Ward. Ruhm also used his newspaper, the only German daily ever published in the South outside of New Orleans, to promote better education.

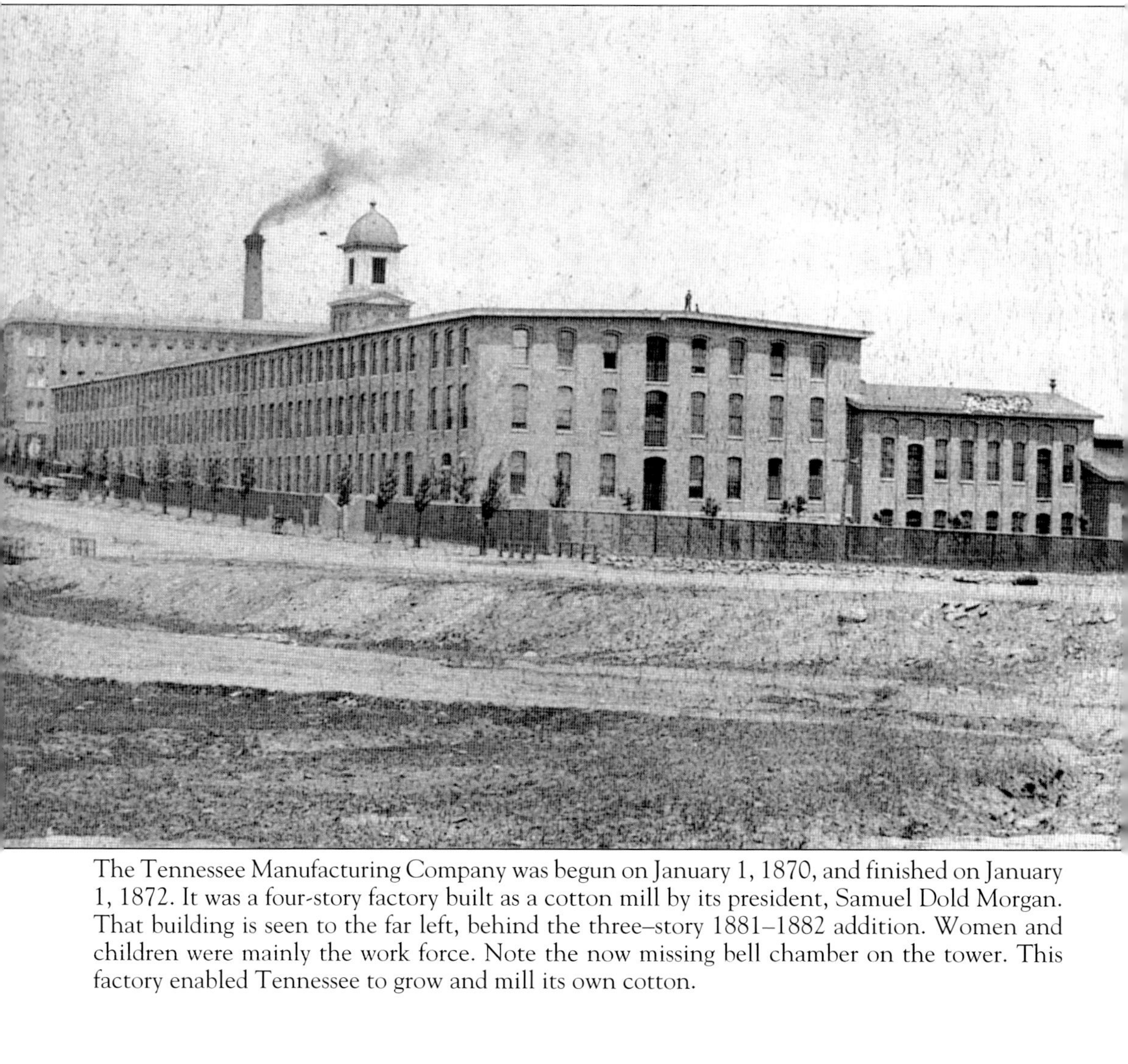

The Tennessee Manufacturing Company was begun on January 1, 1870, and finished on January 1, 1872. It was a four-story factory built as a cotton mill by its president, Samuel Dold Morgan. That building is seen to the far left, behind the three–story 1881–1882 addition. Women and children were mainly the work force. Note the now missing bell chamber on the tower. This factory enabled Tennessee to grow and mill its own cotton.

Seven

Belle Meade: Queen of Tennessee Plantations

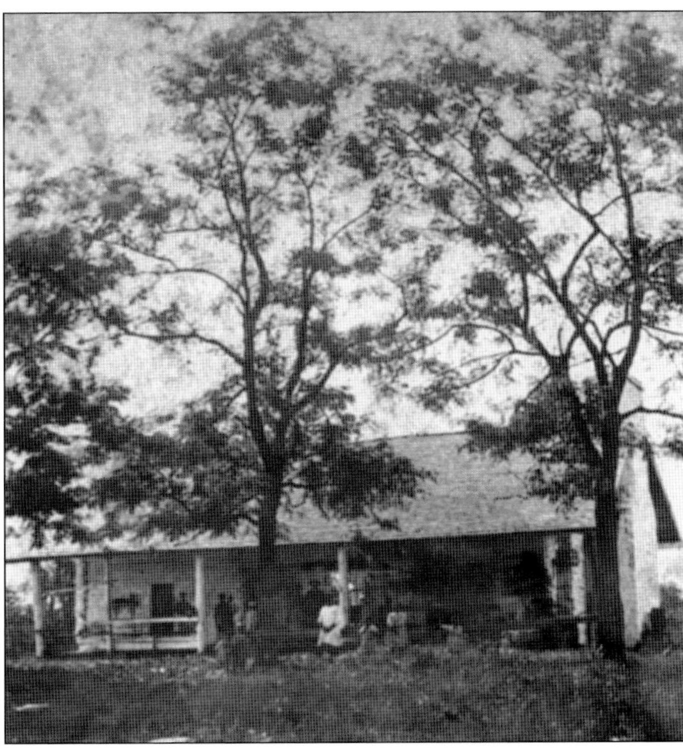

The birthplace in 1808 of William Giles Harding, this dog-trot cabin, in part, predates the Hardings living on this stretch of Richland Creek. Daniel A. Dunham built one crib to the double cabin around 1792. Bob Green, head hostler at the Belle Meade thoroughbred stud farm, lived here from 1884 to 1885 and is seen here with his family. Bob Green married when he was nearly 50, and by the time he was 67, he and his wife had eight children.

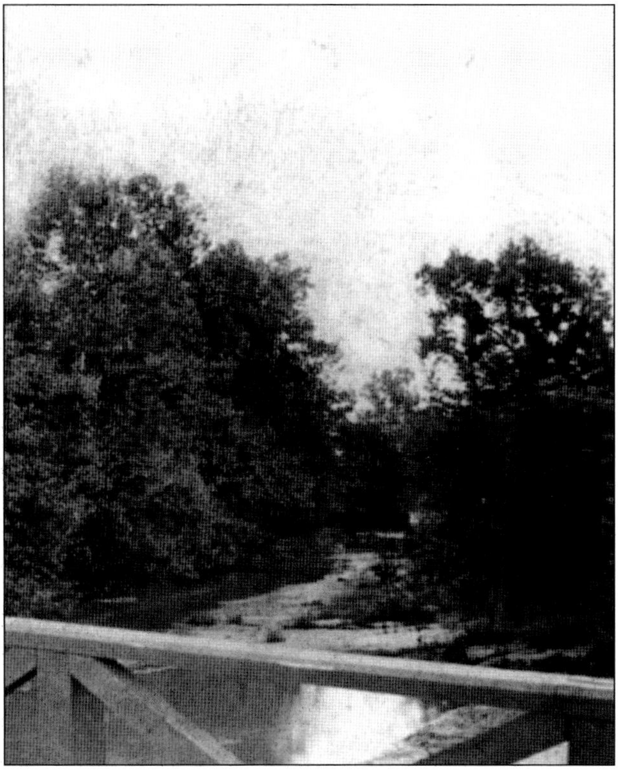

This bridge crossed Richland Creek from the Harding Pike to the Harding home. In 1807 John Harding purchased part of the Dunham land grant. He boarded horses there for such people as Sam Houston and Ralph E.W. Earl. John Harding served as the president of the Nashville Jockey Club in 1830.

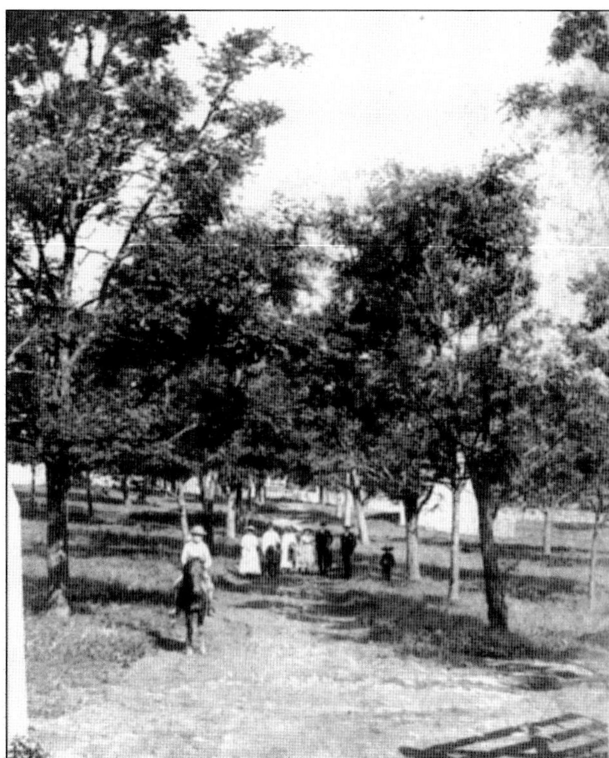

In 1839 John Harding turned over the management of Belle Meade to his son, William Giles Harding. By 1820 John Harding had built a two-story, two rooms over two rooms, brick home. In 1853 the depth of the house was doubled, and a limestone entablature and six stone columns were added to the facade. The 1880 census shows the farm totaling 4,462 acres, with 110 horses, 40 asses and mules, and 250 tons of hay. It had become the premier thoroughbred stud farm in Tennessee. Here, the family gathers for Otto Giers to photograph them in *c.* 1885. In 1886 William Giles Harding died, and his son-in-law, the spendthrift William Hicks Jackson, took over the management. The large indebtedness that he ran up bankrupted the farm, and it was sold for debt payment after his death in 1903.

This view shows the lawn in front of Belle Meade, which leads to the bridge across Richland Creek and the Harding Pike.

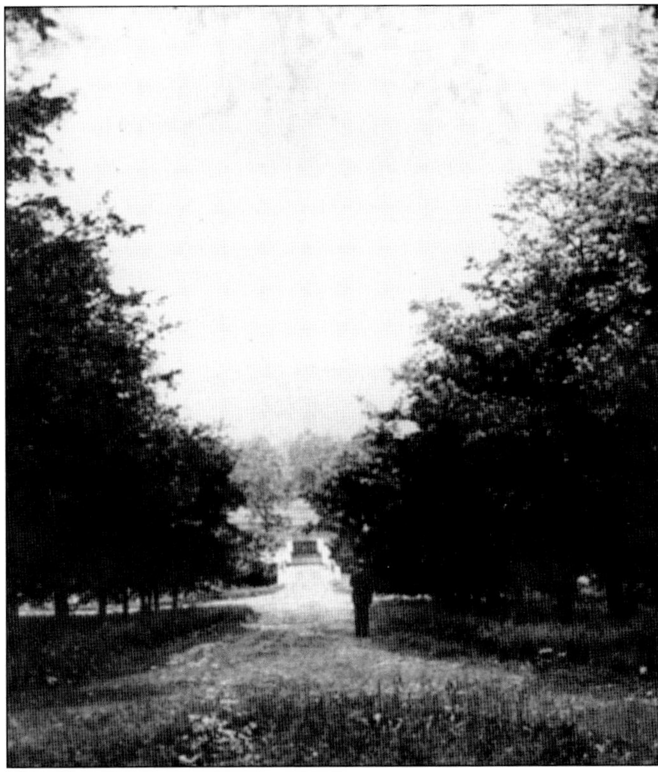

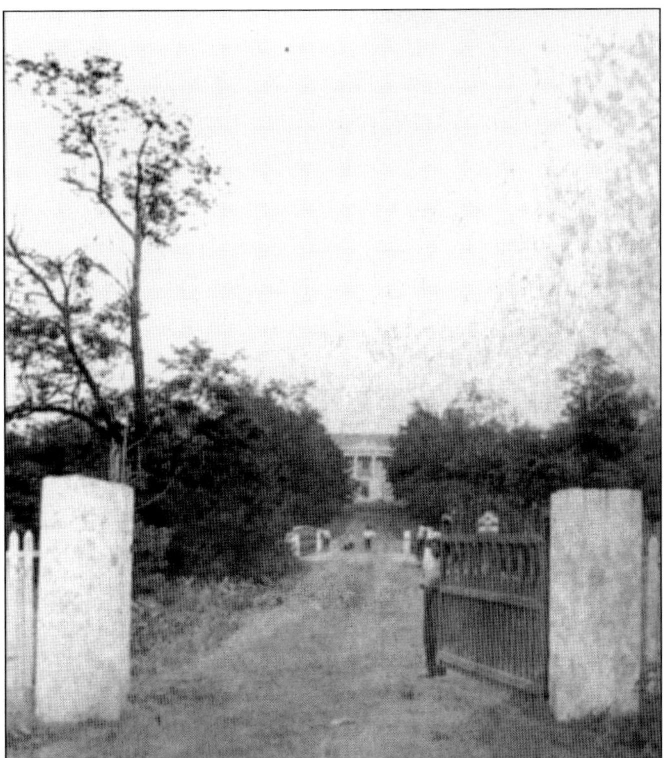

Looking from the front gate, this photograph captures a scene along the pike toward Belle Meade.

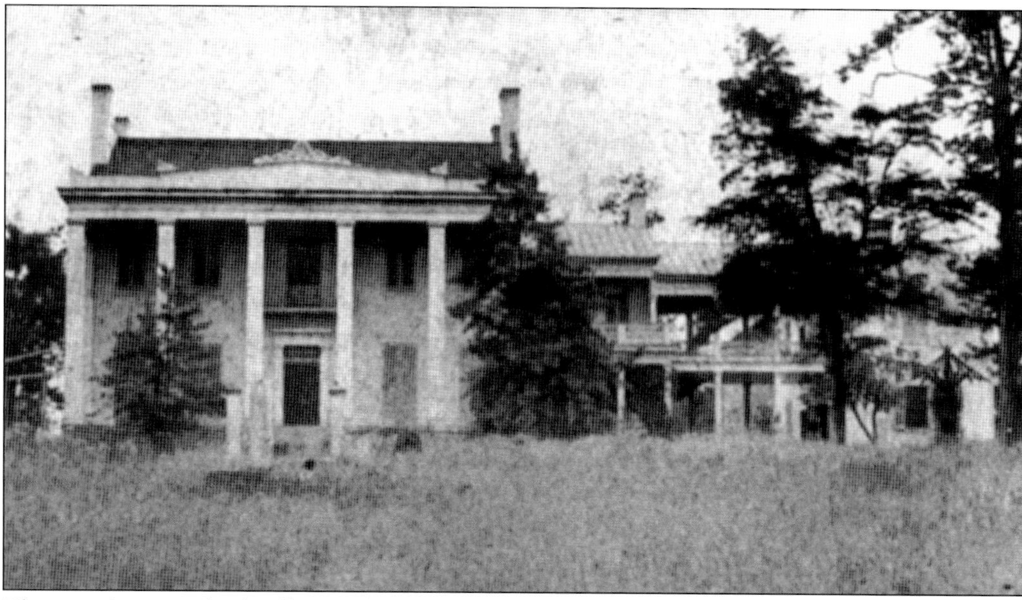

This is a photograph of Belle Meade in the summer, before lawn mowing became fashionable on such a large scale. Notice that the house is shuttered and that the porch connecting the kitchen house (on the far right) to the main house is not yet enclosed. The house has a beautifully designed porch.

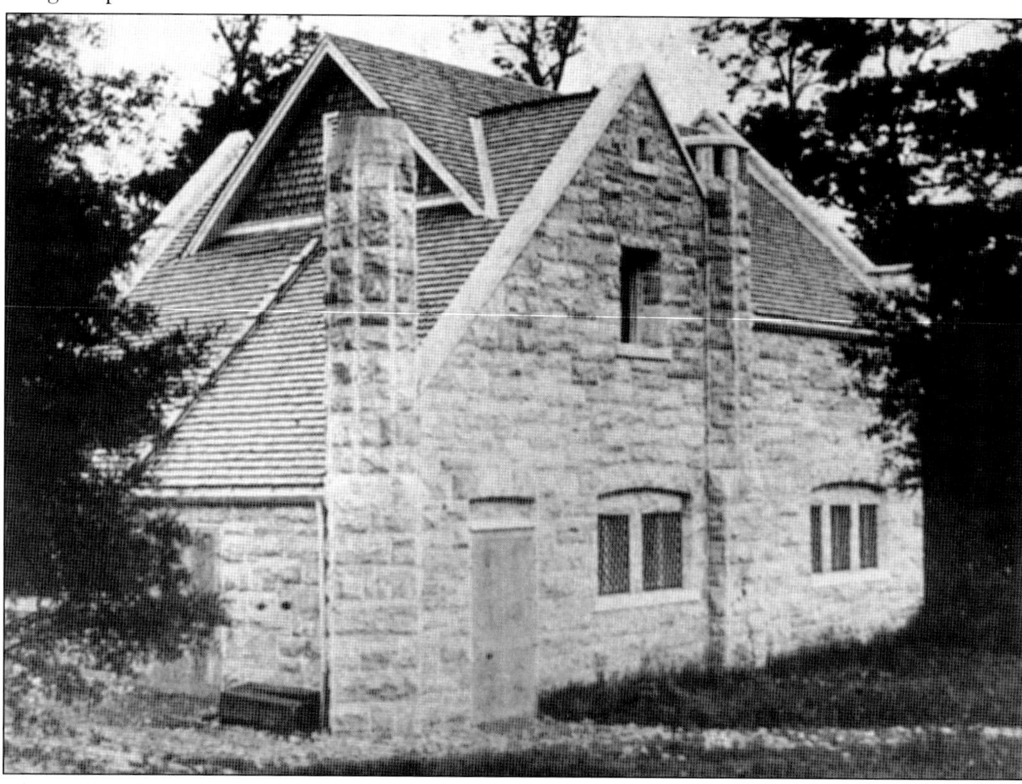

The Belle Meade dairy house was begun in 1884 and opened in the spring of 1885. Here it stands, newly completed.

The Belle Meade Yearling Sales Barn, which stood across present-day Leake Avenue from the house, was built in 1878. This view shows the front of it.

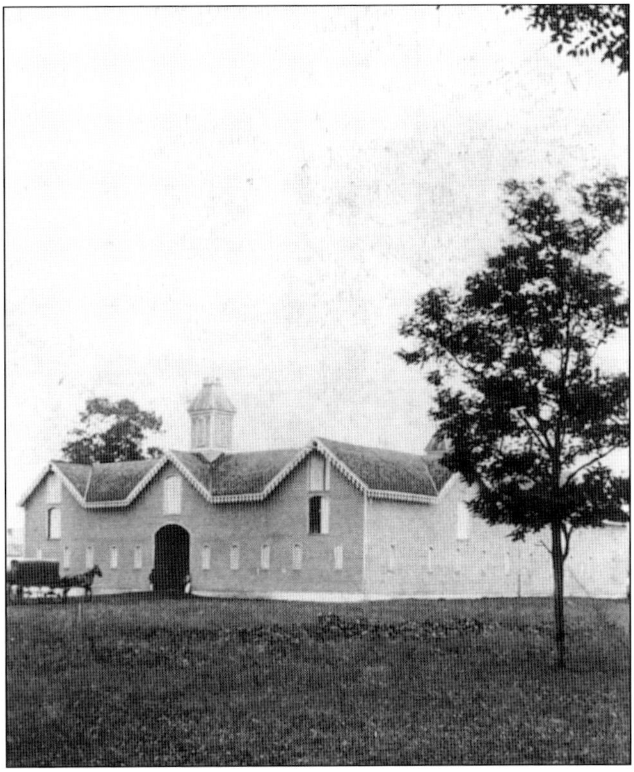

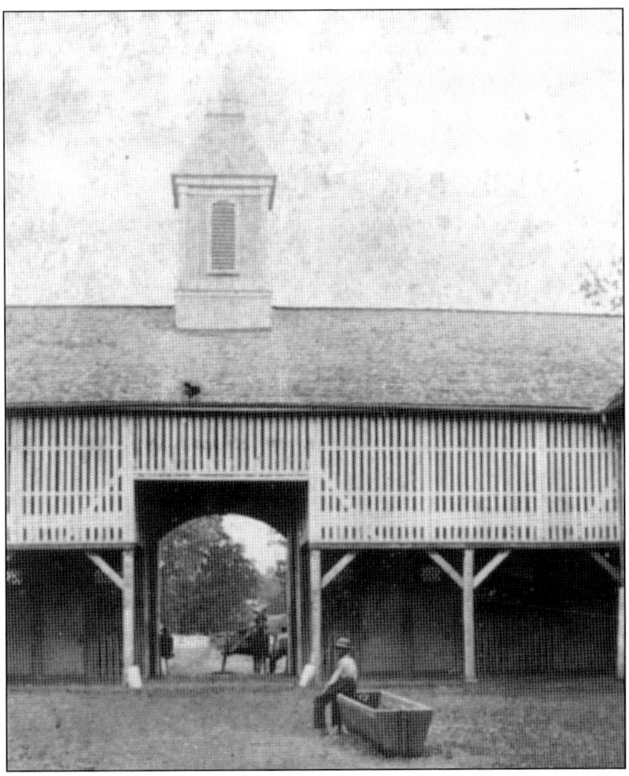

The Belle Meade Yearling Sales Barn courtyard is seen here, photographed by Otto Giers.

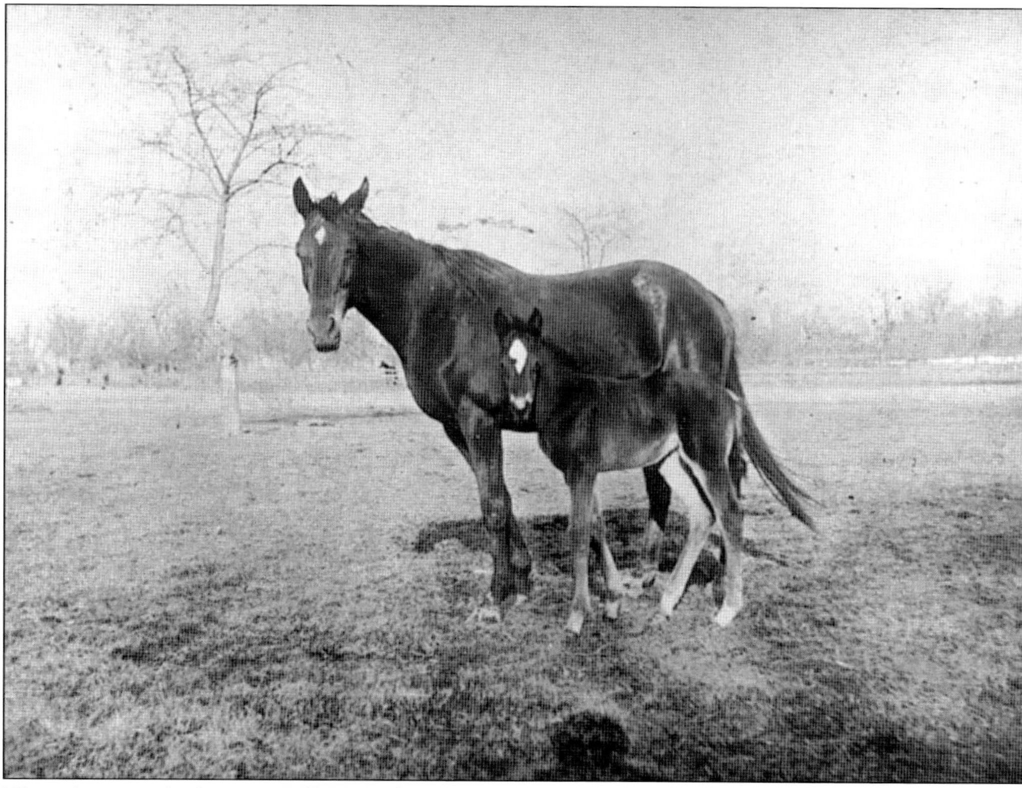

This photograph shows a Belle Meade mare and colt in a pasture on the farm.

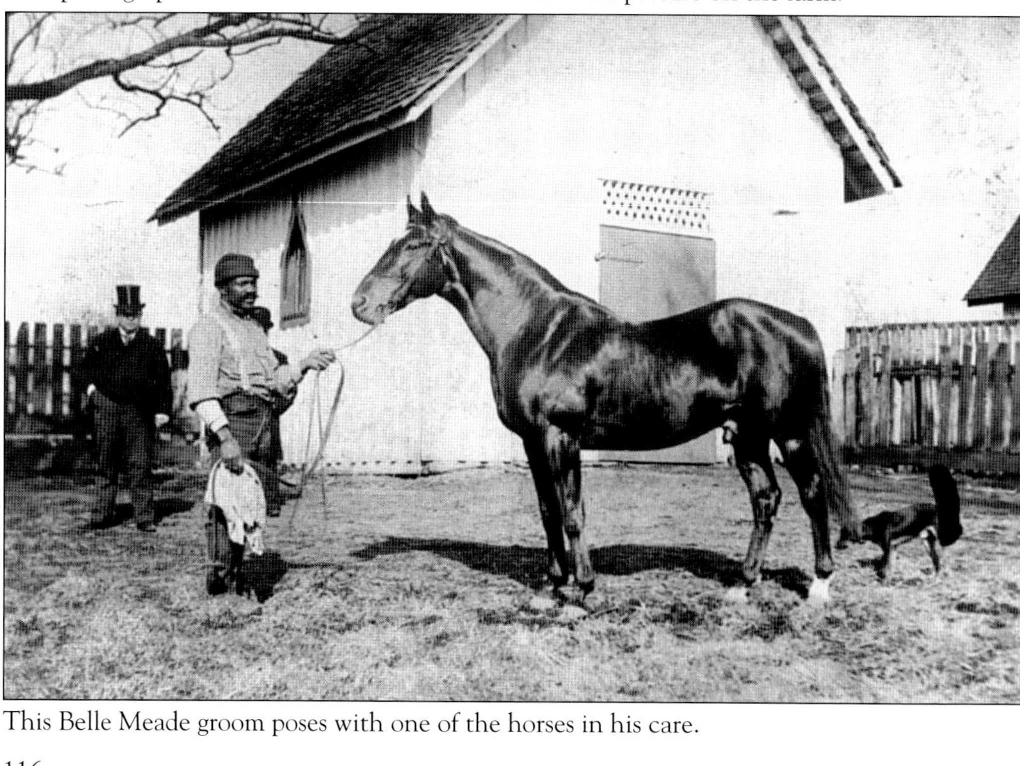

This Belle Meade groom poses with one of the horses in his care.

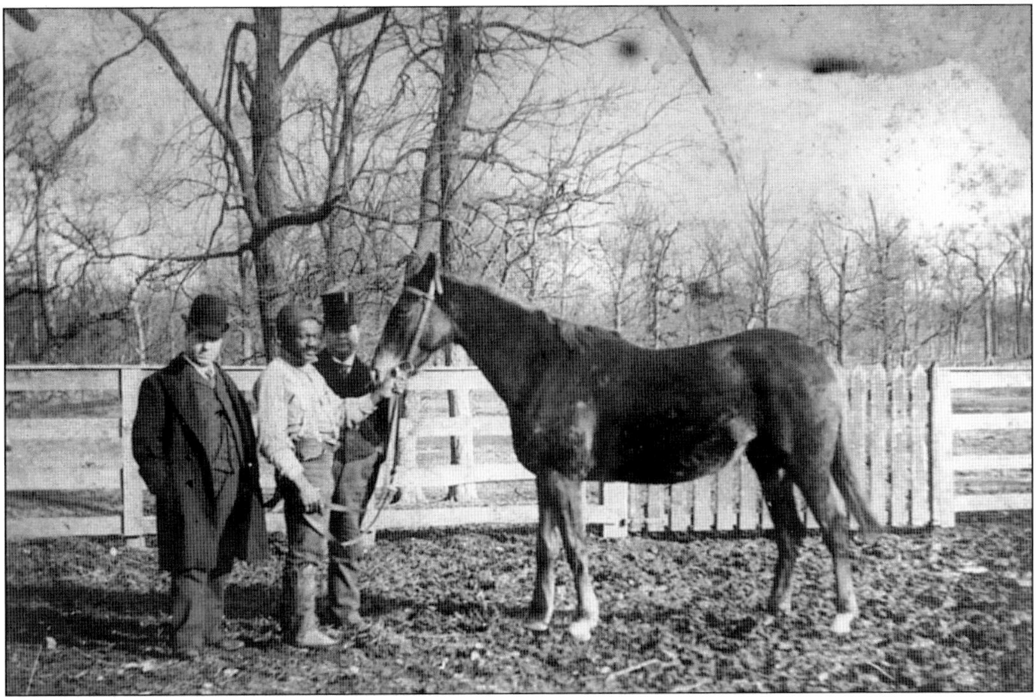

By 1902 Belle Meade totalled 5,200 acres. Here, the same groom poses with another horse.

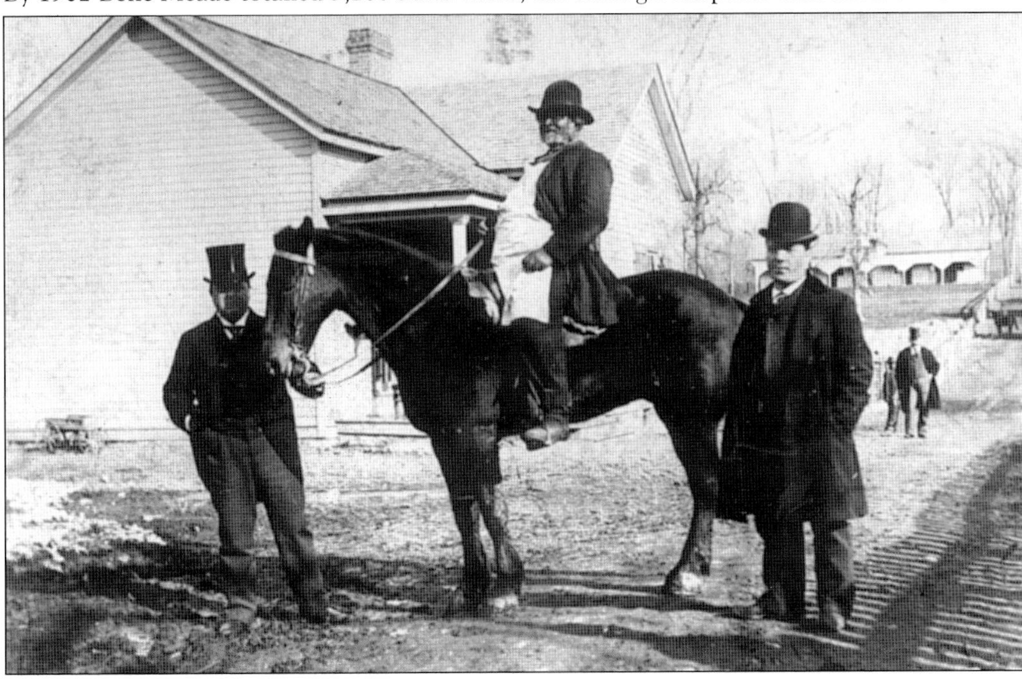

In 1881 the French government sent representatives to inspect horse breeding in America. Their report stated that "the best specimens of the thoroughbred horse we found at General Harding's Belle Meade, in Tennessee. Indeed, we saw a crop of thoroughbred yearlings there that surpassed anything we had ever seen in England or France." Bob Green sits here on one of those horses.

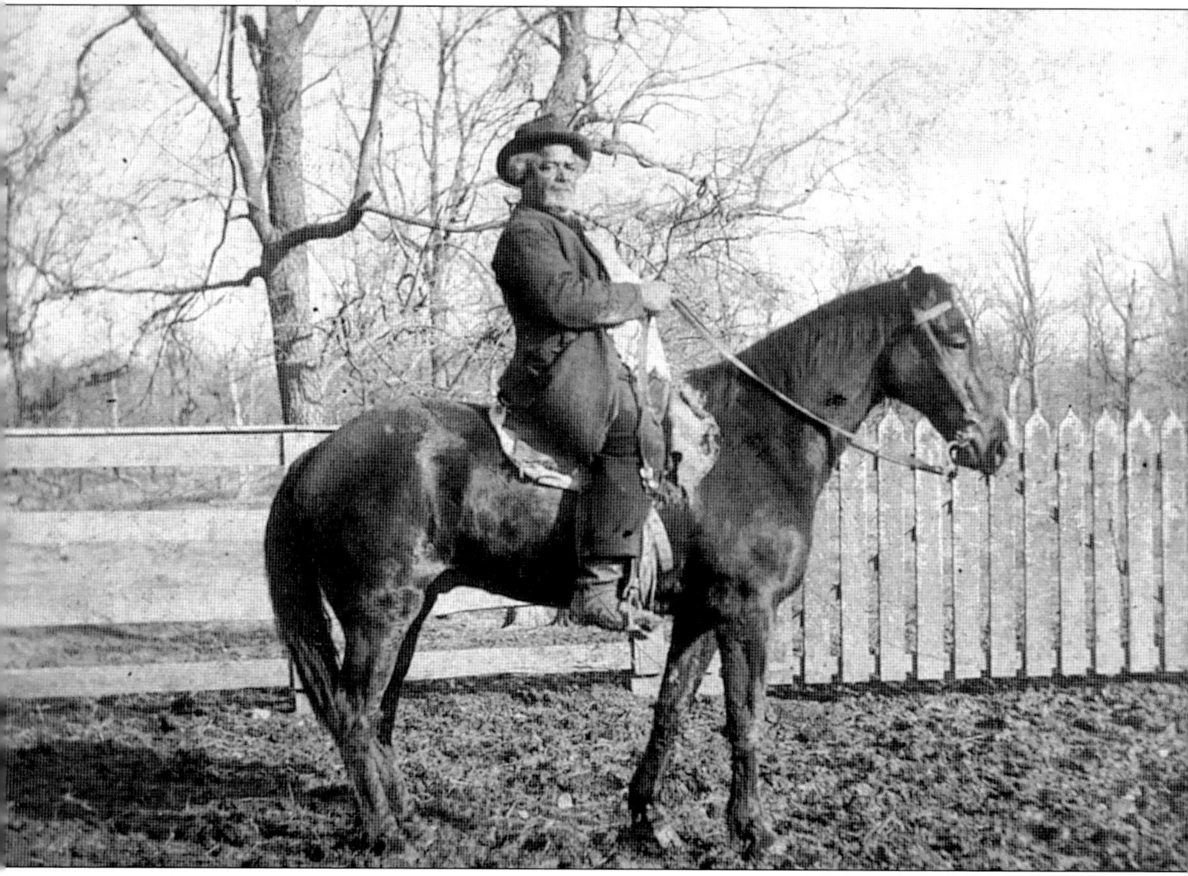
Bob Green, seen here, was the head hostler of the Belle Meade stud.

Eight

Home of Presidents

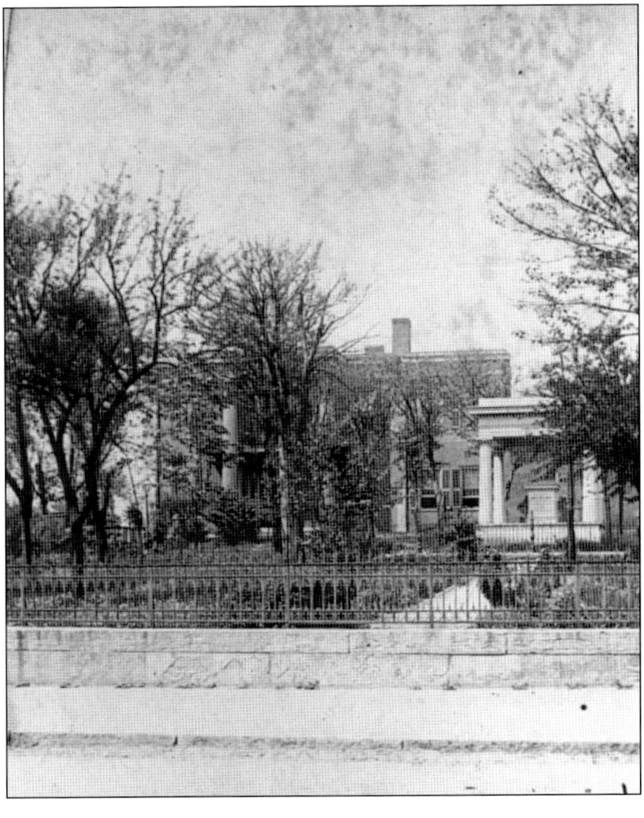

Polk Place originally had as its lot the area bounded by Church Street and Union Alley, and High (Sixth) and Vine (Seventh) Streets. By the 1880s, Mrs. James K. Polk had sold off the frontage on Church Street for Colonel Cole's home and the Nicholson House Hotel, retaining her old drive as Polk Avenue. This photograph shows the side entrance along Vine Street and also former President Polk's tomb in the garden to the right.

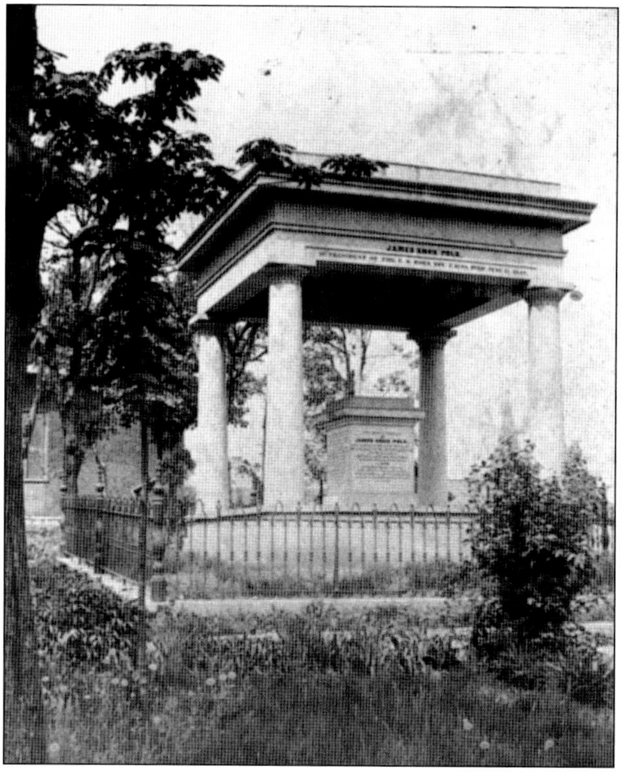

The Polk tomb, designed by William Strickland, was in the garden at Polk Place until 1891, when Mrs. Polk died. At that time, their heirs sold the home to Jacob McGavock Dickinson, and the State of Tennessee moved the tomb to Capitol Hill, thus adding a Polk monument to the one already there commemorating Andrew Jackson.

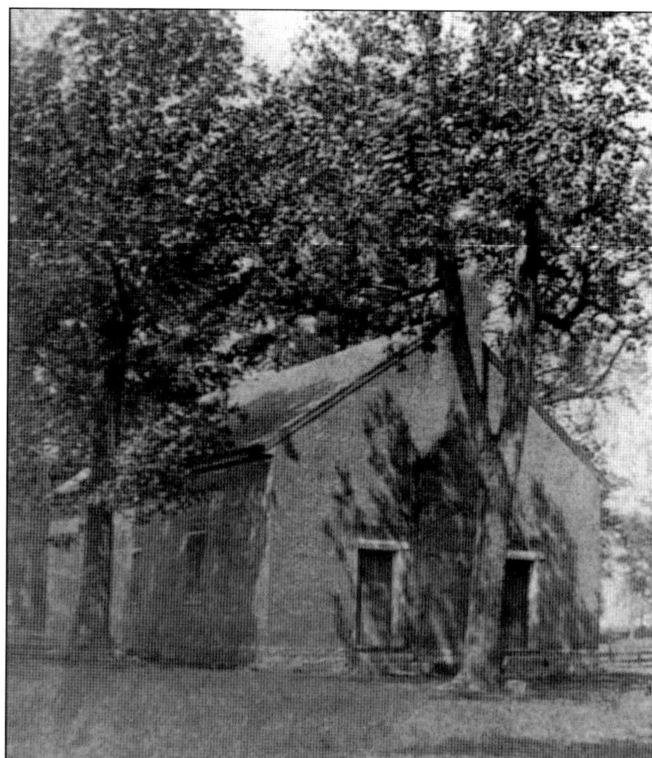

The Hermitage Presbyterian Church was built on the Lebanon Pike by Andrew Jackson in 1823, for his beloved wife, Rachel.

In 1804 Andrew Jackson bought a farm that he named The Hermitage. It would be his home for the rest of his life. He and Rachel lived there in a two-story clapboarded log house until 1819. That year, they built a two-story brick home, which, in time, evolved into the house we see today. This is the front gate.

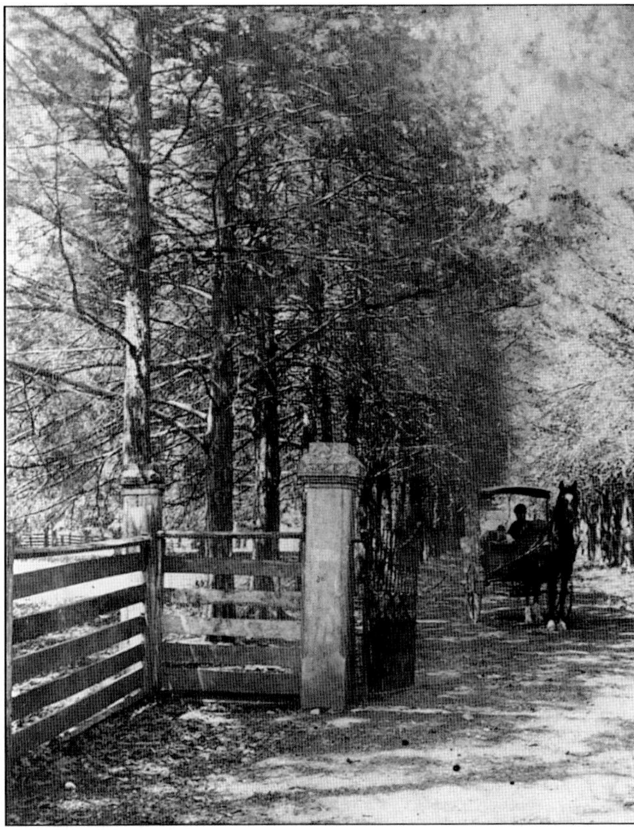

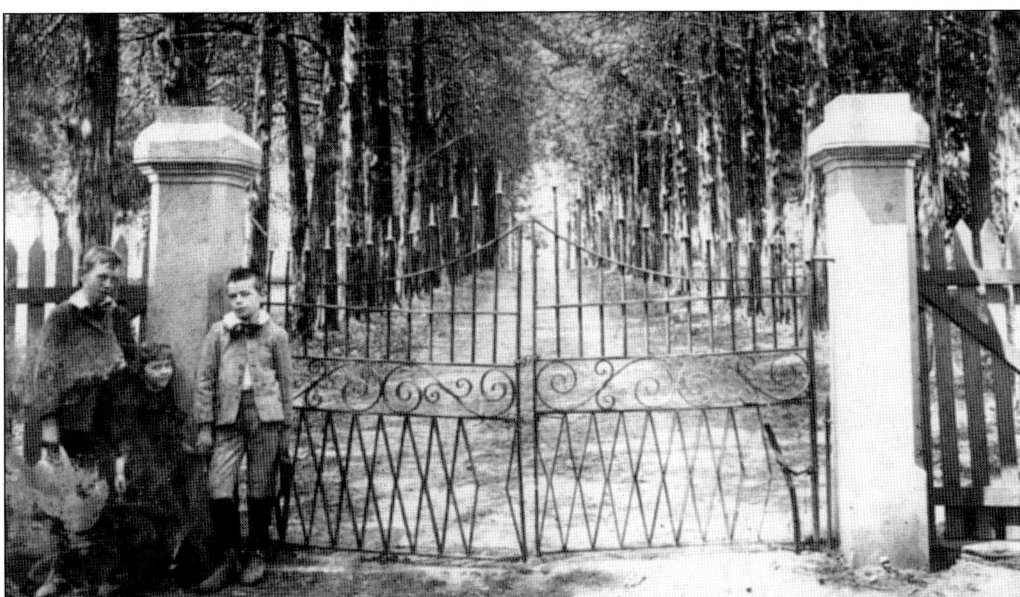

The drive leading up to the house is laid out in the shape of a guitar. Jackson planted eastern red cedars to line it.

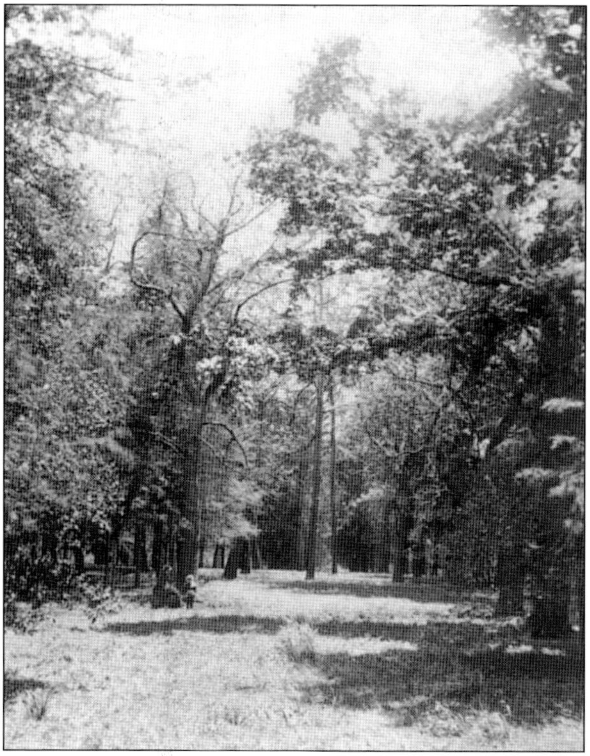

By the 1880s, the once open farm yard around The Hermitage was turning more sylvan, in keeping with the name. In 1856 the State of Tennessee purchased the house and 500 acres. It was proposed to be turned over to the federal government as the site of a national military academy. In 1858 Jackson's nephew moved out, but the regional tensions prevented a move there by the academy from West Point, and Andrew Jackson Jr. moved back in as a tenant at will in 1860. In 1889 the Ladies Hermitage Association formed and has administered the site since then. In 1893 Andrew Jackson III moved out and sold the contents.

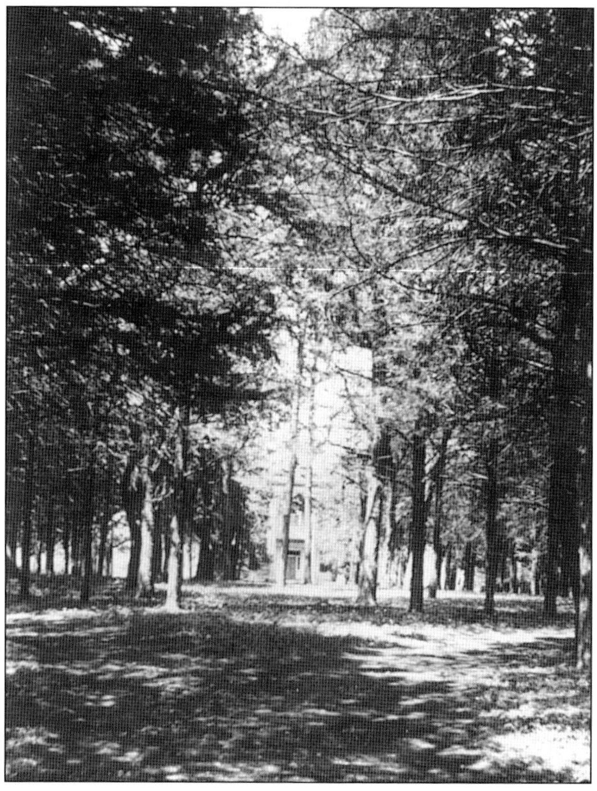

This is the guitar-shaped drive leading to The Hermitage. The 1998 Nashville tornado destroyed most of the cedar trees lining it.

In 1831 Andrew Jackson added two one-story additions onto The Hermitage. A fire in 1834 damaged some of the house, and William C. Hume and Joseph Reiff of Philadelphia were hired to remodel the home. They added the two-story portico we see today.

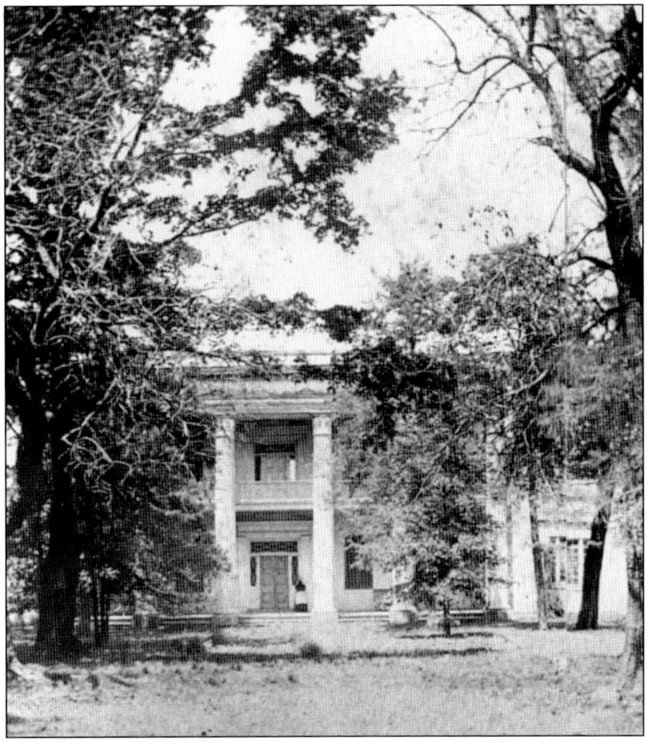

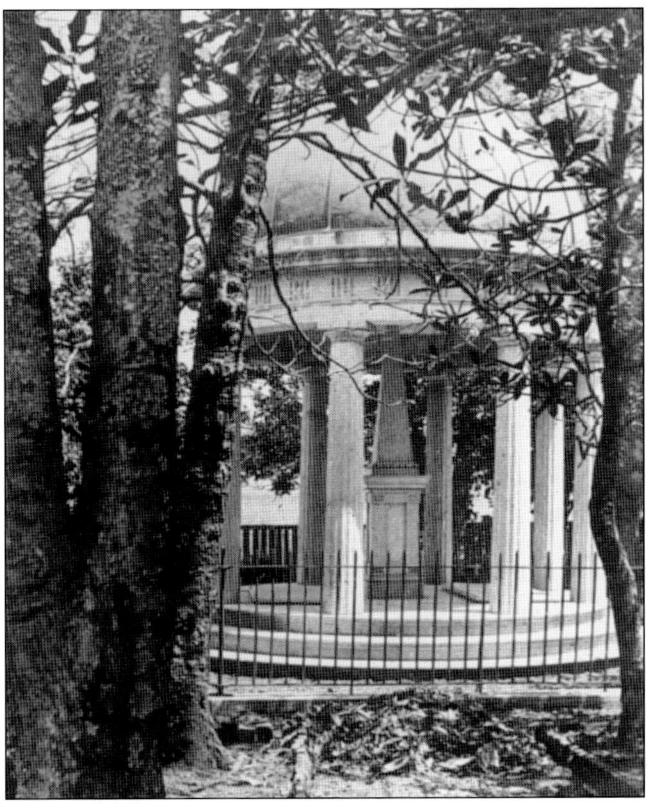

The family cemetery at The Hermitage is tucked into a corner of the garden that Rachel Jackson laid out. Her tomb was placed there in 1831 and was designed by David Morrison. After his own death in 1845, Andrew would lie here as well, with his Rachel.

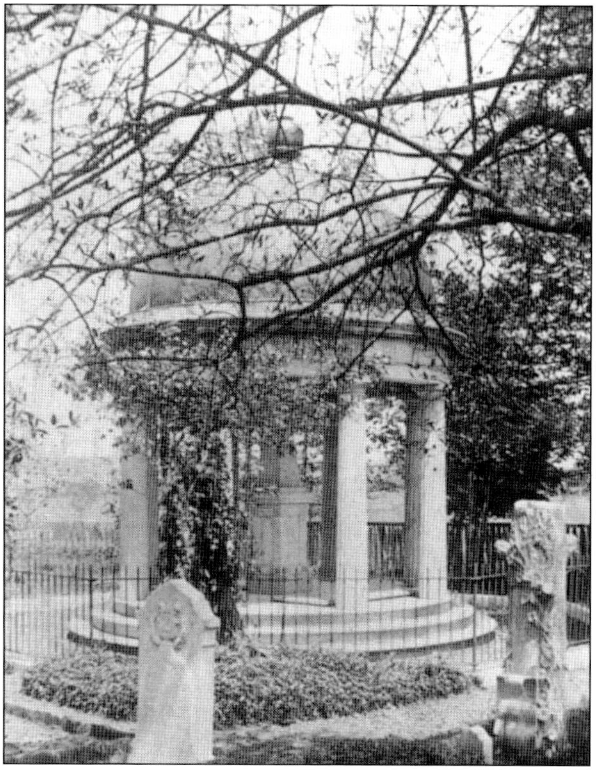

This is the family cemetery at The Hermitage. Its first burial was that of Rachel Jackson, followed by Ralph E.W. Earl, Andrew Jackson, and many other family members. In 1901 Alfred Jackson, the general's former slave, was also buried there.

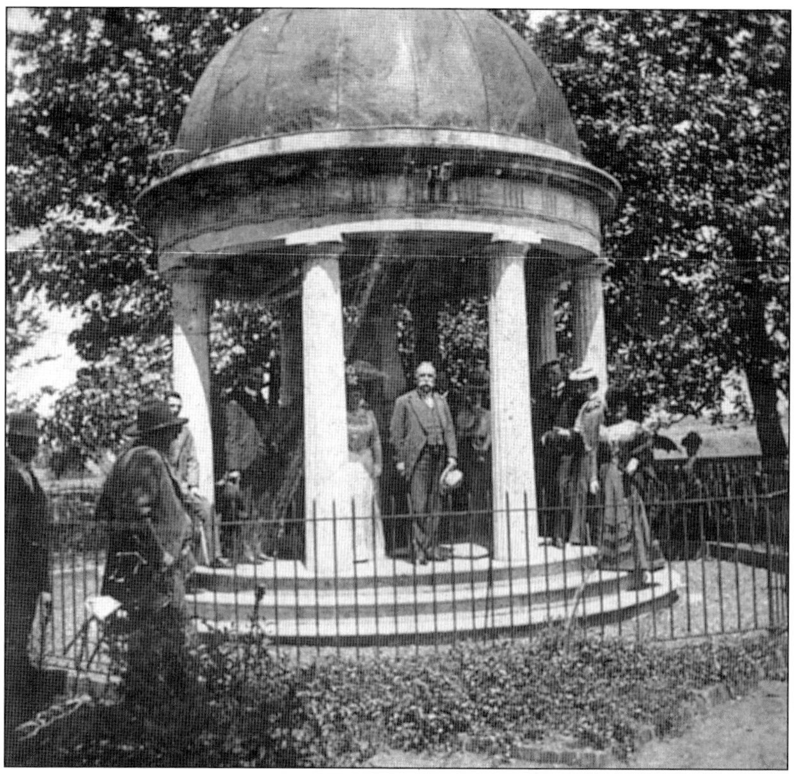

Many distinguished visitors had their photographs made at the tomb of Rachel and Andrew Jackson.

The Ladies Hermitage Association lays a wreath at the tomb every March 15th to commemorate Andrew Jackson's birth and every January 8th to commemorate the Battle of New Orleans.

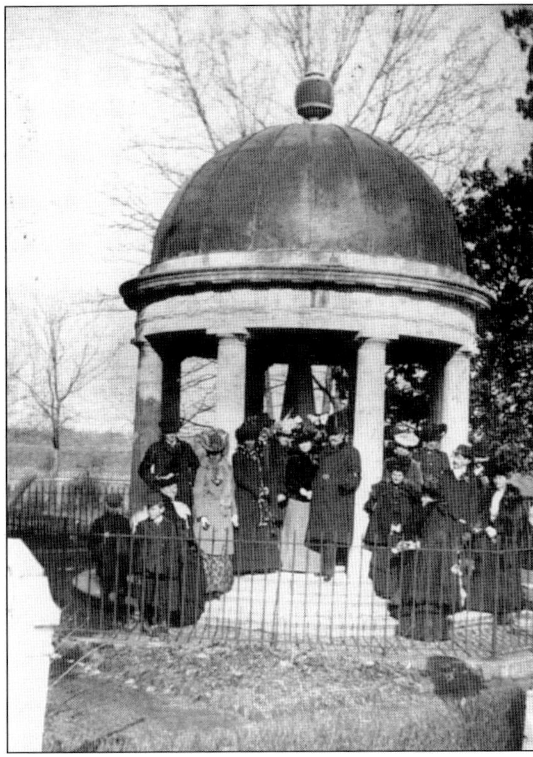

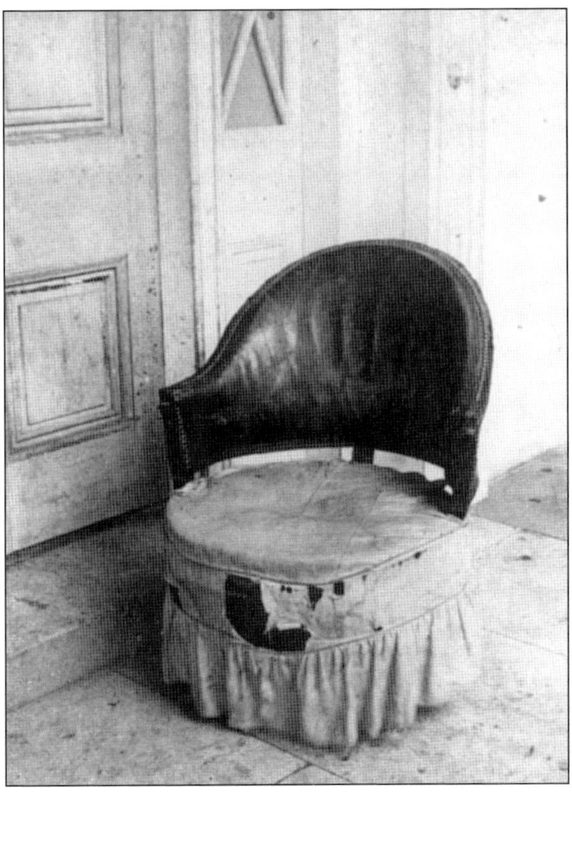

George Washington's desk chair was bequeathed by him to his physician Dr.James Craik, who had attended Washington at the time of his death. Craik's granddaughter's family gave it to Andrew Jackson. In 1905 Jackson's family returned it to Mount Vernon. Here it is photographed on the porch of The Hermitage, beside the front doors.

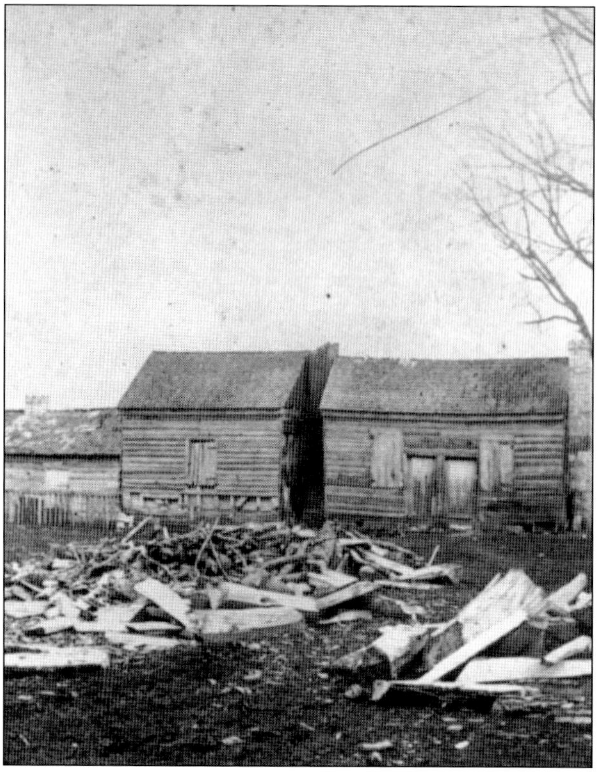

This image shows the slave cabins at The Hermitage, which no longer exist.

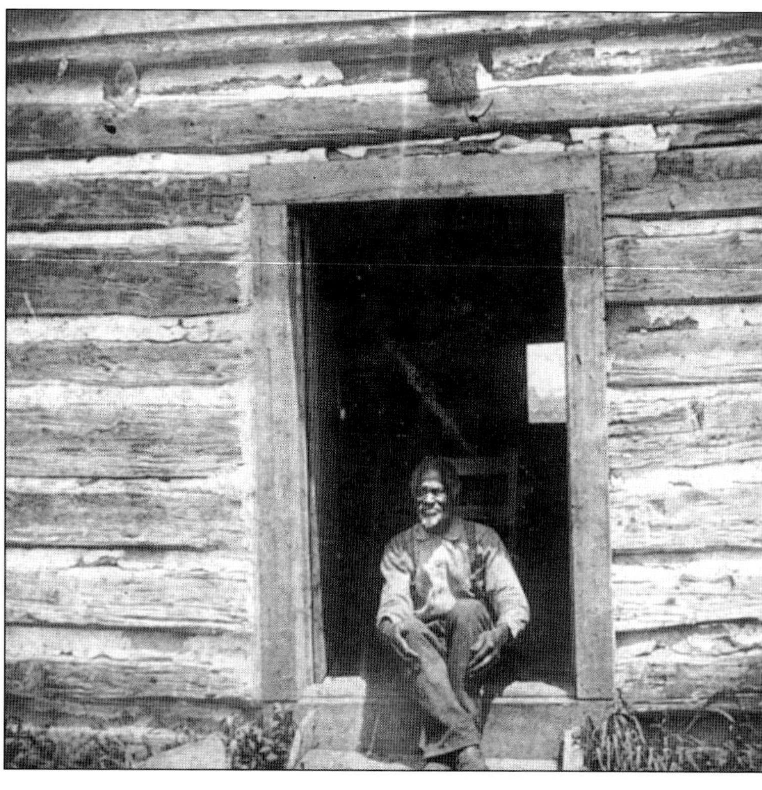

Alfred Jackson, the president's former slave, sits in the doorway to the cabin in which he lived, behind The Hermitage.

Alfred Jackson stayed on at The Hermitage after the president's death. He greeted visitors and gave personal tours. Two years prior to his own death in 1901, he went into Nashville to have Otto Giers photograph him.

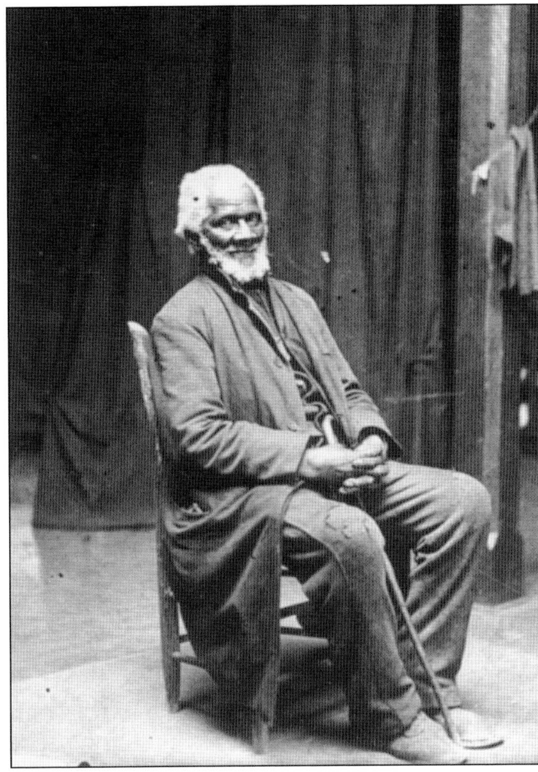

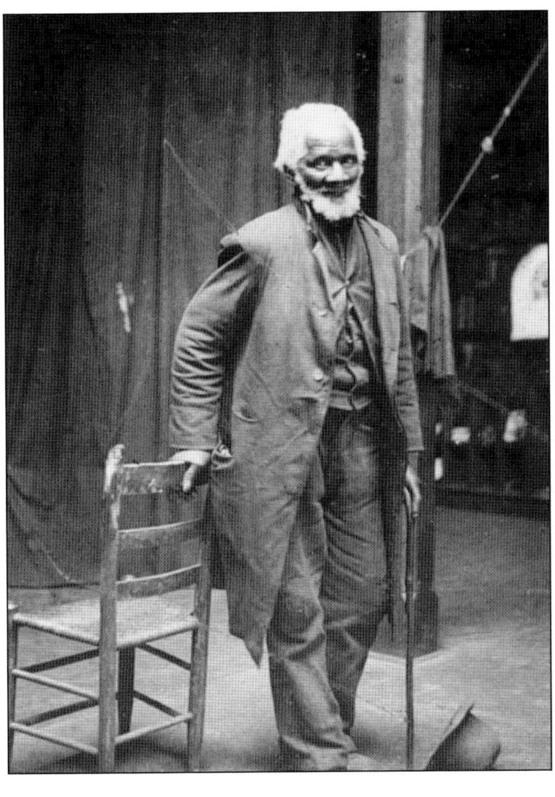

Alfred Jackson, former body servant to Andrew Jackson, died September 4, 1901, at the age of 96. He had been born there shortly after Jackson purchased the land for The Hermitage. Alfred married his wife, Gracey, in the hall at The Hermitage, and they remained together for 50 years. He was at Jackson's bedside when the president died. Alfred and Gracey alone stayed at The Hermitage with Sarah York Jackson during the Civil War. He served as the guide there from the time of the war until his death. He lies now near Jackson in the family cemetery.

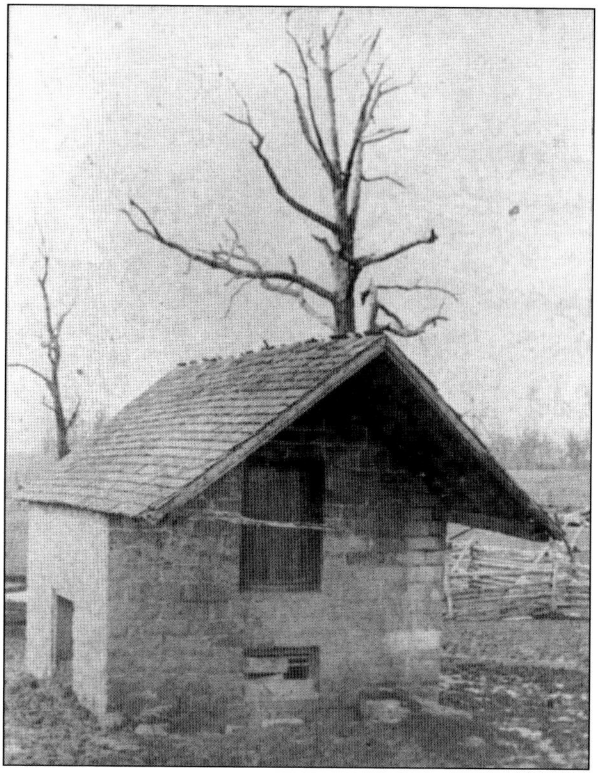

This is the Spring House at The Hermitage, which still stands at the rear of the property.

Bibliography

Brumbaugh, Thomas B. *Architecture of Middle Tennessee.* Nashville: Vanderbilt University Press, 1974.

Clements, Paul. *A Past Remembered: A Collection of Antebellum Houses in Davidson County.* Nashville: Clearview Press, 1987.

Connelly, John Lawrence, ed. *North Nashville and Germantown: Yesterday and Today.* Nashville: The North High Association, 1982.

Crabb, Alfred Leland. *Nashville, Personality of a City.* Indianapolis: Bobbs-Merrill, 1960.

Davis, Louise Littleton. *Frontier Tales of Tennessee.* Gretna: Pelican Publishing Co., 1976.

Douglas, Byrd. *Steamboatin' on the Cumberland.* Nashville: Tennessee Book Co., 1961.

Gadski, Mary Ellen. *Tennessee State Capitol Historic Structure Report.* Nashville: Tennessee State Building Commission, 1986.

Graham, Eleanor, ed. *Nashville: A Short History and Selected Buildings.* Nashville: Historical Commission of Metropolitan Nashville/Davidson County, 1974.

Hoobler, James A. *Cities under the Gun: Images of Occupied Nashville and Chattanooga.* Hong Kong: Rutledge Hill Press, 1986.

McGaw, Robert A. *The Vanderbilt University Campus: A Pictorial History.* Nashville: Vanderbilt University Press, 1978.

Minnix, Kathleen. *Laughter in the Amen Corner: The Life of Evangelist Sam Jones.* Athens: University of Georgia Press, 1993.

Nashville City Directories. Nashville: Marshall & Bruce Co., 1883–1886.

Official Records, Private Plans and Actual Surveys. Philadelphia: G.M. Hopkins, 1889.

Patrick, James. *Architecture in Tennessee: 1768–1897.* Knoxville: University of Tennessee Press, 1981.

Seven Early Churches of Nashville. Nashville: Charles Elder, 1972.